BEING

EXTREME

Thrills and Dangers in the world of High-Risk sports

BEING EXTREME

BILL GUTMAN

WITH

SHAWN FREDERICK

CITADEL PRESS
KENSINGTON PUBLISHING CORP.
www.kensingtonbooks.com

CITADEL PRESS BOOKS are published by

Kensington Publishing Corp.
850 Third Avenue
New York, NY 10022

All Kensington titles, imprints, and distributed lines are available at special quantity discounts for bulk purchases for sales promotions, premiums, fund-raising, educational, or institutional use. Special book excerpts or customized printings can also be created to fit specific needs. For details, write or phone the office of the Kensington special sales manager: Kensington Publishing Corp., 850 Third Avenue, New York, NY 10022, attn: Special Sales Department, phone 1-800-221-2647.

First printing: November 2002

10 9 8 7 6 5 4 3 2 1

Printed in the United States of America

Library of Congress Control Number: 2002104321

ISBN 0-8065-2353-0

In memory of a treasured friend, Phil Berger, whose sport was basketball and who played the game with the same kind of passion exhibited by the athletes featured in this book.

—Bill Gutman

This is for all the dedicated photographers and athletes around the world who continuously put themselves in harm's way in pursuit of their dreams. And to my family and friends, thank you for all the unwavering support throughout the years. You're the best.

—Shawn Frederick

CONTENTS

Acknowledgments		ix
Introduction		1
1.	There Were Always People Being Extreme	13
2.	The Psychology of Risk	23
3.	The Adventure of the Extreme—Jumping and Flying	41
4.	The Adventure of the Extreme—Climbing	81
5.	The Adventure of the Extreme—Riding	125
6.	Coping With and Overcoming Fear	165
7.	The Addiction of the Rush	185
8.	Life, Injury, and Death	201
9.	The Extreme With a Higher Calling	217
10.	Why Smart People Sometimes Do Stupid Things	229
11.	Earning an Extreme Living	249
12.	Living on the Edge—The Lifestyle of the Extreme	269
Websites		281
Index		283

ACKNOWLEDGMENTS

There is only one way to learn about the world of high-risk adventure sports—sometimes referred to as extreme—and that is to speak with the participants themselves. Previous literature on the subject can give you background, basic information about the various sports, and descriptions about some of the individuals who perform highly skilled and dangerous feats on a regular basis. To fully understand why these people have chosen a lifestyle filled with challenges and danger, there is no substitute for the real thing. That wasn't always an easy task, because so many people who follow a high-risk lifestyle are often traveling to every corner of the globe to pursue their sport. Time constraints made it difficult to speak with all the people we might have liked.

When available, however, these were people who were gracious, open, honest, and candid about what they do, how they came to do it, and why they continue to pursue activities that have altered, and sometimes ended, many lives. The authors would like to thank, with the deepest gratitude, the following people who took time from active and busy schedules to provide the information for the major portions of this book.

They include climbers Kim Csizmazia, Abby Watkins, Craig DeMartino, Chris McNamara, Carlos Buhler, and Sharon Wood; skier and cinematographer Tom Day; skier and climber Kristen Ulmer; snowboarders Rob daFoe and Circe Wallace; ski diver and aerial photographer Tom Sanders; sky diver Jim McCormick; BASE jumper Mick Knutson; sky diver and BASE jumper Kevin Quinn; sky diver, BASE jumper, and rope flyer Miles Daisher; skier and BASE jumper Shane McConkey; big wave surfers Mike

Parsons and Archie Kalepa; tandem surfer Bobby Friedman; kayak waterfall jumper Scott Feindel; motorcycle jumper and stunt rider Seth Enslow; and freestyle motocross rider Mike Metzger.

In addition, the authors would like to thank Dr. Robert Leach, who is a sailor and rock climber, but who has worked with and treated high-risk athletes for many years, as well as contributing photographers Rob Gracie, David Pu'u, Dave Nagel, Joni Kabana, Sylvain Cazenave, Christian Pondella, Bernhard Spottel, and Ulrich Grill. Lastly, the authors would like to thank Barbara Serhant of Red Bull, for graciously providing photographs from her company files, Rick Erkeneff for helping to arrange several important interviews, and Bob Shuman, our editor, who put up with us through numerous delays in tracking down these globe-trotting athletes and then moved the manuscript through the necessary early pre-production stages with skill, professionalism and, most of all, speed. Thanks Bob.

BEING
EXTREME

INTRODUCTION

*T*HE *huge, snow-covered mountain stands supreme, jutting more than 28,000 feet into the sky, a natural monument to the creation of the earth, formed and shaped over millions of years. At the top the air is so thin and so cold that nothing can survive there for more than a short period of time. When looked at from the base, the mountain is beautiful and majestic, appearing unspoiled and almost surreal. In fact, in both mythologies and some ancient religions, mountains such as this were said to be homes to the gods that gazed down upon us from a place where people simply didn't belong.*

In the context of the life of the planet, humans have been on earth for a relatively short period. And for most of that time, those living in areas around mountains simply stared at them in wonder, maybe even worshiped them. Nothing more. Humans, after all, were too busy trying to survive, finding food and shelter, trying to protect themselves from wild animals and other enemies. There was no earthly reason for anyone to even remotely want to ascend to the tops of mountains. The magnificent peaks, so high that they were sometimes covered by clouds or enshrouded by fog, seemed so distant that they appeared to be in another, forbidden world. Climbing them was not only unthinkable, but considered impossible.

No one really knows when the first man looked up at a mountain and wondered what it was like at the top, wondered if there was a way he could climb up and maybe commiserate with the gods or simply look out from the summit and view the entire world. Humans have always been a curious lot. The more people who looked up at the mountains over the centuries, decades, years, the more they began wondering what it would be like at the very top. It really wasn't until the twentieth century that some adventurous souls began to feel that the great mountains were there to be climbed. No one yet knew what to expect, especially as one reached the upper sections and slowly moved into more difficult terrain, steeper slopes, ice-covered rock faces, crevasses that could give way and swallow up anyone crossing them, and finally into air so devoid of oxygen that it would make people extremely ill before ultimately killing them.

It would take tremendous skill, physical fitness, tenacity, determination, and luck for anyone to climb such a mountain. Once humans ascended past 25,000 feet, they would enter a different world, one that would come to be known, in the second half of the twentieth century, as the death zone. Why, then, would anyone in their right mind do such a thing? After all, reasonable people who looked at the mountains and thought about climbing them would probably begin counting all the ways there were to die.

In the late twentieth century and into the twenty-first, more and more people are traveling to locales such as the ones described above and attempting to stand on the summit of the world's greatest mountains. These daring adventurers represent a segment of a rapidly growing subculture in American society. Besides climbing the world's highest mountains, there are other similar challenges being met. Some ski or snowboard down vertical slopes; others ride surfboards over the largest waves the mighty oceans can produce. Still others leap off the sides of cliffs and bridges, looking to pull the handle of a single parachute only seconds before landing, or fly through the air on a rope nearly 1,000 feet long. Today, thousands of people are forging an alternative lifestyle in extreme sports and challenging creations of nature or obstacles of their own making, such as trying to jump a motorcycle more than 200 feet through the air. Either way, it is the kind of life that is often fraught with risk and danger. For the most part the people engaged in these activities are highly trained athletes who think very deeply about their sport. Instead of playing baseball, basketball, football, volleyball, tennis, or one of the other so-called mainstream or conventional sports, they practice high-risk, alternative, radical sports. While these New Age athletes are leaving a legacy of achievement, they are also playing with the possibility of being seriously injured or even killed.

In fact, it is the potential for disaster that is the common denominator of all these sports. Every time a man or woman goes out to pursue them, there is the chance of not coming back at all. This is a prospect that would be quite daunting to most people, but to these very special athletes it simply comes with the territory. It is a risk they fully acknowledge and are willing to take. The reasons may vary somewhat, but the bottom line is always the same: They love what they are doing, enjoy the visceral feelings generated as they perform, and always get a special kind of satisfaction from completing the task at hand. At the end of the day, the people who pursue extreme sports feel they are living life to the hilt. As one of the world's best big wave surfers, Laird Hamilton, once told an interviewer:

"You're never more alive than when you're near death. The slightest mistake can cost you your life. That's living!"

Life and death. This is the accepted dichotomy for those who have taken these sports to heart and they are very much aware of the possible consequences. Many have lost good friends or have seen some of the ultimate practitioners of their particular discipline come to a tragic end. Yet given this reality, for the most part they go on, continuing to do that which has become part of their lives, knowing full well that it all could end at any time.

The various sports that are often called *extreme*—a label that many of the athletes have come to dislike—vary greatly in their duration and intensity. An expedition alpine mountain climber might spend two months or more navigating up a difficult route of Mount Everest, K2, Makalu, or Kanchenjunga. A BASE jumper leaping off the top of El Capitan in Yosemite National Park will free fall for only several seconds before opening the chute and looking to land safely. Someone making a death-defying motorcycle jump or going over a waterfall in a small kayak will succeed or fail in just a matter of seconds as well, while a big wall climber might spend several nights sleeping on a porta-ledge, a structure bolted to the side of a rock face several thousand feet above the ground. All pursue these diverse activities with a similar passion not always seen in everyday life, and all seem to have an affinity for continuing in the face of danger and tragedy.

"I don't think the ability to hunker down [in a crisis] is something you develop," said radical freestyle and stunt skier Kristen Ulmer. "It's something you either have or you don't. There are some people who, when there is a fire in the house, just run around like chickens with their heads cut off. And then there are people who say, 'Okay, where's the cat? Is everybody out of the house?' You either have that ability to focus or you don't.

"I've been caught in five avalanches. When you're in the avalanche, you're not thinking, *Oh, my God. I'm gonna die.* Your every instinct is to fight to survive. You're thinking, *What can I do to stay alive?* I continue to do it because I'm really good at it. And when you're really good at something, you feel good about yourself."

BASE jumper, sky diver, and rope flyer Miles Daisher describes the feeling he has just before he jumps off a cliff or bridge with a parachute strapped to his back.

"I just love it so much," he said. "There's no feeling in the world like it. You're standing on an object, you jump off it, you're weightless. You have zero gravity. Then the wind . . . you have subterminal air that slowly begins to pick up. My favorite part, though, is when you are on the object and you lean over to the point of commitment, when you can't stop and turn back. I'm just nuts for that feeling, that feeling of pushing off and totally going for it. I don't know, to me it's like a feeling of being alive. You're not sitting around watching movies. You're actually out there and doing it."

Though he feels his sport is very safe and his own approach is one of meticulous care and preparation, longtime sky diver Jim McCormick said it is the knowledge of what *can* happen that often adds to the overall mystique of jumping.

"I know that with every sky dive, every time I leave the plane, I could die," McCormick explained. "What is the chance of that happening? Extremely slight. Hence, it's an acceptable risk to me.

I also know that every time I leave the plane, I could get hurt. What are the chances of it? Very, very slight. That, too, is an acceptable risk.

"Yet I would contend that if those two elements weren't there, the attraction would go away for more sky divers. There's a great joy in it, but the truth is, in a perverse sort of way, we know that every jump could be our last. We all know that intellectually, but sky divers know it more than other people because we live it. It results in a passion for life and a great joy for every passing moment and every passing day, because we're betting everything on a regular basis. All of this leads to a vibrancy for life. That keeps us sharp and is part of what inspires us."

As with most people who decide to become involved in a high-risk sport or recreational activity, these athletes all think long and hard about the ramifications of what they are doing, both the positive and the negative aspects. Most, in fact, have experienced tragedy firsthand.

Miles Daisher was with the legendary free rope swinger Dan Osman when Osman decided to make one last jump in the twilight at Yosemite. That's when the unexpected—the unthinkable—happened. His rope snapped, causing him to plunge to his death. Osman was a hero to Daisher and his friends. For a while, they didn't think they could cope with his loss, until they realized a greater tribute to the life of Dan Osman would be to continue doing what they all loved.

Kristen Ulmer climbed mountains with Alex Lowe, a man she described as the Michael Jordan of mountain climbing. Lowe was later killed in an avalanche, leaving Ulmer shaken but still willing to go on. One of the world's best mountaineers, Carlos Buhler, once came upon the frozen body of a fellow climber while trying to conquer Makalu, the world's fifth highest peak.

"When you see a frozen guy lying in the snow and realize you could be him in just the next ten or twenty hours," Buhler said, "and to see him there for an eternity like a frozen piece of meat, yeah, it really makes you think."

For BASE jumper, sky diver, and renowned aerial photographer Tom Sanders, the tragedy hit even closer to home. Sanders watched as his wife, Jan Davis, BASE jumped in a protest demonstration off El Capitan at Yosemite National Park. As Sanders and the others who were gathered there that day stood in horror, Davis's parachute never opened and she plunged to her death. Yet Tom Sanders continues to live the life that he and his wife had embraced for so long.

"It's hard for me," Sanders said, "because as you get older, you have more people who die. But I've also had friends who have died of cancer and in car accidents, as well as BASE jumping and sky diving. I'm not going to quit driving on the freeway because somebody wrecks their car, and I'm not going to change my lifestyle because somebody made a mistake BASE jumping.

"All I can say about Jan is that she died at fifty-eight years of age, a beautiful woman. She was vibrant, and it rips my heart out every day. But she died doing something she loved. If I could be so lucky dying while doing something I enjoy and not die from some stupid cancer, I'll consider it a definite success."

While there has always been a small, hard-core group of people living by their own rules, pushing the envelope, and constantly stepping off the edge, in the past this was often done in anonymity, without fanfare and publicity. Only when a particularly dramatic event occurred, such as Sir Edmund Hillary and Tenzing Norgay becoming the first men to make it to the summit of Mount Everest in 1953, did the world of high-risk sports become known to the general public. Even in the recent past of the 1970s, the quintessential *daredevil* was Evel Knievel, who would do some near impossible stunts for large audiences, many of whom began anticipating another Knievel crash which would add to his ever-growing dossier of broken bones. Before long, many of his stunts were fodder for made-for-television extravaganzas.

All the while, a small group of dedicated athletes were pursuing various forms of high-risk sports and activities, yet it really wasn't until the late 1980s and into the 1990s that these sports slowly broke into the mainstream consciousness and began to proliferate. Media exposure, improved equipment, and adventurous people looking to explore their own limits brought the catchphrase *living on the edge* into many living rooms across the country.

For better or worse, the marriage of media and corporate America to the world of extreme sports has made it possible for many of these outstanding athletes to pursue their lifestyles and earn a living at the same time. The changing media climate, which included the advent of cable and satellite television, also served to introduce high-risk activities to a general public not fully aware of the kind of training needed to cope with the dangers that accompany the pursuits. New sports were being created, while older ones morphed into something different, and almost always more dangerous, such as a conventional open-the-chute-right-away parachute jump becoming a free-falling sky dive. Along with these changes came more wannabe extreme athletes, some looking to permanently alter their lifestyles, but others simply looking for a one-time challenge or for a good story to tell their family and friends.

Mountain climbers, for example, traditionally had trained for years before taking on the rigors of high-altitude climbing; now relative amateurs are looking for guides to take them up Mount Everest. Kids who used to play baseball and basketball are now learning all kinds of tricks on their skateboards, taking up snowboarding at an early age, or riding their BMX bikes over ramps and jumps. Skiers who used to train to race through the gates of a slalom course now prefer to ski down unchartered routes on high slopes, where they can express their creativity and freedom in a world where a small slough can quickly become a dangerous avalanche.

Reality shows, the newest form of made-for-TV specials, are inviting people to all corners of the world to participate in high-risk races over different types of dangerous terrains. The adventure-travel trip has become a status symbol as well as a challenge for many Americans. Perhaps the essence of the trend was best described by Richard Bangs, an adventure-travel pioneer who later became an editor of an online adventure-travel magazine.

Said Bangs, "I am continually amazed that people will spend enormous amounts of money up front to go to places that are defined as risky, with people they have never met and guides they know nothing about."

All this hard-core adventure has actually served to make the
ESPN X Games, one of the first venues that showcased the so-
called extreme sports, a rather tame and relatively safe showpiece
when it comes to sportspeople challenging self and the elements.
Partially owing to this increased media exposure, the longtime,
skilled extreme athletes have been joined by people who are taking the same risks, but without the training. There are first-time
risk takers jumping out of planes, off cliffs and buildings, climbing
high mountains, running white water rapids, surfing huge waves,
and looking for other kinds of potentially dangerous adventures.

Many can't even fully explain why they suddenly have the need
to do something they have never done before, especially when it's
an activity that brings so many risks. Some step out to the edge just
one time. After that, the need or curiosity is gone and they return
to their previous lives. There are a few, however, who find the thrill,
or rush, of a high-risk activity to be almost addictive, and they
begin pursuing additional high-risk adventures. They are, in effect, moving farther out on the edge, their lives having taken a
sudden and unexpected turn.

One of the major catalysts in the spread of high-risk adventure
occurred in 1996 when three different expeditions set out to climb
Mount Everest, located in Nepal's Annapurna range. The tallest
mountain in the world, Everest has long beckoned seasoned adventurers looking for the ultimate challenge. Only this time, something went wrong in the form of a severe and unexpected storm as
all three groups converged on the summit. In the fury that followed,
eight people died, including a pair of very experienced climbing
guides, American Scott Fisher and New Zealander Rob Hall.

The story might have hit the papers and then quickly disappeared had it not been for Jon Krakauer. A journalist and a
climber, Krakauer was commissioned to join one of the expeditions and then write about it. Because of the magnitude of the disaster, Krakauer penned *Into Thin Air*, which chronicled the
tragedy, became a longtime best-seller, and is considered one of
the most successful books on mountaineering ever written. Yet
while it told the tale of a tragedy and described the many inherent

dangers that even experienced climbers face in tackling a mountain like Everest, the book had a strange effect on its readers. Instead of confirming the fact that Everest was a potential killer, a place for the average person to avoid like the plague, which was the author's intent, it seemed to bring the mountain back to life. The book imbued it with a mysterious and almost mystical quality that made people want to climb the 29,000-foot-plus peak all the more. Even author Krakauer couldn't understand the effect his book had on so many people.

"Attempting to climb Everest is an intrinsically irrational act," he said. "Any person who would seriously consider it is, by definition, beyond the scope of reasoned judgment. I get all this mail from people who say, 'I know it's crazy but I still want to climb Everest.' Everest has this amazing pull. It causes people to leave their senses."

The pull, irrational and mysterious as it might be, comes from other mountains as well. Not so long ago three friends, middle-aged women from Manhattan Beach, California, decided they wanted to try climbing. Both Deborah Lynn and Nina Redman, like so many others, had been seduced by *Into Thin Air*, and decided that they, too, were ready for Everest. They convinced another friend, Susan Hall, to join them, eventually modifying their challenge and setting their sights on Mount Rainier, a 14,410-foot peak in Seattle, Washington.

Though climbers could theoretically scale the mountain and return in twenty-four hours, Rainier is still fraught with significant risks. There are potentially massive ice falls and very high winds, climactic conditions similar to the peaks in the Himalayas. In fact, Rainier is often considered a training ground for climbers planning to tackle Everest. None of the three women had ever climbed before, so they took a three-day course in basic mountaineering skills, then set about getting themselves in tip-top physical shape for the climb.

When they joined sixteen other amateur climbers in June 1998, they felt they were ready. Sure enough the climb, though difficult, was accomplished without incident. It was on the way down when the unexpected happened, something even the most experienced mountaineers fear and are powerless to control. The entire group was caught in a sudden and potentially catastrophic avalanche. Though it was a harrowing and life-threatening ordeal, all three women were rescued, though one member of their party died on the mountain.

By stepping out onto the edge, the three women were almost killed. At the hospital, Nina Redman was checked for head injuries and subsequently released. Deborah Lynn suffered hypothermia, but recovered within a few hours. Susan Hall crushed two fingers, which required nine hours of surgery and temporary wires to stabilize the bones. For a month after the avalanche, she was so exhausted that she didn't even want to leave home. When their story appeared in the *Ladies Home Journal* the following May, both Lynn and Redmond, who had initiated the idea, were ready to let it go. Susan Hall, however, the one most seriously hurt and exhausted from the ordeal, appeared to have taken the high road. She said she would make plans to tackle another mountain, this time Alaska's Mount McKinley, which is nearly a mile higher than Rainier. "Physically, Rainier got the best of me," she said. "But next time I'll be stronger."

Examples of these types of situations are everywhere, even in Hollywood, the land of movies and make-believe. A number of Hollywood executives have decided to take dangerous "power trips," where they are engaged in one form or another of a high-risk extreme sport. Producer Charles Schlissel found himself three-quarters of the way up the 6,000-foot mountain face known as the Eiger Nordwand in the Swiss Alps several years ago. Sitting in a porta-ledge with the windchill outside some 40 degrees below zero, his left foot throbbing from a bruised tendon, Schlissel finally assessed his situation by thinking, "I'm a little over my head here."

Though he ultimately completed his journey, and went on other trips that included rock climbing, scuba diving, and white water rafting, Schlissel told a magazine interviewer that his numerous forays into the extreme were similar to his need to succeed in Hollywood. "Generally the people who have the most success in this town are the people who really push their way through things," he said. "The whole premise of this industry is 'I can do whatever I want, I can achieve whatever I want.' "

If you believe that, is it really difficult to accept the same person trying to climb the Eiger Nordwand? Of course, there aren't always Hollywood endings. A onetime Warner Brothers president, Frank Wells left his job to try to scale the Seven Summits, the highest peaks on each of the world's continents. He ultimately conquered all but Everest, then returned to another top executive position with the Walt Disney Company. A short time later Wells was killed in a helicopter crash while heli-skiing in the back mountains of Nevada.

What is it, then, that gets into the blood of those who live on the edge? What makes people want to go higher, faster, find more difficult climbs, jump in new and more dangerous ways, and increase the rush that makes them feel good? This is a multilayered question that can't be answered with one definitive statement, or by examining only a single group of athletes from a single sport.

Freestyle snowboarder Rob DaFoe believes, "When you're on a mountain and looking for a cliff to jump, you try to pick the hardest line to go down. Anybody can take the easy ones. It's both a poker game and a personal challenge. The best feeling is to go where no one else wants to go. It's the idea of competing, finding challenges, and having a personal fight with yourself. You're almost fighting your own mind, looking to push yourself. And in a sense, it's still somewhat of a dare—*I can do something you can't.*"

It's apparent, however, that not all athletes are the same, and all the risk takers, even the one-timers, have different motivations, drives, and desires. Some may be trying to overcome a fear, a fear that has absolutely nothing to do with a high-risk sport. Others may want to exorcize some personal demons, free themselves to make other decisions or live a different kind of life. Then there are those who simply want the rush, the exhilaration that comes with putting it all on the line. Some of them eventually choose to make their high-risk pursuits a lifestyle. These are the people who feel they are truly alive only when hurtling down a mountain, or free falling from a plane, or striving to reach the summit of an angry mountain.

That's what makes the high-risk lifestyle so fascinating, and even mysterious. The average person is not about to jump from an airplane and free fall several thousand feet as the ground rushes up at him with seemingly increasing speed, or try to take a surfboard into a killer wave sixty feet high and ready to break. In fact, many people are very hesitant even to climb aboard a nasty roller-coaster at a local amusement park. Yet the numbers of those heading out to the edge are increasing at a steady rate. In fact, many of those who have studied and dealt with people who participate in a high-risk and adventurous lifestyle feel that these endeavors may eventually become the major spectator and participation sports of the new century. As psychologist Frank Farley of Temple University, who has made a study of high-risk behavior and those who seek it, said:

"Baseball will become a minor sport. Sports that involve speed, variety, and change will replace it. Sports that are closer to the central character of this country."

1

THERE WERE

ALWAYS PEOPLE

BEING EXTREME

There is a romantic quality about participating in high-risk sports. It almost takes the place of things that happened in the past, such as the majesty of sword fights with the winner the one who gets the girl.

— Rob DaFoe, freestyle snowboarder

UNTIL a relatively short time ago, there were no extreme sports. In fact, when you consider the whole history of mankind, organized sports of any kind have existed for a very short time. Human nature, however, hasn't changed that much since man first walked on the earth. In those earliest of days, nearly everyone lived on the edge simply because every day was a matter of survival. Would the hunt for food be successful? Would a family or group fall prey to hungry wild animals? Would a violent storm spring up when there was no adequate shelter close by? Just staying safe was a huge task in itself. Whether the species' penchant for taking risks and putting themselves on the line has been a function of the human personality since the beginning is certainly a viable thesis. Back in prehistoric days, there was no choice. Life or death was a daily crapshoot and the choice to remain safe and secure was rarely available. Like the animals they lived with, mankind had a simple daily task—survival.

Once civilization began encroaching upon various parts of the world, people began feeling safer. There were, however, still worlds to conquer and new frontiers to explore. Only now people had choice. It was only the most adventurous who decided to go out to the extreme. In America, these were the original explorers who arrived from Europe. These were men and women who were willing to brave the dangers of the oceans by sailing in small, wooden ships looking for new lands that were not on an existing map. Those who settled then explored the new land were going out on the edge as well. They courted danger with every mountain they crossed, every stranger they met, every step that took them farther away from civilization.

Settlers who left fairly secure homes in America's East to travel by wagon train in search of new lives in the West during the 1840s also embarked on a high-risk adventure. The safety of an entire family might be at stake during this long and arduous journey. What was it that separated those who decided to take the plunge and go, from those who didn't want to risk life and limb and chose to stay home? Maybe some heard stories of unclaimed riches in the West, gold there for the taking, or perhaps unsettled fertile lands that could be claimed for farming. Those with the strongest motivations decided to brave the dangers and take the plunge.

This sense of high-risk adventure continued as long as there were frontiers to tame and conquer. The image of the Western lawman, walking resolutely down the main street of town to face a villain in a gunfight, still piques the imagination of armchair cowboys everywhere. How many films have been made about the Gunfight at the OK Corral, in which the Earp brothers and Doc Holiday faced down a group of allegedly evil villains? The romance and risk of the Old West often meant living on the edge with a Colt-45 strapped to your waist.

Early in the twentieth century, America was quickly becoming more civilized and increasingly mechanized at the same time. Conventional sports such as baseball, basketball, hockey, and football were beginning to attract young people as a way to have fun. Eventually, they would also offer a way to make a living. Though it took a great deal of physical skill and talent to excel at these sports, and there was a risk of injury, the stakes rarely rose to the level of life and death. That was left for other kinds of pioneers. Despite an increasingly safe society, people continued to step out onto the edge in new and different ways. Sometimes it was to test innovative and potentially dangerous manmade machines, such as aircraft. In the years following the Wright brothers' success at Kitty Hawk, aircraft technology improved rapidly. Test pilots were needed to fly new and often experimental machines. These were pioneers willing to risk it all for the combination of their love of flying and the opportunity to earn some money. Flyers and test pilots are not so different from extreme athletes today, and they continued their own high-risk traditions, which led to piloting the first jet planes, breaking the sound barrier, and eventually flying into outer space and walking on the moon.

Other aviators also looked for "firsts" in a young industry that was attracting increasingly more attention among the general public. When Charles Lindbergh climbed into the cockpit of his plane, *The Spirit of St. Louis*, in 1927, and became the first man to fly alone across the Atlantic Ocean, he also became a national hero. His unprecedented flight somehow captured the imagination of those on both sides of the ocean. Today, Lindbergh is remembered not only as a pioneer of aviation, but also as a man willing to go to the extreme for something he believed possible and important. He knew full well what the consequences could be. Just a single engine malfunction, an unexpected violent storm, a miscalculation in his course, and Lindbergh would not have made it. Instead of being a national hero, he would have become just another guy who was killed doing something "crazy."

With life becoming safer and society more protective, those who opted to continue taking risks often had their sanity questioned, something that is not uncommon with extreme athletes today. Then, as now, such labels weren't enough to stop people. Amelia Earhart proved that when she began making solo flights. Although she, along with navigator Fred Noonan, disappeared in 1937 while trying to fly a small plane around the world, Earhart is rarely referred to as crazy, but rather as courageous. Perceptions can change very rapidly, altered by the slightest shift in circumstance. The crazy people went over Niagara Falls in a barrel (a common stunt undertaken back in the 1920s); the courageous ones tried to fly around the world. Both, however, were going out to the extreme by their own free choice.

Exploring new and dangerous parts of the world has always fascinated people with the propensity to go out to the edge. Two of the last desolate and largely unknown areas were the North and the South Poles. Explorers reached the North Pole for the first time in 1909, and not surprisingly, the South Pole became the next goal shortly after that. Located deep within Antarctica, most of the area is covered by ice frozen solid by winter temperatures that can plunge to minus 120 degrees Fahrenheit. Winter darkness there lasts six months and the winds often roar across open and unprotected ice.

Two separate expeditions set out in 1911, each wanting to be the first to reach the pole. One was led by Norwegian Roald Amundsen, the other by Englishman Robert Scott, and to make things more interesting, the two expeditions approached the Pole from different directions. Amundsen's team had the luck of traveling in better weather, and they reached the Pole on December 14. Scott's group, however, was besieged by blizzards and bad decisions. For example, they had brought ponies instead of dogs, a fatal error in a harsh climate that resulted in the animals' deaths and little help to them. Despite all the hardships, they finally made it to the South Pole on January 17, 1912, only to find that Amundsen had already been there and gone.

The Amundsen team made it back safely, actually sledding and skiing part of the way. Scott's return trip, however, turned into a disaster. The fuel they had brought for fires leaked from its containers. Supplies left along the way for the return trip couldn't be found, as blowing snow covered the markers. The men faced frostbite and scurvy, and soon team members began to die. Those remaining struggled into March when blizzards came again. Everyone else, including Scott, finally succumbed, the last ones dying just eleven miles from a supply of food and fuel.

The lesson is simple. Those who are the most fully prepared have the best chance of survival. For example, dogs and not ponies were the correct animal to bring to Antarctica. Fresh seal meat (Amundsen's choice of food) was a better source of vitamin C than the canned meat brought by Scott's team. It prevented Amundsen's men from contracting scurvy, kept them healthier and more vigorous. Then there was pure luck. This time, weather turned out to be the X-factor. It was good for Amundsen, free of storms and blizzard; yet just the opposite for Scott. These are all factors that expedition mountain climbers, for example, must be aware of, even today.

Perhaps the extreme behavior from the early days of the century that most closely foreshadowed the future was the desire to climb mountains. Not surprisingly, the mountain that received the most notoriety in the early years was Everest. As far back as 1852, the Great Trigonometrical Survey of India determined that Everest was the highest mountain in the world. It got its present name in 1865, named after British Surveyor General George Everest, but it wasn't until 1920, however, that Westerners could begin scaling it. That was when the thirteenth Dalai Lama opened Tibet to outsiders and allowed people to enter the country for the sole purpose of trying to climb Mount Everest. The first attempt came in 1921 by a British team that included a man named George Mallory. They weren't successful, but three years later Mallory returned to lead another expedition, the one that would result in the beginning of the legend and the mystique that has characterized the mountain ever since.

At the time of Mallory's 1924 attempt, no climber had been above 24,600 feet, and it was still not known if humans could survive any higher without supplemental oxygen. For this second try, Mallory took oxygen bottles, but no one was sure how well they would work, or whether they might leak, rendering them useless when they were needed the most. Without using the oxygen, the team failed to go above 28,125 feet. Then on the morning of June 6, Mallory and twenty-two-year-old Andrew "Sandy" Irvine decided to make one last assault on the summit, taking the oxygen bottles with them. They started from the top of the North Col, at 23,100 feet, with the feeling they would need three days. They were last seen through the mist in the early afternoon of June 8, by a geologist named Noel Odell, who had followed behind for support. Odell said he saw two black figures, the size of dots, approaching and then climbing a rock step, called the Second Step. It was near the base of the summit pyramid. Odell felt they looked strong enough to make it, but then clouds covered them and they were never seen again.

To this day, some feel that Mallory and Irvine made it, but were lost when they tried to descend back to camp, something that has happened to many climbers since. In 1933, an ice axe was found at 27,750 feet, right along the route they were taking. It had three nick marks on it, characteristic of marks Sandy Irvine was known to put on some of his equipment. Then in 1975, a body was found 750 feet below where the ice axe was discovered, but there was no direct evidence that the body was that of Irvine or Mallory. The two simply disappeared into the mythology of the mountain. Everest was finally conquered by Edmund Hillary and Tenzing Norgay in 1953, and the lure of the mountain has only grown since, especially in recent years as more people than ever seem to be captivated by the prospect of climbing Everest, and decide they want to try to reach the summit. The story of Mallory and Irvine, had it happened elsewhere, would undoubtedly be largely forgotten by now. Because it happened on Mount Everest, however, their names are well known today to almost everyone who wants to attempt the world's highest peaks.

Obviously, behavior that is considered risky and dangerous has been part of the human condition for thousands of years. Since the beginning of time, for example, man has been captivated by flying. The artist and scientist Leonardo Da Vinci tried to find a concept for a flying machine as far back the fifteenth and sixteenth centuries. Even after the Wright Brothers flew the first successful airplane, man continued to think about free flight, a way to emulate birds. Obviously, those willing to go to the extreme for their times wanted to "catch air," in the same way sky divers, para and hang gliders, and BASE jumpers do today. BASE jumper Mick Knutson, in fact, has documented the earliest recorded jump from tall objects as being way back in the Middle Ages. Daredevils of the time jumped off towers with various designs of free fall inhibitors, usually made with some sort of rudimentary wood frame. Sadly, in most of these early cases, the know-how and skills weren't enough to design a safe way to break the fall, especially not with the raw materials available then. The majority of these early attempts ended in disaster.

Through the years the groundwork for the extreme lifestyle was being set forth by brave and adventurous men and women who wanted more than a routine, everyday existence. They wanted to explore the unknown and try to achieve something that others said couldn't be done. The bottom line is simply that the nature of man hasn't changed much. The extreme was always there. Those stepping out on the edge today are combining what has been with what is, and are determined to take it to a place they want it to be.

2

THE PSYCHOLOGY

OF RISK

The biggest risk is definitely death. That's how extreme this sport is. It can kill you. Beyond reason, beyond doubt, that wave can kill you. But on the same note, that's what drives a lot of us to do extreme things, that rush of knowing that you did something that was on the edge.

—Archie Kalepa, big wave surfer

EVERYONE takes risks. While that is simply an undeniable fact of life, it certainly does not mean that every risk poses the same amount of danger. What is it then that makes some people take the bigger risks—the ones where the odds of something going wrong rise dramatically—as opposed to the everyday risks that are just part of normal living? Kids take risks almost from the time they are born. The first time they get up the courage to walk up stairs on their own, they are unwittingly taking a risk. When they climb up on their toy box and decide to jump off instead of climbing down, they are taking another. It is recognized by experts on child development that risk plays a major role in the maturation of adolescents and young adults. Writing in *Camping Magazine*, Bob Ditter explained how risk taking is a necessity for youngsters as they grow.

"Risk-taking is the way that children expand their horizons," Ditter wrote, "learn about new worlds, stretch themselves beyond their current sense of their own abilities, and, in short, gain mastery over new challenges . . . Those children who engage in successful, healthy risk-taking are the ones whose self-esteem tends to be strongest and most resilient."

At some point in the growth process, however, risk begins to divide into two distinct categories—healthy and unhealthy. Healthy risks for adolescents include activities such as participation in sports, the development of creative and artistic abilities, contributions to family and community, volunteer work, making positive friendships, continuing to learn, and setting goals. By contrast, negative or unhealthy risks include drug, alcohol, and tobacco use, unsafe sexual activity, committing misdemeanors and/or crimes, reckless driving, getting into fights, and choosing undesirable friends. Healthy risk can expand the horizons of young persons, helping to propel them into early adulthood where they will make sound decisions, continue to take positive, healthy risks, and live an overall productive and fulfilling life. Unhealthy risk can, pure and simple, only lead to more trouble. At least that's the way it's supposed to work.

Where, however, does degree of risk fit into the world of extreme sports? Can you make a case that those who follow a high-risk adventurous lifestyle come from a group who took the so-called bad or unhealthy risks as youngsters? Or perhaps high-risk adults always took bigger risks, even as children? As with so many other professions, occupations, and hobbies, the participants come from a myriad of backgrounds. In some of the cases, however, the risks taken growing up are definitely higher and more potentially dangerous than those taken by the other youngsters. However, with the exception of the fact that the high risk might lead to injury, it doesn't necessarily have to be considered negative behavior.

Not surprisingly, though, there were some future daring athletes who came out of that bad risk background, their early problems dictated by the same personality traits that would eventually lead them into the world of the extreme. Radical skier Kristen Ulmer says she wasn't very athletic as a child and admits she made some bad choices early. "I got into drugs and alcohol at an early age," she said. "It was very unusual at that time because I was just thirteen. Then, at age fourteen, I quit all that. When I did it, though, I did it one hundred percent. So I think I have the tendency in my personality to be an extreme person. Though I was always very aggressive, I wasn't focused. The focus came when I discovered skiing."

Miles Daisher, who would become a multisport high-risk athlete, remembers his early years as an Air Force brat, traveling with his family from one base to another, both in the United States and abroad. It didn't always make him happy.

"I played a lot of soccer and baseball when I was young," Daisher said, "but when I was in Greece with my family, I failed history and wasn't allowed to participate in school sports. That's when I guess I started being a bad kid. I was so mad I couldn't play that I began turning into a rebel."

Some of that rebelliousness led him to begin taking risks. He became a big fan of the Burt Reynolds stunt man movie, *Hooper*, and soon was trying to emulate his hero.

"I used to have all these rope swings in my front yard," he said, laughing at the memory. "My friends and I would jump off the roofs of our houses, jump our BMX bikes off a ramp into the water, and dig giant ditches so we could come out of them on our bikes and fly through the air. As a result, I was hurt a lot as a kid. I broke my ankle a few times and once broke my pinky so bad that I had a cast almost all the way up my arm. I was injured a lot until I got into college. When I look back at it, I think where I am now is a culmination of everything I did as a kid growing up."

Alpine mountaineer Sharon Wood was another who was searching for an outlet early on to offset what she remembers as extreme boredom. "I grew up in Vancouver [British Columbia], played a few team sports, but was always more attracted to individual sports," she said. "I was hungry for adventure from an early age and used to go off on long bike trips, all by myself, just ride across the city and find new routes. But I was also stuck in this suburban environment, which was very frustrating to me. So I didn't really express this adventurous attitude as I could have. When I was younger, I was right on the brink of juvenile delinquency.

"I was definitely searching for an outlet to express what I felt was my essence. I loved situations that involved adventure. I defined it as embarking on a journey where the outcome was uncertain. I like what that brings out in me. My father was as aircraft carrier pilot, which was pretty high risk. He always encouraged me to pursue my own interests and I think some of the best advice he ever gave me was don't wait for your friends to do with you whatever it is you want to do. Go there and meet new people."

Snowboarder Circe Wallace feels that discovering her sport at an early age (fourteen) became a healthy outlet for her. She, too, began opting for higher risks and it could have gone the wrong way.

"I grew up in Eugene, Oregon," she explained, "and there was a real drug and hippie culture there in the 1980s. That made it a difficult place to grow up. I was a little bit of a troublemaker and skateboarding became a healthy outlet for me. I did ten years of dance, modern and jazz, starting when I was two or three, but I also remember taking chances. I was always breaking stuff from friends daring me to do things. I broke my scapula after someone dared me to run down a slide, and I totally banged myself up a few times on roller skates, including a time I was clotheslined racing to a swing set and had to get ten stitches in my eye.

"But the first time I strapped a snowboard on, I fell in love with it. That was the ultimate healthy outlet. I think I've always been one of those people who want to push the limits of my own abilities. I have competitive tendencies and I've always had friends who were a little bit older and who were pushing me to test the limits of my strength and ability."

With the kind of personality she now realizes was always there, Circe Wallace is undoubtedly fortunate that she found the right outlet when she did. Not all high-risk athletes, however, followed the same route. Climbers Abby Watkins and Kim Csizmazia, for example, were both products of active, athletic families who did things together. For Csizmazia, the very nature of their activity involved risk.

"My parents were really active," she said. "We started out alpine skiing together, then my parents got into cross-country skiing. I grew up among very active kids, both girls and boys, and we were all doing very active stuff. It isn't necessarily risk, because I don't think kids consider things risky. I think it's more of a personality thing. But it seemed as if most of my friends were pretty go-for-it. So I grew up in that atmosphere."

Australian born Abby Watkins grew up surfing, swimming, playing tennis, running track, and spending a great deal of time with gymnastics. "I had a long and very intense gymnastics career, sometimes seven hours a day in the gym," she recalled. "I started climbing when I went to college at Berkeley and it got me back into the incredible outdoors. But I've never felt that I took unnecessary risks."

Big wave surfer Mike Parsons remembers being extremely competitive as a youngster. "I was always the kid that if we bombed a hill on a skateboard, I would definitely bomb it higher than the other guy and make sure I went faster than anyone. I wound up in surfing because it was the most fun. But no matter what I did when I was young, I never considered the possibility of getting hurt. I thought I was indestructible."

For freeskier and BASE jumper Shane McConkey, the risk as a kid involved one primary thing—catching air. "I can't really put a finger on when I realized I liked catching air," McConkey said. "I just found fascination with it. I don't know why. My earliest recollection of high-risk activities is jumping off cliffs into water. I did it with my friends. It's always better to do fun stuff with your friends. Otherwise, you don't have anyone to show off with."

Kevin Quinn, who played professional hockey, and has skied, sky dived, kayaked, and para glided, as well as serving as a guide for big game hunters before starting his own heli-skiing business, comes right out and says he was a high-risk kid. "Yeah, I took a lot of dares growing up in Alaska. I used to build up the snow under the second-story balcony off our deck, then jump off the deck," he said. "When I was about seven or eight, I was jumping off big cliffs into the water. It was just for fun, to be able to fall. When I jumped off the balcony of our deck, I'd do flips and all kinds of things, and never even think about the landing consequences."

Sky diver Jim McCormick and BASE jumper Mick Knutson both became involved with their sport initially to overcome a fear. Neither remembered taking dares as a kid or engaging in high-risk behavior in their early years. But once they became involved in sports that can certainly be risky, something clicked.

For Tom Day, the extreme attitude seemed to come early. A longtime skier who now adds extreme cinematography to his résumé, he followed his family tradition of skiing, hitting the slopes at the tender age of five. Maybe it was because he started so young, but Day never felt that what he was doing was dangerous.

"I was challenged to push myself," he said, "but I don't think I looked at it as a danger. It was more of a let's-give-it-a-try kind of thing. I would look at something and say, 'I think I can do it.' But I also knew that if, for some reason, I didn't make it, I would probably get hurt. I remember breaking my arm in the eighth grade and just losing a single day of skiing. For the next three weeks I went out every day with one pole."

Freestyle motocross rider Mike Metzger was another who followed a family tradition. Both his grandfather and father rode motorcycles and Mike was being given his initial rides while still in diapers. He was riding and racing at an early age, and never thought about risk or injury. Riding was already just a natural part of his life.

"I always had the personality for it," he said. "Looking back to when I was a kid, the risk factor never meant much to me. I never thought about what the risk would be if I didn't do something successfully. It was like I'm going for it, no matter what the risks are. I'm just going to try it because I want to do it."

In contrast to Mike Metzger, who courted risk almost from infancy, there is Carlos Buhler, who grew up in affluent Westchester County, a suburb of New York City, and later attended a private school in Connecticut. No one could have guessed then that Buhler would become one of the world's most accomplished expedition mountaineers, a man as familiar with the "death zone" above 25,000 feet as anyone on the planet. If it weren't for spending summers at a family member's New Mexico ranch, young Carlos may have never discovered the outdoors. Yet he demonstrated virtually no high-risk behavior until he went on a five-week, thirty-five-day wilderness expedition the summer of his fifteenth year.

"It was a wonderful experience," he remembered, "and a total departure from everything I had ever thought about."

It certainly appears that most, but not all, of these high-risk athletes exhibited a tendency toward some kind of higher-than-average risk taking as youngsters, or had a period when their choices included the so-called bad risks. It also seems that most of them already had the kind of personality that would lead them to focus with a rigid determination on whatever they chose to pursue. Most adolescents, whether they are driving a car ninety miles per hour, taking a dare, or jumping off cliffs into water, feel they are indestructible, that nothing can happen to them. As people age, that feeling usually wanes slowly, and a more realistic view of possible consequences evolves. Is there something about these athletes that keeps many of them continuing with their high-risk sports into their thirties, forties, and even beyond? Some think there is.

One theory that has received a good bit of attention says, simply, that America has become too safe for many people, hence the need for increased risk. Some of this may have changed somewhat after the terrorist attacks on the World Trade Center and Pentagon in September 2001, but the theory was developed before that as more people began stepping out on the edge and pursuing high-risk endeavors. Dr. Michael Apter, in his book *The Dangerous Edge: The Psychology of Excitement,* says that "risk taking is essential to human beings. But our safe society has made it more difficult to attain. The safer you make life, the more people feel the need for excitement. Doing extreme sports is one way to feed the need."

Another author, Michael Bane, who wrote *Over the Edge: A Regular Guy's Odyssey in Extreme Sports,* also feels that some people are looking for a kind of life that used to exist, but doesn't anymore. "The trend in society is to eliminate risk," said Bane. "It's gotten to the point where there are no more swings on the playgrounds. At the same time, people are saying, 'Where's Indiana Jones?' People need adventure in their lives."

Snowboarder Rob DaFoe touched on this very same subject when he said, "Life is easy now. There are sometimes no tests at all, so people have to test themselves in other ways. People need that. Your family cat can still go out and hunt, then bring you home a trophy of his adventure. People have to create their own excitement."

Even if this theory is true, and it obviously is to some extent— science and technology have helped create creature comforts that didn't exist 300, 200, 100, and even 50 years ago—those who want more action, adventure, excitement, and risk can certainly find it. But there is a choice. The majority of people still opt to live within the parameters of the day, enjoy their comforts, and venture outside them to whatever degree they choose. That doesn't mean, obviously, that everyone becomes a mountain climber or a BASE jumper, or decides to ski down the most vertical slope they can find as opposed to enjoying a leisurely ski weekend.

One man who feels that personality plays a large role in the risks an individual will take is psychologist Frank Farley of Temple University in Philadelphia. Professor Farley uses the term *Type-T* or *Big T* personality to describe people who tend to be risk takers.

"These people are motivated by risk, uncertainty, novelty, variety," he said. "They thrive in ambiguous situations. They like intense experiences. They are inner-directed. They believe they can control their fate. Whatever comes up, they believe they can handle it."

By contrast, Farley's *small-t* personalities are risk-averse. He says they would never try something such as climbing Mount Everest or any other mountain. Rather they are motivated by certainty and predictability. They are more comfortable repeating familiar experiences as opposed to seeking out new ones. However, Professor Farley feels that the majority of people fall somewhere in between the two types, that they are somewhat adventurous, somewhat willing to take risks, but within reason. That still leaves the so-called extreme athlete as a solitary figure out on the edge. Though most of them can tell you why they actively pursue very dangerous endeavors, risk is only part of the equation. It is a combination of other factors—the by-products of risk—such as the satisfaction or rush, and their overall philosophy of life, that makes the risk worthwhile. So it appears there is no one answer for why these people are willing to take high risks.

Kristen Ulmer, for instance, feels that taking big risks is just part of what she needs in life to find satisfaction.

"I'm addicted to excitement," Ulmer explained. "I have to have something interesting happen every day. It doesn't have to be an adrenaline thing. I don't have to go out and risk my life. That would be really sad if I was like that. Excitement for me can be simply meeting an interesting new person or going shopping to find the perfect leather jacket."

Yet Ulmer has courted death and pain for many years, having been caught in avalanches and having endured seven knee surgeries. Despite everything, she continues to take risks. Perhaps an incident in Alaska not so long ago showed the essence of Ulmer's desire for excitement and adventure. She had gone there for some heli-skiing and the weather wasn't cooperating. Nine days had passed and she wasn't in the air or on her skis once.

"I was starting to get really, really antsy," she explained. "As I said, I'm addicted to excitement and nothing was happening. I won't say I was bored, because only boring people get bored. But I was just craving stimulation of some kind."

What happened next was totally unexpected. Ulmer was hitchhiking back out to the helicopter pad because she had decided to leave and had some business to take care of first. She picks up the story from there.

"I didn't think twice about hitchhiking because everyone does it in Valdez, Alaska. "That's how people get around. This guy in a van picks me up and at first he appeared very nice, said he wasn't doing anything and would give me a ride to the pad, then back as well. It was on the drive home that he really lost it. Apparently, he had just gotten out of prison, been in jail for two years. Suddenly, he started threatening to kill me, rape and sodomize me. He was screaming at the top of his lungs."

Most women in this situation, as high a risk scenario as they could possibly imagine, couldn't be blamed if they panicked and totally freaked out. Many would simply become paralyzed with fear, a totally justifiable reaction under the circumstances. Ulmer's response was completely opposite.

"My first reaction when he started going off on me was, thank God, something interesting is finally happening to me. I mean, I really needed something to show me I was alive after nine days in Alaska." Instead of panicking, she quickly assessed the situation. "I felt, okay, he wasn't saying he *was* going to do this to me and he wasn't pulling the van over to do it. What I did was show a nonchalant, ho-hum attitude toward him while he was screaming. I wasn't giving him a power trip. I just kept up a conversation with him as if I knew him. He had already told me about his life so I just made small talk with him while he was screaming at me. When women aren't totally frightened, it's no fun for a rapist. So I just decided I wasn't going to be scared by him."

Eventually, the man stopped the van and allowed Ulmer to get out. Through his entire tirade, he hadn't touched her. It seems that her experience in dealing with risk, crisis, and in making quick decisions had served her well.

"Sure, I could have possibly been raped and killed," she continued, "but I wasn't, so now it's just an amusing story. I often find it funny that people get so traumatized by things. If I was in a near fatal airplane crash where the plane was going down and then landed, and we were all okay, I'd tell the story with a huge grin on my face."

In other words, you take the risk, know the consequences, deal with it in any way you can to survive, and then it's over. Period. The fact that you have lived to see another day and take another risk—at least in the world of Kristen Ulmer—is the only way to go.

There have been additional theories for extreme behavior. Some feel many of these high-risk personalities are trying to overcome feelings of low self-esteem, but that wouldn't explain why so many have been doing it nearly their entire lives. There is also a theory that people taking high risk have a need to attract attention to themselves, to be admired. In a media-hungry society there may be some truth to that, but then again, people who just want to attract attention to themselves usually do it for the immediate fame and/or the money it can bring. Then it's over. The hard-core athletes in many of these sports, however, are often doing it more for themselves and continue to do it over a lifetime.

To this point, sky diver Jim McCormick remembers a day when a film crew from a TV station showed up at the jump zone to do a story. McCormick, there to spend the day doing what he loved, began chatting with one of the cameramen, who made the following comment:

"We don't call this a camera in our business," the man told McCormick. "It an AM, an *asshole magnet*. You put this on your shoulder and every asshole in the group will introduce himself."

McCormick laughed at the comment. "Then I thought, you put some people on camera and they won't behave any differently," he said. "But you put other people on camera and they'll be like a five-year-old who wants all the attention. I think, however, that it's just a small group that behaves in that manner."

Other theories of risk include one that says people are trying to fend off aging and stay perpetually young; that they are looking for a need to feel omnipotent, conquering the elements they are challenging; or the one with the most finality, that they have a subconscious death wish. On the other side of the coin, yet another theory espouses that high-risk athletes flirt with death in order to chase away their ultimate mortality. You can obviously make a case for all of them, but as with most theories, they simply aren't universal—they don't apply to everyone. High-risk people, especially the athletes, often have personal reasons for what they are doing. In most cases, the risks they take are closely allied with fear, danger, and the satisfactions their sport ultimately provides.

There does, to an extent, seem to be some correlation between risk and age, especially the kind of physical risk needed to pursue the so called extreme sports. Some of the sports, such as radical skiing and snowboarding, freestyle motocross, and big wave surfing, require the strength and athleticism of youth. When athletes in these sports began to feel they are losing some of their skills to age, they will scale back the degree of risk. In some of the other sports—sky diving and BASE jumping, for example—participants can continue much longer and, if they desire to push the buttons, will continue to take the same kinds of risks they took when much younger.

A few athletes will also curtail the degree of risk they are willing to take when their lifestyle changes, such as marrying and perhaps having children. But again, there is no set formula, for this is strictly up to the discretion of the individual. Alex Lowe, the superb mountaineer who was killed by an avalanche in 1999, once explained why he continued to take such enormous risks on some of the highest and most dangerous mountains in the world after becoming the father of three boys.

After his first son was born in 1988, Lowe began to have second thoughts about the kind of climbing he was accustomed to pursuing. Climbing with an old friend in Nepal, Lowe asked the other man, who had a son about five years old at the time, how he felt about continuing dangerous, high-risk climbs. The other man told Lowe a story about his own childhood. When he was about twelve years old, he was out with his father, who ran into an old friend. The friend asked the father if he still scuba dived. His answer was no, not since I had children. At first, Lowe's friend felt proud, picturing his father in scuba gear and exploring the world under the sea. Then he began thinking about what he had heard, and before long he began to feel something akin to guilt. Suddenly, he realized he was the cause of his father no longer doing something he had once loved. That's why he continued to climb, hoping to share his experiences with his kids as they got older.

Lowe listened and soon adopted the same philosophy. His friend said he would teach his children to make good judgments and enjoy risky activities in a positive way. Explained Lowe, "That sums up my philosophy. I don't see myself being out of control in doing what I do in the first place. And I want to turn my kids on to the same pleasure I've experienced in pursuing things like that."

Like many others, Alex Lowe felt that he was controlling the risk. His skills as a mountaineer were so well developed that he did control his situation most of the time. No one, however, can control the weather or the sometimes fickle quality of the snow, and an avalanche ultimately claimed his life. Hopefully, Alex Lowe's three sons will grow to understand the love their father had of the mountains and why he continued to pursue a sport that is considered one of the riskiest on earth.

While risk, indisputably, goes hand in hand with all of the sports discussed so far, there is an interesting feeling among some athletes about the way authorities in the United States look upon their rights to take risks and to choose what they wish to do. Much of the controversy revolves around BASE jumping. Because the practitioners of the sport jump off fixed objects, such as buildings, bridges, antennas, and cliffs, it is illegal in many places. BASE jumper Mick Knutson, who studies all the technical aspects of his sport with the same kind of precision that he exhibits as a trained engineer, feels that there is a hindering mind-set in America that continues to make his sport illegal in many places.

"Every BASE jumper knows there are illegal jumps," Knutson explained. "Most of the outlaw jumps are in the United States. Other countries have really opened up. As of now, I'm going to Malaysia for my second trip. The Malaysian government invites us over to do demonstration jumps off this building. It's fully legal. They've given permission. This is also happening in Germany and Finland, and we are trying to set up jumps in Italy and England. People don't see it like they do here.

"In the United States, everybody wants to be protected. Everyone is afraid of their own self. Everyone wants a big, quick buck. If I died jumping off a building or an antenna, my parents would never think about suing someone because of how I died. They know me. The people I associate with are just like me and I feel fortunate to have friends who think as I do. If I slip and fall, no one is going to sue for a million dollars because the wet floor sign was turned sideways and I couldn't see it. You have to take control of your own life. You've got to take responsibility for your life.

"I don't want the government to take control of my life. I should be able to do anything I want to myself without having someone to protect me. I don't need handrails; I don't need a walking chain. I need to live my life as I choose to live it. Every other country except the United States believes in that. If you were to do something like jumping off a cliff and you broke your leg, in America they have this stupid notion that *we* didn't stop you from jumping. *We're* responsible. That's bullshit. It's stupid and it's wrong. I know what I'm doing. I know the risks and responsibilities that go along with that. I don't put a burden on anybody."

Aerial photographer, sky diver, and BASE jumper Tom Sanders has a similar feeling. He watched his own wife, Jan Davis, plunge to her death at Yosemite's El Capitan when her parachute failed to open, yet he has been hired repeatedly to set up high-risk stunts for major motion pictures. He continues to work in a high-risk profession and follow a high-risk lifestyle, and he feels that in certain situations people in America are being held to too many restrictions.

"America is a great country and I love it," Sanders said, "but I'm not really impressed about it always being the land of the free. This past summer I traveled to France, Italy, and Switzerland. They don't really care if you're para gliding with a parachute off a cliff, or hang gliding, or climbing up the side of a mountain, or if you're lounging by a pool. Whatever you want to do as long as it doesn't hurt anyone else is perfectly fine with them. BASE jumping fits right in there. They're really into all the adventure sports.

"What they are really supporting is the human spirit of adventure. In America, we have this society that believes you're not allowed to get hurt or die, and if you do, it's somebody else's fault. The policy in America is you could get hurt doing that stuff, so you shouldn't be doing it."

Kristen Ulmer's interpretation almost echoes Peter Finch's Academy Award–winning portrayal of the mad newsman in the 1976 film *Network*, who implored everyone to say, *I'm mad as hell and I'm not gonna take it anymore.* Ulmer also questions America's attitude toward risk.

"There is always this notion in America that nobody should take risks," she said. "The toilets are clean, the hamburger meat is cooked to X degrees, and there are a lot of lawyers. American culture is a real scaredy-cat culture, and people are sick of it."

Risk, obviously, is a constant with extreme sports, but at the same time a complex issue. People take risks for various reasons, many of them without category, and the degree of risk varies, as does the perception. Some don't consider the risk to be very great when it actually is. Many feel they can control the risk, when they really can't. Others keep the risk in perspective and make sure they don't step across a certain line. All, however, feel the risk is worth it or they wouldn't be taking it on a regular basis. Dr. Robert Leach, who has treated both conventional as well as high-risk athletes, has watched people take various degrees of risk firsthand for many years. He himself is a lifelong rock climber and sailor who has been in a number of potentially dangerous situations. Dr. Leach feels there are high-risk athletes and then there are *high-risk* athletes. He explains.

"I don't think a lot of these people—at least in my dealings and discussions with them over the years—minimize risk. They don't say, *There is no risk*. The majority fully understand the risk. What they seem to have in common, however, is a feeling that the risk is worth it. And I don't usually find these people stupid. I find people who are ranging from very intelligent to reasonably intelligent.

"However, I think as people go up the skill ladder, that a little division is formed. There are a group of people who are highly skilled and who simply stay where they are, but there is another group who have the same skills, who push the risk level higher. And then there is [a third] subgroup that gets careless a bit. These are the ones I find dangerous, because they endanger others and then endanger themselves. The larger group continues to take the risk and they do it reasonably well. The small group goes on and becomes more dangerous because they become careless, making it an inevitability that something will happen. That's the group I want to really stay away from.

"I don't think that this group is trying to die. I distinctly don't. I think they are planning when they do things, but they continue to put themselves at risk beyond which seems excessive."

According to Dr. Leach, the world of high-risk sports is made up of many diverse individuals, pursuing their sport with different motivations and taking different degrees of risk. To more fully understand this, the sports themselves and the people who pursue them need to be examined. Before that, however, here's yet another reason for taking risk, one that might well neutralize all the others.

Asked why he is involved with two separate sports (freestyle

skiing and BASE jumping) that both pose a high risk, and if something in his personality always brings him to a place where risk is
continually a partner, Shane McConkey answered quickly.

"People have done a lot of studies that say high-risk people
have traits in their genes. I don't know if that's true or not. But for
me, it's simply the need to have fun. It's how I enjoy my life. While
it's totally sports, I also see it almost as art."

3

THE ADVENTURE OF THE EXTREME— JUMPING AND FLYING

We were all part of the rope flying in Yosemite. I had one jump and it was one of the craziest, neatest things I had ever done in my life. I look back and say, man, I'm glad I had that opportunity. But I can tell you hon-estly, I don't ever want that opportunity again.

—Kevin Quinn, skier, sky diver, BASE jumper

THERE are a number of adventure sports that come under the general category of jumping and flying. There is sky diving, by far the most popular, and perhaps the safest overall. Then there is BASE jumping, where the participant jumps off a fixed object, rather than out of a plane. Most radical of all, perhaps, is the sport of rope free flying, a sport the late Dan Osman described as "flossing the sky." Let's look at the most popular of these jumping and flying sports, the dangers involved, and what it takes to pursue them successfully.

Sky Diving

Before there was a sport called sky diving, parachute jumping was associated with the military. World War II paratroopers jumped into battle using round parachutes over which they had little control. In the years following the war, civilians slowly began to discover parachute jumping as a sport. Since then, jumping has changed dramatically. As with so many of the adventure sports, improvements in equipment have given the practitioner more control, more latitude, and the ability to do more things. Rectangular-shaped chutes now allow sky divers to control their canopies and not be victims to the vagaries of the winds.

There have also been dramatic changes in the way people approach the sport today When it was still called parachute jumping, a person would simply leave the plane, deploy the chute immediately, and float to the ground. That can be quite an experience in itself for someone who has never done it previously. Before long, however, veteran jumpers began to feel it wasn't enough. What if, they thought, we don't deploy the chute until we are much closer to the ground? Thus a new element was added—free fall—and the sport of sky diving was born. The jumper could now fall thousands of feet through the air at high speeds before deploying his chute and landing safely. Jim McCormick remembers reading about how commandos were trained when he was maybe ten or eleven years old. Before he went to college, he established a list of life's goals and making a single sky dive was one of them. Though he admits that jumping from an airplane was not something he was predisposed to do, McCormick finally decided to take up the challenge of fulfilling the goal he had set years before.

"I wanted to have the experience, prove to myself I could do it," he said, "and I wanted to bolster my courage and my confidence. That was what was driving me to do it."

Then something unexpected happened in the time it took McCormick to reach the ground on that initial jump. "My first words when I landed were, 'That was great; I want to do it again.' I said it was phenomenal immediately. I didn't know what had taken place emotionally, but I knew I wanted that same experience again. I wanted to try it one more time. I wanted to experience more of it than I was able to experience the first time. With so much happening at once, the body has trouble processing the various inputs simultaneously."

McCormick had experienced something that occurs in a number of high-risk sports, a phenomena called sensory overload. "Your body shuts down some of its inputs because you can only process so much," he explained. "People told me to keep going because I'd have a so much richer experience the second, third, and fourth time.

"What happens with sensory overload is that some people just stop accepting input from some of their senses. A classic example is if a person feels frightened, he'll close his eyes. It doesn't make anything go away, but it's one less thing that's being activated. People will land after a first sky dive and say things like, 'I don't think I was breathing.' Obviously, they were, but they just weren't aware of it. Their sense of smell may go away, or their sense of hearing may stop functioning. Sky diving is very loud. You're traveling at 120 miles an hour, but it's just like there is a traffic jam at the central processing unit, and some of it shuts down. You may not hear the wind at all."

McCormick has admitted that having the knowledge that each jump may theoretically be a jumper's last is often one of the elements that attracts people to the sport. Yet, he also feels that conventional sky diving as practiced today has become relatively safe . . . if it is done right and the jumper follows all the rules of safety. "From the unschooled eye, you see someone hurling themselves out of a plane," he said, "and if everything goes right, they open a parachute and maybe live through the experience. That's a commonly held perception of what's taking place and it's very far from the truth."

To explain his sport more fully, McCormick began by praising the planes, saying that recreational sky divers in the United States are now lucky enough to have quality aircraft at their disposal that will allow the sky diver to jump from 13,000, 14,000, or 15,000 feet. Not only does that give the jumper a lot of time in free fall, but if something goes wrong, there should be enough time to correct it. McCormick also said that virtually every sky diver leaving the plane has a visual altimeter, either on the chest strap or on the wrist. He or she also has an audible altimeter inside their helmet, connected directly to their ear. This will activate at three predetermined altitudes and can be set by the jumper to remind him just where he is. However, that isn't all.

"More than fifty percent of the sky-diving community has automatic activating devices in their rig," McCormick explained. "If you get past a certain altitude and you're still in free fall, it will automatically open your reserve parachute. Every sky diver who jumps legally in this country has to have a second parachute. We all jump with a reserve. It has to be fully inspected and repacked every 120 days by a Federal Aviation Administration (FAA)–licensed rigger. It may take me ten minutes to pack my main chute, but it will take the rigger a couple of hours to repack my reserve chute. Then it gets closed, sealed, and signed. Whenever we show up at a jump facility, we have to show the documentation that the reserve chute has been repacked in the last 120 days. That's the level of detail involved in the sport."

Another aspect of sky diving that most people don't understand is how different the ground appears from 15,000 feet. People may think that as soon as a jumper leaves the plane and begins descending, he sees the ground coming at him like gangbusters. Mick Knutson, who began sky diving before he switched to BASE jumping, says that nothing is further from the truth. "In sky diving, you don't lose your stomach," Knutson explained. "You don't get the sensation of falling at all, and you don't get a visual falling either. Your eyes can only gauge what we call ground rush within 2,000 feet of an object. So if you're jumping at 15,000 feet and you open at 3,000 feet, you never really see the ground coming up at you fast. Never."

Tom Sanders, the aerial photographer who has all kinds of sky-diving and BASE-jumping experience, began when he took a class designed to build self-confidence. One of the assignments was to find a challenge, something he really didn't want to do, and then go ahead and do it.

"That was in 1978. I was a carpenter then," Sanders recalled, "and sky diving wasn't a popular sport. In fact, people were still using the round parachutes. I initially jumped to overcome a fear of heights, and soon after began photographing other sky divers out at the jump zone. I've been doing all kinds of things in the air and with my cameras ever since."

Sanders, of course, has gone through all phases of sky diving and BASE jumping, both as a photographer and a participant. As far as taking a leisurely sky dive now, he doesn't look upon it as anything dangerous at all. "To me it's pure human flight," he said. "Almost all regular sky dives are relaxing and satisfying. It's very peaceful, a lot of fun, and an incredible experience to body surf across the sky. The parachute ride is quiet and peaceful, allowing you to enjoy the scenery. It's a very satisfying sport."

As with the other high-risk, adventure sports, there are various degrees of sky diving, various ways sky divers can test themselves and push the envelope. Jim McCormick says there is a very broad line separating the recreational sky diver from those who pursue the sport on a regular basis for many years. "I think it's important to know that ninety-nine percent of people sky dive just once," he said. "One percent jump more than once. That leaves just a small percentage who become regular recreational sky divers. So you can imagine how few take it to other levels."

Jim McCormick, for one, has. Besides just going out to the jump zone and enjoying a day of leisurely sky diving, McCormick has done both exhibition sky dives, for which he is paid, and has also jumped from very high altitudes, something he has done for himself. In both cases, however, he plans his jumps very carefully. "In exhibition sky dives, high-altitude sky dives, and even in large formation sky dives (multiple persons jumping together), you're adding additional risks, no question about it," McCormick explained. "Each time you do it, you're dropping the odds and you have to be looking at all the variables involved. It's a matter of how well you prepare yourself for it."

McCormick says he hates to hear stories about sky dives that go awry because he feels that, for the most part, it's a lack of preparation, human error. "I will never do an exhibition sky dive without walking the landing area first," he said. "When it's a sky dive out of town, before I assess whether it's even possible, I have to receive an aerial photograph, and I'll commonly talk to sky divers who live in the area and ask if they are familiar with the location, ask what they think of it, and whether there is something I'm not noticing on the photo.

"I'll do things like have smoke canisters open when my parachute opens so I can tell what direction the wind is blowing, what speeds it's blowing at, what characteristics it's showing, such as any swirling effects. Sometimes before I go to the airport for an exhibition dive, I'll release helium balloons one at a time and watch what they do as they ascend. What is happening on the ground and what is happening in the air can be different. One of the things that's a concern to me is knowing that every time I do an exhibition jump, I'm an ambassador for the sport. It pains me to see people not doing things well because it discredits the sport and makes us look like a bunch of goofballs that have a death wish. Nothing could be further from the truth."

Though Jim McCormick's approach to his sport is one of careful preparation, check and double-check, he still takes an occasional turn on the edge, though still with a step-by-step plan. His desire to jump from high altitude was just such a turn. "I fly a lot commercially," he said, "and I thought it would be a joy to look out the window of a commercial airliner and say, 'Yeah, I jumped from this altitude.' Prior to that, I always wondered if I could jump from way up there."

Way up there was 31,000 feet, and it does take some unique preparation and equipment. The first thing McCormick needed was an FAA medical certificate that stated his body was in sufficient condition to withstand the forces that a sky diver will experience jumping from that height. Once he had that, he went through a day of flight physiology training provided by the Air Force, then he had to go through depressurization simulation in a high-altitude chamber, the same as used by Air Force pilots who fly at extremely high altitudes. In addition, he went into an oxygen deprivation chamber to see how hypoxia (the term for oxygen deprivation) manifests itself in his body.

"Everyone reacts differently to hypoxia," McCormick explained. "What I learned was that my lips turned purple, the area under my fingernails turned purple, and my peripheral vision became so profoundly limited that it appeared as if I was looking at the world through a cardboard paper towel roll. By doing that, I would be able to realize that if any of those things happened while I was in a high-altitude environment, there was an oxygen problem."

Next he had to do a conventional jump while wearing the high-altitude equipment. That included a military helmet, visor, and mask. After that, he would prebreathe pure oxygen for forty-five minutes, then jump from 24,000 feet, taking the mask off just before he left the plane. That done, he was ready. McCormick actually did two jumps. The first was from 28,500 feet. Weather conditions wouldn't allow the aircraft to go higher. The second time he made his 31,000-foot goal. Since you need oxygen above 24,000 feet, he had a bottle fastened to the leg strap of his parachute rig with a hose leading up to the mask. As he left the plane, he activated the bottle of oxygen.

"It's very cold when you leave the plane, maybe thirty or forty degrees below zero," he said. "You're so high that things look differently. Even the color of the atmosphere is different. You're moving faster but I can't honestly say you have a sensation of it. The free fall last about two minutes and forty seconds, compared to sixty or seventy seconds with an average jump from 15,000 feet. It was quite an experience and something I simply wanted to prove to myself that I could do."

Yet with all the different sky dives he's done, Jim McCormick doesn't consider himself a daredevil. "Evel Knievel is the common perception of a daredevil," he said. "Most people would name him if asked. That really bothers me. While I have profound respect for the man and what he has accomplished, he's doing it in such a way that there is an exceedingly high likelihood of severe personal injury, and that to me is insane. I won't do anything where there is a high likelihood of personal injury."

Jim McCormick is a fine example of an athlete who participates in an acknowledged high-risk sport yet takes extreme care and preparation to minimize that very risk. Many longtime sky divers follow similar patterns. Yet because sky diving was one of the first of the adventure sports to become popular, there was sometimes a perception that sky divers—or anyone doing something risky that was considered out of the norm—had some kind of death wish. A world champion sky diver, Cheryl Stearns, feels that she minimizes risk by always being in control.

"People think sky diving is death-defying," she once said. "But it isn't, unless you don't respect the sport. I know what I'm doing. I have two parachutes. I pack them; I choose when to jump. I don't do anything stupid. I stay in control. I realize the sport isn't for everybody and that it takes a special person to jump out of a plane. You need self-assurance, an open mind, and an affinity for excitement. But not, I was surprised to learn, a desire to go out in a blaze of glory. I don't have a death wish. I am not trying to endanger my life."

Yet as with all sports, both the conventional and the high-risk, improvements in equipment and young athletes with "attitude" are taking them in new and different directions. With adventure sports, this sometimes means more danger. Tom Sanders has seen this happening in sky diving firsthand. He himself has set up extremely dangerous sky-diving stunts for films such as *Drop Zone* and *Point Break*. Because of his work, he makes sure he has a thorough knowledge of all the new developments in the sport, as well as closely observing the youngsters who are beginning to sky dive.

"In a sense, sky diving has become more of a mainstream sport and is so safe in many ways that there are many more people trying it who would not have dared in earlier days," Sanders said. "The sport is easier, the equipment is smaller, and the new chutes land softer. So there is a different caliber of people who now sky dive and a kind of sky diving going on today that we would never have thought of twenty years ago. There are, however, two sides to it. Kids are always on the edge of every sport. They look to set new records and they're definitely taking the sport into areas that are phenomenal and great, and that can be done safely. With the equipment, it's a natural progression. So it's possible for someone to do something that might be considered crazy today that five years from now will be considered mainstream again. But unfortunately, there's a flipside to that.

"We have more people killed sky diving under a perfectly good open parachute than any other way simply because the parachutes are so fast now. That's part of the sport that is appealing to a lot of people, because the chutes are capable of turning very low to the ground, then flattening out the glide so that the sky diver can skim across the water or ground very low, almost buzzing it. It works great if you're really, really good and don't make mistakes."

Sanders explained that the advent of the rectangular parachute initially gave the sky diver much more control and steerability. Today's chutes are even more maneuverable. "It's really a big step further. They have a different type of airflow and tend to be much smaller and go much faster. It now like they're Ferraris and Porsches, where they used to be Cadillacs. Before that they were Volkswagons. The round parachute was good and reliable, and got you to the ground. But you thumped pretty hard, and they weren't very steerable if there was any wind. Now the parachute has progressed to a very efficient airflow, and it's very fast and very deadly. That's where we have most of our fatalities now, the jumper making a mistake under a very fast chute. He's either trying something he hasn't practiced enough but maybe watched someone else do, or he just gets careless."

So while conventional sky diving is now, in many ways, a very safe sport, just the nature of the act still invites participants to look for the extreme and the danger, and it doesn't always turn out well. In February 2001, six sky divers decided to jump from a plane at the South Pole. They went on an organized adventure trip, undoubtedly with the desire to sky dive in a different locale, maybe to look for a greater challenge. Something went wrong and three of the six were killed; their parachutes never opened. The consensus was that the accident was not caused by equipment failure, but rather by a terrible error in judgment. Conditions at the South Pole are very different from most other areas. Antarctica is not California, or even Minnesota. Prior to the jump, very few people had sky dived in that area, so very little was known about jumping conditions. Yet people are drawn there, even paying thousands of dollars to be taken on an organized trip. Nadia Eckhardt, who works for a company that takes people to Antarctica, didn't mince words when it came to the danger involved.

"It's totally unpredictable [in Antarctica]," she said. "It really is the last frontier. The weather might be calm and suddenly the winds are up and the weather is bad."

Yet people who might not be totally prepared decide they want to sky dive there. Even the knowledge that three sky divers were killed sometimes serves to bring others to the same place. Again, it's the adventure, the challenge, the risk. As Eckhardt also said, "It's sad, but that's part of the appeal."

Mike McDowell, who is the director of Adventure Network International, a London company that takes people to Antarctica, is also very much aware of the risk. He insists people on his tours carry insurance since a rescue can cost upwards of $100,000. "It's a different breed that comes down to Antarctica than those who go on a weekend hike," he said. "You better be prepared, for the chances of something bad happening are significantly higher. It's the most wonderful place in the world. When you come down here, you get polar fever. It's spectacular. You feel very free down there, but you also feel very, very small."

In the case of the three sky divers who were killed, they had obviously decided to take their sport out to a dangerous edge, a place where the avid sky diver who emphasizes safety first would never go. Again, that's what seems to happen with all of the adventure sports. People work hard at them, learn all the skills, know all the safety measures that should be taken, and still sometimes decide to test both the limits of the sport and the limits of themselves. Tom Sanders, for one, has seen many changes in the sport over the years. While he feels that many people still perceive sky diving as a trip from a plane to the ground, he knows there is a lot more to it than that.

"It's even pretty elementary today to leave the plane, body surf across the sky, and fly over to friends to build formations," Sanders said. "But sky divers don't always fly in the traditional belly-to-earth style anymore. As a cameraman, I fly on my back a lot of the time, underneath a formation as if I'm in a lounge chair so I can film the people's faces. Some prefer head-down flying, and from the moment they leave the plane to when they open the chute, they are in a head-down position and that way can move vertically across the sky, or even horizontally. Some use a feet-down or sit-down position, that looks as if they are sitting in a chair. There are all different ways sky divers are now flying. A head-down dive will be up to speeds of 180 miles per hour and you don't have to go straight down. You can move horizontally over to a friend and both fly together in the head-down position, as if two people were standing on their heads in a living room. So there is some incredible new flying that is going on."

Miles Daisher, who numbers sky diving among several adventure sports he pursues, says that this new style of high-speed free fall has recently spawned contests where the participants do all kinds of tricks while free falling and before pulling their chutes. "You're able to get a lot more movement at the higher speeds,"

Daisher explained. "You can move forward, backward, up or down a lot faster. You've got a lot more wind going by so you can use the wind to create more movement. That allows the jumper to do a whole different range of ricks. This is another up-and-coming type of competition."

It is, however, a competition certainly not for the faint of heart. Tom Sanders credits modern equipment with bringing about a revolution in all the jumping and flying sports, enabling people to enjoy them, enter competitions, as well as pushing for new limits and new ways to fly. "I've hang glided for many years," he said. "Sometimes you find birds just flying along with you. It's amazing what modern materials have created and enabled us to do. These sports weren't available to people in the 1920s. Only climbing was. I still consider sky diving to be in its infancy. It evolved out of the military and wasn't done as an active sport until maybe the mid-1960s. So it has only been around some forty years or so."

Sounds as if there's still a long way to go.

BASE Jumping

Perhaps no sport in America has caused as much controversy in recent years as BASE jumping. The premise of the sport is simple: Instead of jumping from an airplane, the BASE jumper leaves a fixed object, free falls for a very short period of time, then deploys a single parachute—usually at the last possible safe second—and descends to the ground and hopefully a safe landing. The object can be a **B**uilding, an **A**ntenna, a **S**pan (bridge), or **E**arth (cliff). Hence, the acronym **BASE**. By the very definition, it's easy to spot controversy number one. Are the authorities going to stand by as someone jumps from the Empire State Building in New York City or off the Golden Gate Bridge in San Francisco? Obviously not.

Because of the vary nature of the sport, which began evolving slowly in the mid-1970s, BASE jumping has been declared illegal in many of the favorite venues in the United States. Even at Yosemite National Park, where jumpers love the high cliff called El Capitan, Rangers are ready to arrest anyone attempting a BASE jump while, at the same time, rock climbers, hang and para gliders, even free rope swingers have pretty much free rein to pursue their sports. The very fact that BASE jumping is an illegal activity in so many places could be one of the reasons some people are drawn to it. However, it has also led to several well-publicized tragedies, such as the deaths of Frank Gambalie and Jan Davis at El Capitan in Yosemite National Park.

That doesn't mean that BASE jumping is practiced by a bunch of footloose, one-step-ahead-of-the-law extreme athletes who don't care whether they live or die. There continues to be some misconceptions about the sport. In fact, one quote often associated with BASE jumping says, *The most common injury is death.* That, in itself, isn't about to serve as a poster-ready invitation to the sport. BASE jumpers, however, dispute that quote vigorously. The numbers of fatalities over the years may not be stated with certainty, but many of the sport's top practitioners say that it's only about forty, and many of those occurred in earlier years, when the chutes weren't as good and the jumpers not quite as careful. That notwithstanding, BASE jumping is not for the one-time thrill seeker. Unlike sky diving, there is not a lot of time to adjust and hopefully solve a problem that might arise. Miss pulling the chute on the first try and you might not get another. Yet those who pursue the sport will tout its virtues whenever asked, and will literally travel the world looking for new and interesting places to jump. Versatile athletes who participate in more than one of the adventure sports will almost always say they love their other sport or sports, but nothing can compare to BASE jumping. The sport seems to catch people by the short hairs and never let go.

Writing in his baselogic.com website, which is devoted to BASE jumping, Mick Knutson, one of the most thoughtful and erudite practitioners of the sport, described a BASE jump in the following way: "It has to be one of the most powerful experiences ever. You are standing on the edge of a deep and forbidding chasm that seductively draws you in. Vertigo nests solidly in the pit of your stomach, but your spirit soars. The tension is unbearable, your heart goes apeshit, and liquid energy courses through your veins. You become detached from the real world, extraneous information around you disappears, and time stands still. It's quiet—very, very quiet. Ready, set, go! You step out into the void that is deep, beautiful, and calm. Euphoric shock warps time and you can't believe what you are seeing as your surroundings gain momentum and the wind starts to roar in your ears. You know that the longer you hold out before deploying your parachute, the more incredible the experience will be, but those last moments become eternally long as the ground rushes up at you. Faster, faster, faster, the energy builds, ignites, and explodes within. Seconds from impact. Groundrush! Not yet, not yet. NOW! You fire the pilot chute, the canopy crashes open, the earth stands still, and reality floods back."

This passionate description comes from a man who began sky diving at twenty, converted to BASE jumping after some 200 sky dives, and never looked back. Because he has studied so much about his sport and goes about planning and scoping out his jumps much like a scientist planning a flight to the moon, Mick Knutson also knows much about the history of jumping. "My uncle was a paratrooper in Vietnam," he said. "He used the old round parachutes and jumped with eighty pounds of gear. You would never get me to do something like that. But things change. The new chutes give the jumper so much control and that's pretty much the only thing that allowed BASE jumping to happen. Those advancements. Because you have to land in such a small area every time, it's very important to have that type of equipment."

Knutson agreed to try BASE jumping after talking to a man named Adam Filippino, who was already into the sport. Because Filippino talked about the sport in an engineering sense, a language Knutson could understand, he figured he would try it once. Filippino had told him, however, that unlike sky diving, in BASE jumping you always have the feeling of falling.

"I just trusted this guy and talked to him about it for hours and hours on end," Knutson recalled. "He helped me on my first jump, which was a bridge, a 685-foot-high span in northern California. It wasn't a legal jump, but I went anyway, jumped, pulled the chute, and was flying down. The whole thing, from jump to landing, only lasted thirty-five or forty seconds. But while you're jumping, everything slows down. That forty seconds seemed more like four minutes. I just thought it took forever for the parachute to open, and once it did, I just thought it took forever to get to the ground."

Knutson says that because the duration of BASE jumping is so short, that it begins and end so quickly, that time is always incredibly compressed. "Most people think in seconds," he said. "That's the smallest minute amount they can comprehend. Sky divers don't even comprehend anything less than a second. But in BASE jumping we talk about splitting things up into an extra half-second for the parachute to open, then compensate for that. Unless you've BASE jumped, it's hard to explain to you or justify what those little quarter-seconds can mean to your brain. Your brain is going a million miles an hour. When I jump off things, I can feel the hairs on my arm stand up within the first three-quarters or one second, as soon as I start to gain a little bit of air speed. That's just amazing. To me, it's a kind of euphoric and powerful feeling to realize the sensations of your body or your mind."

Miles Daisher who, like most BASE jumpers, began as a sky diver, makes a very succinct comparison between the two sports. "In sky diving, you jump out of a plane with two parachutes," Daisher said. ""If you have to cut one [chute] away, if you have a malfunction on your main canopy and cut it away, now you're BASE jumping. Now you have just one canopy and you've got to make it work for you. In addition, you're a lot lower. When you jump out of a plane, you're really not worried about anything, but when you're BASE jumping and go off an object, you only have so many seconds before you hit the ground. Everything is sped up a lot faster in your head. Everything is also a lot tighter. Sky divers have a big open field in which to land. No problem. You can land almost anywhere. On a BASE jump, you usually have to put it in a single, small landing zone. Maybe on a single track or a road, with trees everywhere and obstacles all around you. It's a totally different world."

If BASE jumpers are in familiar territory, a place where they have jumped before, chances are they will just check weather conditions and jump. But if it's a new jump, a place they haven't seen before, the smart jumper will spend as much time as necessary to scope out the jump, the wind conditions, surrounding topography, and the landing. This is something Mick Knutson has done many times. "We were at this cliff in Moab, Utah," Knutson recalled. "Most of the cliffs there are between three hundred and five hundred feet tall. Because we hadn't jumped there before and it being a cliff there would be a rock face behind us on the jump, we started looking at it with laser range finders. We'll also use binoculars sometimes, and use four-wheel drive vehicles if possible to check out different angles of the cliff. Then we'll look at the landing area, and put up wind indicators at the top and bottom to keep tabs on the wind conditions. I've done studies on meteorology and micrometeorology so I can understand what kind of thermal activity will have an effect on our jumping. Depending on the location and type of jump, we'll do anything from an hour to a month of research."

Some BASE jumpers aren't quite as scientific. Miles Daisher and Shane McConkey once went to scope out a 400-foot cliff jump they hadn't done before. It was called Lover's Leap in South Lake Tahoe, California. There was a big bulge of rocks at the bottom, called the talus, which can obstruct a jumper's landing. Daisher and McConkey didn't have any scientific equipment with them, so they did it another way.

"We did a series of snowball tests," Daisher said. "We just starting throwing snowballs over the side and then looked to see where they would land. If we threw them really weak, they would bounce off the bulge of rocks. Since we didn't want to bounce off the rocks ourselves, we knew it would take some speed to clear that bulge. We sat up there for maybe an hour, just throwing snowballs. Finally, we figured if we got a running start and pushed further away from the edge as we jumped, we could make it. I know my good friend and mentor, Frank Gambalie, had made the jump and said it was one of the most technical he had ever done. I'll tell you, it was the most dangerous I'd ever done and very scary. But we made it."

There aren't a whole lot of BASE jumpers when compared to other sports. Estimates say there are upwards of 1,000 regular jumpers in the United States and maybe 5,000 worldwide. The sport has been accepted by only a small number of sponsors, and organized activities are few and far between. But those who do it and love it hope that someday the general perception will change. "We're tired of being branded as careless, reckless outlaws," said BASE jumper Dennis McGlynn. "A monkey can jump off this bridge and the parachute will open, but it takes skill to fly a chute and land without getting hurt."

Henry Boger, a sky diver and professional daredevil, looks upon BASE jumping as a hobby, albeit a sometimes dangerous one. "We love life and don't have death wishes," he said. "We realize every time we get on the cliff and we jump off, I mean, theoretically, we've committed suicide until we make a conscious decision to save our lives. It's suicide without the commitment. It's true. Yet there are so many people I've talked to that have dreamed about, 'Oh, I'd love to step over the edge of cliffs and jump off.' We actually do that."

Joe Webber, a dentist from Indiana, says that his profession provides him with the funds to pursue his real love, BASE jumping. "One second to me here [at the cliffs above the Colorado River near Moab, Utah] actually feels like a minute," Webber said. "Your senses are heightened. It's an incredible awareness."

Miles Daisher, a man of many extremes and many sports, has said, flat out, "There's no feeling in the world like BASE jumping. I just love it so much. If something happened to me and I couldn't walk, I'd just roll my wheelchair off the end of a cliff. I'd still do it somehow. That's how much I love it."

There have been several organized BASE-jumping competitions. Bridge Day, an annual event in Fayetteville, West Virginia, draws about 200,000 visitors each year. The problem is that the sport continues to be banned in many other places. Permits are rarely issued, even when requested, and when a death or serious injury occurs, the negative publicity seems to far outweigh the positive stories of a hundred successful jumps. Thus active BASE jumpers will sometimes seek out new jumps in places where most people wouldn't even imaging going. Mick Knutson will never forget a jump he made in Mexico several years ago. He feels it really caught the total BASE experience, the real essence of his sport.

"I'm just one of forty people in the world who have jumped into this fourteen-hundred-foot cave down in Mexico," he said. "It's called the Cave of the Swallows and it's the largest cave in the world. While it draws a lot of visitors, only forty people have ever been down inside it. It's just an incredibly beautiful place. There must be literally millions of swallows who live in it, millions of parakeets. It took us three hours to drive to this little village in the middle of the jungle. I don't even think it has a name. Just a village in the middle of nowhere. But to be able to jump there, then get hoisted out by rope—it's an experience that so few people have. I feel so fortunate that I get to experience all these things and have to thank BASE jumping for it."

The Outlaw Image

It is the negative publicity generated by BASE jumpers who continue to go off objects illegally that has caused so much of the furor about the sport. One of the favorite jumping points in the United States is El Capitan in Yosemite National Park. Unfortunately, it is also an illegal jump zone, and because so many people jump there, the park rangers are always ready to intercept them. The result has been several tragic accidents that have probably slowed the sport's acceptance and made other venues continue to oppose the jumpers. This is also one of the reasons why so many people perceive of BASE jumpers as people who almost don't care if they live or die. Why else, one could reason, would someone sneak up to the top of a skyscraper, or walk out onto a popular bridge, or hike up to the top of a cliff at night so they won't be seen and then jump off at first light, hoping to land successfully and then escape being caught or captured? Yet when you take a look at a jumper like Mick Knutson, you know, for the most part, that these are not careless people. In fact, Alistair Gosling, an avid BASE jumper and also a businessman who founded the world's first twenty-four-hour alternative sports network, Extreme Sports Channel, feels that BASE jumpers have a quality that many other athletes don't, one that is necessitated by the very nature of their sport.

"[I believe] BASE jumpers to be the most disciplined of all athletes," Gosling said. "They're very together, very sorted as they, and no one else, are dealing with their own lives."

Unfortunately, they also have to deal with it on another edge, the edge of the law. When a jumper leaves an object illegally and is caught, he is often charged with trespassing. He can be fined several thousand dollars and also have his gear confiscated. That gear is very expensive and, because of the dangerous nature of the sport, very personal. There are many BASE jumpers on probation (for being caught jumping illegally), and some have actually gone to jail for short periods of time. This being the situation, there is nowhere else where the battle lines have been more clearly drawn than at El Capitan. The cliff is approximately 3,000 feet high and, with the surrounding beauty of the area, always a favorite of BASE jumpers. Soon after the sport began in 1980, Yosemite decided to try allowing jumpers to go off the cliff legally. The experiment lasted just two or three months. BASE jumping off El Cap has been illegal ever since.

Back in 1980, however, some of the new jumpers convinced the United States Parachute Association (USPA) to establish legal jumping guidelines in conjunction with the National Park Service (NPS). The guidelines included the issuance of permits, license requirements, and times for jumping. After a short time, however, the experiment ended. According to the park, there were a whole set of problems created, including people leaving trash behind, damaging the environment, and not behaving responsibly. Still, during this time there were no fatalities, no serious injuries, just a few minor hurts on landings and a couple of rescues by park rangers.

Mick Knutson remembers those days and still doesn't think it was quite fair. "Basically, a permit system was put in place. It's still there, but they just don't issue permits anymore," he explained. "Otherwise, they wanted us to pick up trash and jump at allotted times. Yes, people were leaving trash there, but rock climbers are now doing that worse than ever. I've always picked up any trash I've created, but that was one of the beefs back then. We were also jumping at sunrise and sunset, instead of in the blocks of time they allotted. It's a beautiful valley and a beautiful time to jump, and often the time I want to be jumping. So I guess some people didn't follow the time constraints. They also allowed for just one jumper at a time, and some people were doing multiple jumps. I think a four-way was the biggest. People like to jump together. It's fun and very safe. I was once part of a twenty-five-way jump, a world record, though not at El Cap. So there were some rules being broken, but I think, also, they just didn't like the people."

Then there was the flatbed truck incident. Some jumpers decided they didn't want to hike all the way to the top of El Cap, which can take up to eight hours, and drove up an old logging road as far as they could. According to Mick Knutson, the rangers gave them permission, but when they drove back down, a squad of rangers was waiting for them. At that point they allegedly denied having given permission for the truck to go up there. Other sources say the USPA tried to help the overall image of jumpers by expelling those who drove up in the truck. The jumpers then sued the USPA, claiming they had no right to regulate BASE jumping. The USPA dropped the action against the jumpers, but by then the National Park Service decided it was best to outlaw BASE jumping in national parks.

As with any dispute, there are always two sides. Still, almost all BASE jumpers feel they are being treated unfairly. Tom Sanders is another who thinks jumping should be legal in many places. Though he lost his wife in a BASE jump at Yosemite, he nevertheless feels that the authorities are not following a logical way of thinking. "I've had friends go to jail because they were BASE jumping," he said. "One friend spent three months in jail because he helped organize a group of jumpers. They went out and rented a houseboat and were jumping off cliffs out in the Lake Powell area. It's a huge artificial lake that was created by the construction of the Glen Canyon Dam on the Colorado River, though the lake is mostly in Utah. The odd thing about Lake Powell is that water is designated as landing area for aircraft. Any kind of plane can land there at any time. Unfortunately, someone had died during that trip, and because my friend had organized it, he was thrown in jail for three months. But it just seems to me if five guys paddle out to a pipeline and one guy drowns, they're not gonna throw the other guys in jail.

"With my friend, they said it was illegal to BASE jump in the park system and there was a big fight over it. They actually won one legal battle when the judge agreed it was a designated landing area. Then it was reversed, and it went on and on, finally going to a higher court and they lost. The whole thing was a nightmare. Think about it. If you were jumping off those cliffs without a parachute, it would be legal but you'd die. If you jump off with a parachute and you live, it's against the law and you get arrested. Because some guy BASE jumped and died, my friend went to jail. It wasn't murder. He didn't pack his parachute, but he was charged."

This story would come back to haunt Tom Sanders. Before that fatal day when his wife died, there was another event that would be part of the equation. It was the death of expert BASE jumper Frank Gambalie, a beloved friend to many in the sport. Gambalie was twenty-eight years old, a veteran of more than 500 BASE jumps and a man who totally loved his sport. Flip-siding the usual rationale of living, Gambalie once said that the scariest thing he'd ever done was work at a nine-to-five job. A security systems designer by profession, Gambalie began bungee jumping to relieve stress. Then he began working with the bungee company so he could jump for free. "One day, a couple of guys just walked up and jumped off the bridge with their parachutes," he said. "I knew immediately that's what I was meant to do."

Soon, BASE jumping became his career. "It's not a hobby or an activity," he said. "It's a lifestyle. You have to be fully involved in it because of its intensity and risk. Yet the chances of my parachute malfunctioning in a manner I can't correct are far less than getting hurt in a car accident. I would never jump off something if I thought I was going to die. BASE jumping is portrayed as being a reckless sport, but years of training go into making a safe jump." Like so many others, Gambalie studied every aspect of his sport, learning just how his chute would react under different wind and weather conditions, how to leave the object to avoid hitting a rock ledge or other obstacle on the way down, and how to gauge and control his jump and chute to be sure of landing in the usually small, safe, hand-picked landing areas.

Gambalie loved to tell people about the biggest thrill he ever had jumping. "I had a twenty-six-second free fall from the Troll Wall in Norway," he said. "It's the tallest cliff I know of in the world. I didn't know it was going to be a record until I did it." He also recalled a leap from a famous skyscraper in New York. To do that, he had to hide out in the building all night. Then he jumped at 5 A.M. "That was the pinnacle of my career," he was fond of telling people. "It was amazing to be able to stand on a building with so much character and class."

That was the essence of Frank Gambalie, a man of character, courage, and care. He didn't feel he took unnecessary chances. He was also a friend and mentor to aspiring jumpers and athletes. One of them was Miles Daisher. "My first sky dive was in September of 1995," Daisher recalled. "I was living with three roommates, all of whom had sky dived before. One of them was Gambler [Daisher's nickname for Frank Gambalie]. He would show me videos of his BASE jumps and sky dives. I was really taken by it. At that time I was doing some bungee jumps and working as a landscaper. Gambler would always ask me, 'Do you love landscaping?' I'd say yeah, I like it a lot. And he'd repeat himself. 'But do you love it?' Then I'd admit no, not really. Then he'd say, 'If you don't love it, you've got to stop doing it and do what you really love.' Gambler kept telling me if I wanted to make a living out of something, I had better love it."

On June 9, 1999, Gambalie was going to make yet another jump from El Capitan. The story has it that the rangers were given a tip that he would be jumping and were waiting at the landing area to arrest him. The jump went fine, but when Gambalie saw the rangers coming for him, he tried to escape. He decided to try to swim across the Merced River. However, he didn't realize the river was swollen by runoff from heavy rains and was rushing past with swift currents. His good decisions while BASE jumping turned into a bad decision to try to swim across the river. His attempt failed and Frank Gambalie drowned.

"Yeah, he was running," Miles Daisher said. "He was really

paranoid about being caught. He had been caught a few times and said that it really sucks. So he ran from the rangers and decided to try to swim across a river . . . but there were class five rapids right behind him. He had never even been hurt on a BASE jump and died running from authorities. It's funny, because there's a video with an interview with Frank that must have been made three years before he drowned. In it, he says, 'The jump doesn't scare me. I have control over the jump. The authorities I have no control over. They scare me.'"

Gambalie's death reverberated throughout the BASE-jumping world. Many in the sport felt that something should be done, that an athlete like Frank Gambalie, so careful with his jumps and so in love with his sport, should not have died in vain trying to elude authorities because of a law they all felt was unfair. In late October, a protest jump was organized for El Capitan. Five BASE jumpers were going to defy authorities and jump from El Cap one by one as a tribute to their late comrade. The other reason for the protest was to show everyone that these jumps could be done safely. It was a beautiful late October afternoon. The park rangers were present, of course, and so were many members of the media, as well as Frank Gambalie's mother, Riccarda Mescola. Mick Knutson was scheduled to be the third jumper that day. Right behind him, fifty-eight-year-old Jan Davis would jump. She was the wife of Tom Sanders, who would not be jumping but would be filming the entire event from below. What happened next was simply horrifying to those watching.

The first two jumps went fine. Knutson was next. His chute opened and he floated down to a safe landing. Next came Jan Davis. She had spent the first part of her adult life in conventional style. Her first husband was a police officer in Santa Barbara and she was a successful real estate broker. When her husband died suddenly, she quit her job and began skiing. When she decided to try sky diving one day, she met Tom Sanders. The two soon fell in love, married, and Jan began embracing her new husband's lifestyle.

"A few years later I got her into the Screen Actors' Guild," Sanders related. "She was a talented and smart woman and occasionally there would be a role in some of the films I did where I could put a female sky diver in there. Sometimes I had her double for men. We did a scene for a movie called *Puppet Masters,* shot at twilight, and we had to land on top of a building. I'm filming Jan and another employee and she was dressed in Delta Force gear. You couldn't tell whether it was a man or woman. She did quite a bit of that and had a lot of fun with it. Jan was also the first woman to BASE jump from Angel Falls in Venezuela, the tallest waterfall in the world. I believe she still has the most jumps from it of any woman, thirteen. It's a very unforgiving free fall because the cliff is overhanging and it's three thousand feet high. The landing area is pretty challenging as well. So Jan really knew what she was doing."

For her protest jump at Yosemite, Jan had borrowed a friend's gear. This is not uncommon when jumpers feel they will be arrested. If they don't want to have newer, more expensive gear confiscated, they'll borrow some older gear that might not be used regularly. According to Tom Sanders, the borrowed gear was "totally airworthy." There was an agreement in place before the demonstration began that the jumpers would land in a designated area, allow themselves to be arrested, and forfeit their equipment. They would then try to oppose the ban on jumping once again in the courts.

Finally Jan Davis was ready and she jumped. At first everything seemed fine. But as she descended, people began screaming, "Open up! Open up!" In just seconds, everyone knew what would happen. The chute never opened and Davis plunged to her death. A grief-stricken Tom Sanders just collapsed, still holding his camera as friends rushed to console him. Though her death still haunts him, Tom Sanders can now talk about it more analytically. Like other jumpers, he wanted to know what went wrong.

"The jump off El Capitan for her was pretty much an easy jump," he said. "The most difficult thing about it was the exit, and she nailed it. In fact, it was the best exit and best track that I've ever seen her do. It appears that she couldn't find the pilot chute. The pilot chute on the container she was wearing was located about six inches from where she was used to it. I couldn't look at the videos, but a good friend who's a coroner and also an experienced BASE jumper ran the video through his crime investigation lab, where they had the frames enhanced. It appeared she touched the handle once, but didn't realize she had it, then went looking somewhere else. Had the jump been legal, she would have used the same equipment she always used at Angel Falls, a sky-diving rig with a dual parachute. I firmly believe that had it been her own rig, she would have been fine, and wouldn't have died.

"Yes, she made a mistake. But I would say that ninety-five per-cent of the fatalities at Yosemite—and there haven't been that many—are due to the fact that jumping is illegal. I don't know of one fatality off the top of my head that wasn't related to the fact that jumping is illegal."

Park rangers were quick to use the tragedy to convince people that the ban on BASE jumping was justified. Park spokesman Scott Gediman said, "This is the sixth death since 1980 due to BASE jumping in the park, and we've had numerous injuries. It's a poor track record. There's going to have to be an investigation to sort this out, and it may take quite some time."

Looking back, Mick Knutson still feels the irony of that tragic day in 1999. "Media-wise, Jan Davis's death did an enormous amount to inform the world to what BASE jumping was, where it had come from, and the fact that it wasn't going away," Knutson said. "But personally, it was the worst thing that could have hap-pened. Everybody knew and loved Jan."

Just two months before Jan Davis's death, the CBS News show *48 Hours* did a feature on rescues at Yosemite. It talked about the new wave of 1990s adventurers looking for high-risk thrills . . . and the high cost of rescuing them when they got in trouble. The focus of the story was a missing free solo climber named Derek Hersey, who had gone out the night before and hadn't returned. The story also emphasized that Hersey had a nickname, "Dr. Death," for helping push his dangerous sport to new heights. Free solo climbers don't use ropes. The tenor of the story, reprinted on the CBS News website, really focused on how taxpayer money was flying out the door to rescue more of these so-called adventurers who kept getting themselves in trouble. It also said that Yosemite, with as many as 30,000 visitors on summer holidays, has the busiest search and rescue center of all the national parks.

"I've, at times, been so tired that I've been afraid that I'd make a mistake that would kill somebody," said John Dill, who was running the emergency unit at the park.

Ranger Scott Bowen was assigned to lead the search for Hersey, and he quickly noted that the type of search he would launch could easily cost more than $10,000. The story also pointed out that there were more than 6,000 search and rescue missions at America's national parks in 1998, a jump of nearly 50 percent from the year before, with the cost some $3.5 million. Bob Andrews, the chief ranger at Yosemite, was quoted as saying, "You talk to the taxpayers who say that, 'Well, you spend a half-million dollars of my money rescuing people who are doing dumb things or dangerous things. That's not right. [The people] should have to pay it themselves.' "

The story ended on a pair of negative notes for the world of high-risk sports. That same day they were searching for Derek Hersey, park rangers had to help a BASE jumper, Chris Hartfield, who was injured during an illegal jump. It said the rescue cost thousands of dollars and that Hartfield felt no guilt and planned to jump there again. "I do pay my taxes like everybody else," Hartfield was quoted as saying. "So I'm glad they're there and they were able to help me out."

One of the rescuers, Cameron Jacobi, fell during the rescue, tore up his foot, and was out of work for seven months. "I was irritated with the guy," he supposedly said of BASE jumper Hartfield. The story closed by saying the rangers found the body of Derek Hersey, who was killed in a fall while free soloing. It also stated that the rescuers hoped his death would serve as a reminder to other "adrenaline junkies" of the potential consequences of their behavior. The final paragraph of the story on the website added this bit of editorial comment:

"The rescuers have missed the point. In this game, death is the opponent, and the Chris Hatfields of the world will tell you all the fuss over risks and rescue will never stop them in their search for an even higher-risk high and the chance to walk away one more time."

Not a very flattering look into BASE jumping, climbing, or any other high-risk sports. As in other similar articles, there is a point to be made, but by using selective examples and quotes, the essence of the athlete is completely lost. They are portrayed as skewed people, looking for some kind of satisfaction that they may never find. So they'll keep getting hurt and killed, and the rescuers will have to risk their own lives, as well as burning the taxpayers' money to find them. Tom Sanders, for one, feels there is an even deeper meaning in stories such as this one, that they are conveying a message that could close things off for even more adventuring sportsmen.

"I think there's a belief that parks like Yosemite should be looked at, but not enjoyed," Sanders said. "They literally do not intend Yosemite National Park to be for recreation. I thought I misheard the chief ranger when he told me no, Yosemite is not de-signed for recreation. There's recreation here, he said, but BASE jumping is not what we want here. They only allow climbing be-cause it was there years ago. But they don't really want it, they don't really want the hang gliding. They pretty much don't want people to do anything but come in with a big tour bus, buy a hot dog, and look. It's unfortunate, because I've met a lot of great rangers."

So the battle continues, especially with the BASE jumpers. Even Mick Knutson, who looks at his sport in such an intelligent, logical way, has felt the sting and seen the incongruities in the way the BASE-jumping community is looked upon. "The rangers get paid overtime to camp out in the valley and wait for BASE jumpers," he said. "They're not waiting for poachers or anything else. They're sitting out there waiting for BASE jumpers to parachute off a cliff. Then there's a two-thousand-dollar fine, a lot of income. Two weeks after I got charged for jumping off El Cap when Jan Davis died, there were two kids, fifteen and sixteen, caught with high-pow-ered rifles and a sack full of dead squirrels. They were arrested, but got just a five-hundred-dollar fine, total. Where's the sense there?"

So BASE jumping remains pretty much on the outside looking in. There have been some predictions that, in time, it will find its place and move into the mainstream. In reality, as long as it remains illegal and jumpers continue to challenge authority at various venues, it will be difficult. Add to that the occasional death, which is magnified many times, and the sport is still perceived as very risky and highly dangerous. For Mick Knutson, however, it's all a product of society and the direction in which everything is moving in the twenty-first century.

"Society is pushing the boundaries in everything," Knutson said, "computers, sports, moneymaking, everything. I think that tends to be a trend in itself. BASE jumping was way ahead of its time when it came out and people have caught up with it. Most people who BASE jump still realize you can't just put on a parachute and jump the same way you can put on a snowboard and go snowboarding. That makes it difficult to get into the sport, but there are a lot of people knocking on the door."

Flossing the Sky

Jumping and flying. Neither act, as practiced in the world of high-risk adventure sports, is endemic to man. Because it isn't natural for man to fly or to jump great distances, those who do it are often looked upon as aberrations by those who don't. And that, in part, is why people engaged in these various sports are often referred to as "crazy." Jumping from a plane, off the side of a cliff or building, flying more than 10,000 feet or more through the air is not something the so-called average person is apt to do. However, those who have discovered a need for this kind of adventure continue to look for new ways either to increase the intensity of what they are doing, or create a slightly different version of their sport. That has been the norm since these sports began coming to the fore.

When sky diving began, for instance, jumpers did what are called *static lines*. That means they would jump from the plane, open their chutes immediately, and float to the ground. Soon, sky divers began thinking of new ways to practice their sport. Why not wait to open the chute? After all, if you jump and open the chute at 3,000 feet, why not jump at a much higher altitude and still open the chute at 3,000 feet. Thus free fall enabled sky diving to reach a new level. Some sky divers enjoy doing tricks as they free fall, doing spins and cartwheels, almost as if they are doing gymnastics in space. An adjunct to the sport was created when someone had the idea of jumping with a small surfboard strapped to the feet. Thus the sport of sky surfing was born. Today, with smaller, faster, and more controllable chutes, sky divers can literally soar across the sky, fly low, and skim across the water, the treetops, or even the ground. As the sport has progressed, the danger has also increased, though the conventional version is still considered relatively safe.

BASE jumping, of course, came directly from sky diving. Most BASE jumpers began as sky divers before discovering that they enjoyed jumping from fixed objects, a shorter fall with a single chute. More dangerous? Probably, since there is less time and no second chute, but as mentioned already, these sports are progressing and changing, with the equipment making it possible to do things that couldn't be done even a short time ago. In the 1980s, there was a sudden craze that spread very quickly, then faded just as fast. Bungee jumping allowed people to leap off a fixed object, often a manmade crane, with an elastic bungee cord attached to their ankles. The jumpers would free fall for a distance and the cord would stop them before they reached the ground. Because it was elastic, it didn't stop them with a bone-shattering jolt, but rather stretched out like a rubber band, then yanked the jumper skyward several more times, each bounce shorter than the one before until it came to a stop. Bungee jumps began appearing at carnivals and state fairs, or were just set up independently in a field somewhere so that people could come get the thrill of jumping and falling, for a price, of course.

The craze, however, didn't last. Bungee jumping did become fashionable for a brief period, perhaps because it was often featured on television then and was set up in public venues where many people could try it for a small fee. There was also a great deal of publicity generated by it, especially when a well-known celebrity would try a bungee jump, yet it wasn't ever considered an extreme sport and didn't seem to make a large percentage of participants turn to high-risk sports on a regular basis.

There was one man thinking seriously about bungee jumping, however, and how it might be modified to suit his purposes. Dan Osman would go on to become one of the most radical of all the high-risk athletes, a man who defied category and actually created his own sport, which is still done by only a few highly skilled brave souls. It's called rope free flying, though Osman preferred to call it, euphemistically, *flossing the sky*.

In a nutshell, rope free flying allows the participant to jump off a fixed object, such as a cliff. Instead of wearing a parachute, the jumper has an elastic rope attached to him by a harness. Unlike bungee jumping, where the jumper is yanked straight up once the rope reaches the end, the rope flyer is able to swing in great arcs because the rope is tied off away from the cliff or the object from which he is jumping. Thus it can be a longer and far more exciting ride.

Osman started off as a rock climber. His skill level was legendary and he was soon doing solo climbs without ropes. One of his best friends, Miles Daisher, marveled at Osman's skills. "Dano was probably the best free solo climber in the world," Daisher said. "He was making these out-of-control climbs without ropes. He would be jumping and catching the rocks above him, maneuvers where you actually leave the rocks, catch air, and you get up a little higher than you can reach, then grab on to something. He was the most fit person I ever met in my life. He had muscles growing out of places you've never seen muscles. In addition, he was as strong mentally as he was physically."

According to other friends, Osman was always a man who marched to his own drummer. He worked odd jobs in construction, just enough to pay his bills and support his climbing. Despite his great physical prowess, he didn't always follow a healthy regimen. If he wanted to drink, he would. If he felt like smoking, he would. If he had a yen for junk food, he followed it. He had a drawer full of unpaid traffic tickets and was habitually late for appointments. His friends coined a term for a special unit of time, the *Danosecond,* saying it was so huge it couldn't be measured. Osman wore his hair long and probably fit most people's image of the wild, high-risk athlete.

Dan Osman, however, was far from out of control. There was always a method to the madness, and you could debate all night long whether it was madness or not. His rope-swinging prowess actually developed for a very logical reason. For all his skills and outward fearlessness, Dan Osman had a fear of falling. Hard to believe, considering the kinds of things he did. Back in 1989, he apparently fell a number of times while attempting a difficult route up a place called Cave Rock. He began to think more about falling, knowing that to fall in certain situations meant to face death. He felt if he could face this head on, he would be able to climb stress free. To accomplish this, Osman decided to try to control the conditions that made him feel that fear. He wanted to be able to experience a long free fall, simulating a possible fall from the rocks. Yet he wanted to choreograph the fall himself, control it, and hopefully conquer once and for all his fear of falling.

That's what brought him to swinging with ropes. He thought about bungee jumping, but felt that it permitted a free fall of only about half the height of the jump since he would begin feeling the pull of the very elastic bungee rope halfway down. By using a less elastic rope, he could free fall the entire distance of the rope while being able to calibrate exactly how far off the ground he would be when he stopped. Once he started working with ropes, Dan Osman found a whole new way not only to deal with his fears, but to create a new and different sport that excited him as nothing else had.

"He got so good with ropes that he was actually teaching Navy Seals some of his climbing techniques, how to climb and use the ropes to the best advantage," Miles Daisher said. After doing some relatively simple rope free falls, Osman began setting up his complex system of ropes that would allow him to free fly. His rope swings became larger and larger. He learned some sky-diving techniques from friends Daisher and Frank Gambalie and began approaching 1,000 feet with his free falls.

"What you do is jump out," Daisher explained, "and you're not even loading up the rope until you get almost down to the bottom. You're free falling for about nine seconds, then the rope becomes taut and you roll over on your back because you're tied in a chest-waist attachment, a kind of harness similar to what people wear when they go big wall climbing. At the end of the nine-second free fall, the rope is starting to stretch. It's a dynamic climbing rope that stretches so it doesn't basically snap your neck when it catches you. We would stretch the rope to fifty or a hundred feet or more, and then it would load up and kind of pull you back up into the air. But we weren't bouncing straight up like bungee jumpers. We were bouncing up at an angle. It was similar to the shock of a bungee cord, except that it was so big and the stretch was so big that it was a smoother shock to take than bungee jumping. That was really overwhelming for me."

The danger, of course, is in the area in which the flyer moves. Sometimes the flyer is close to the ground and swinging between trees. Osman remembered one close call he had while doing one of his rope swings from a bridge. "I did a free fall off this 750-foot bridge and I brushed into one set of bushes, then two seconds later, I went 650 feet across the canyon to kiss the other bushes," he said. "It didn't hurt, it just scared the daylights out of me. I knew I was pushing it, but when it happened, it was *wooeee!* The bushes were only ten or twelve feet high, and when you're coming that close to the ground that fast, it's pretty overwhelming."

Yet by all accounts, Dan Osman was not a careless man. Safety came first and he paid close attention to all kinds of details. He always insisted that all the gear be triple-checked by two people before every jump. "Dano was very methodical," Miles Daisher said. "He would draw things out on paper. He had a dry erase board and would always be drawing his plans out. Get all the length, do all the calculations, do the math. Then he would take it slow at the beginning and finally add more length of rope and get down deeper, deeper, and deeper until he couldn't possibly take it down any more. He was always pushing the limits. Yet there were a lot of times when I'd say, 'Come on. Let's dive right in.' And Dano would tell me to wait a second, then start to look around again. You could almost see him thinking, piecing it together in his head. Sure, there were people he would show his plans to who would say, 'That's nuts, dude. What are you talking about?' Dano would just smile and laugh. He knew what he was doing. He always did."

Osman felt that the higher jumps were even safer than those at lower altitudes because the ride was smoother. It was because he wanted to go over 1,000 feet that Osman and his friends came to the Leaning Tower, which has been described as a sheer-walled thumb of granite on Yosemite Valley's south side. In October 1998, Dan Osman rigged his most ambitious jumping system ever. First a rope was strung out some 1,200 feet and tied to a nearby outcrop called the Fifi Buttress. The rope was straight across and ultrataut. A pulley system was then put in place to make the rope even tauter, with more tension. Miles Daisher said if you plucked it, it would be like a guitar string. Using a pulley, someone then went hand over hand out across the top rope to where he tied off the jump rope. That was the point from which the jumper would swing. The jump line consisted of six 200-foot ropes tied together.

"You couldn't tie the top of the jump line to a rock," Daisher explained, "because that would swing you back into the rock. So what we're doing is getting the jump line out to a point where it will swing you away from the wall. While you are swinging, you have a butt pack and a leg pouch, which contain additional ropes. On the end of the jump rope is a big ring. Once you're done swinging and bouncing, you attach one of the ropes from your pack to the ring at the end of the jump rope and rappel down about two hundred feet to the trees."

Once it was set up, Osman and his friends made some thirteen initial jumps, including one in which Osman made the first jump of more than 1,000 feet. He actually plunged 1,050 feet before the rope stopped him just 90 feet from the ground. The rope swings were documented on video and also attracted the attention of the park rangers. In still another incongruity, the rangers let the jumping continue because there were no regulations prohibiting it. However, if someone had decided to BASE jump off that same cliff, he would have been arrested.

In a strange irony, Osman was arrested in Yosemite Village on October 28, but it had nothing to do with his rope swinging. He was charged with possession of marijuana and driving with a suspended license, and he sat in the Yosemite jail for two weeks until his sister made bail for him. For a while, he went home with her to Reno, but he was concerned about his rigging. On November 22, Osman returned to the Leaning Tower. His sister said he was going to take the rigging down, but according to Miles Daisher, he had always planned to jump again, taking Daisher and several others with him. By then, the rigging not only had stood up to the thirteen initial jumps earlier, but had also been weathered by a month of sun, snow, rain, and wind. Osman felt it would still hold. Both he and Daisher jumped once that day and everything seemed fine. The next day they were there again. Osman inspected the ropes and found the knots to be very tight. He had to hammer then apart and retie them more loosely so it would be easy to adjust the ropes to the length he wanted. He said the knots would be fine. Daisher jumped again, and then Osman prepared for his final jump. This time he would try for about a 1,100-foot jump with no cameras, no one to witness it except a few of his closest friends.

He also decided to turn his jump north, toward a tree-lined boulder field that sloped down toward the valley floor. That direction, he figured, would allow for a 1,100-foot jump. Miles Daisher looked at the landing area and warned his friend to watch out for the trees. Osman answered quickly, "I already thought of that." It was late by then, about six o'clock in the evening. Osman measured out another seventy-five feet of rope and planned to try the biggest jump of his life. It was quite dark already, but he still wanted to try it. Finally, he jumped and Daisher listened for the sounds of the rope whipping below.

"I was waiting, waiting, waiting, waiting. . . . It seemed like twenty minutes passed," Daisher said. "Then the rope made that

FSSSSSHHHHEWW sound, cutting through the air. Then I heard Dano let out a yell, followed by a sound of tree branches, like a huge tree just broke in half."

Like so many others in the world of the extreme, Dan Osman hadn't misjudged his jump or the length of the rope. Rather, an X-factor came into play, something no one expected. The rope broke! It may have been that the time the ropes were up there in the elements had just weakened them, or maybe it was just a freak thing, old-fashioned bad damned luck. But one of the knots gave and Osman fell 200 feet to his death. Daisher was the first to reach him, checked for a pulse, then "just freaked."

"No one knows exactly what happened," Daisher said when asked about the accident three years later. "It was a windy evening and from my best observation I'd say the wind blew the jump line over the taut haul line, which the jump line is tied to, and the jump line broke right near the knot, maybe from the friction. Then the knot hung on the haul line and snapped the jump line."

However it happened, the world of the extreme had lost one of its most skilled and radical practitioners. The accident could easily give those opposed to high-risk sports more fuel for the fire. *He was crazy. He didn't know when to stop. He kept taking more and bigger risks.* Yet those who knew Dan Osman best felt he had lived life as he chose. "We know he went doing something he loved," said his sister, Andrea Osman-Brown. "He wasn't crazy. It was him. It was part of what made up his whole soul." Someone else pointed out that Osman hadn't done the things he did to get rich, or become famous. So much of what he did went unrecorded, was done as almost clandestine events. Osman himself might have touched on his own essence when he said, shortly before his death:

"Society puts these standards on people, saying that this is safe, this is normal, this isn't. I've always been different. People look at me and say, 'You're nuts.' But I do what I do for me, not for anyone else. I'm not suicidal. When you're sitting on the couch watching TV, you're dying. I'm most alive facing my fears."

Though he has lost two of his best friends, Frank Gambalie and Dan Osman, Miles Daisher continues to do the things he loves.

"We still use a lot of Dan's systems," he explained. "We're doing things now like cutting away from a para glider. It flies you to maybe a thousand feet out and six hundred feet up from where you want to cut away and land. You have a BASE rig on. Then we take our safety line off, cut away, and land. When we start falling, we roll over and do a couple of quick tricks, then get flat and stable, then pull the chute. So we're doing cutaways from para gliders using the same system Dan used."

Did Dan Osman leave a legacy? Without a doubt. It is very apparent that he touched in some special way, all those who knew him, especially those who understood the things he did and the passion with which he continued to do them until the very last precious seconds of his life.

The Innovative Wing Suit

There is little doubt about the progression of high-risk sports. People continue to look for new and different things to do. In just the jumping and flying sports, parachute jumping has led to static-line sky diving, pulling the chute almost as soon as you leave the plane; and finally free fall sky diving. Soon, someone had the idea to sky dive off a cliff or bridge or building, and BASE jumping was born. Dan Osman created rope free falling roughly from the fad sport of bungee jumping, and then Miles Daisher used Osman's techniques to cut away from a para glider, in other words release himself from the glider, and begin a BASE jump from there. The people who love these sports are often creative and innovative, and if the risk were not so great, more people might appreciate them instead of calling them names or questioning their basic sanity.

Much of what has happened with high-risk sports over the past two decades has also been the result of new and improved equipment. Along those lines, there is something else, already developed, that might once again alter and change both sky diving and BASE jumping. It's called a wing suit. "A wing suit is made of nylon," jumper/filmmaker Tom Sanders explained. "It's almost like a personal hang glider. There are wings that extend from your wrists to about your hips, and then if your legs are spread apart, there's a triangular piece of material that fills in that whole area. In effect, it's a big webbed area."

Sanders said the wing suit serves to lengthen fall time by virtue of increased surface area. "You can go off a cliff that is normally a twenty-second free fall and you'll free fall for forty seconds. For a human being to stand on the edge of a spectacular cliff in Norway, and jump off and fly away for forty seconds, then open a parachute and fly for another two minutes, now that's a pretty incredible experience. Sky dive in a wing suit, and instead of getting one minute free fall from twelve thousand feet, you'll get a two-minute free fall. The fall rate is twice as slow and it allows you to glide across the sky."

With continuing passion for his sport, Tom Sanders is excited about this latest innovation and feels it will affect the future of both sky diving and BASE jumping very soon. "I really don't think wing suits are a fad," he said. "In the early 1960s guys tried to sky dive with bat wings, which had rigid supports with wood in them. It didn't work because the wing would break. Like a bird with a broken wing, they would die because the equipment failed. But the wing suits now are a reality and I think they will continue to be improved. They're very safe for a real qualified jumper. It's kind of a bold statement right now, but a lot of BASE jumpers and sky divers familiar with wing suits think that we're going to be able to land a wing suit in the next five to ten years, that the design of the suits will eventually allow them to float to the ground without a parachute. People have already left an airplane and then returned to it using a wing suit without even opening their chute. In other words, they made a sky dive and got back into the plane. Pretty amazing stuff."

Has pure human flight been the goal and objective of these high-risk jumpers and flyers all along? Present an extreme sky diver or BASE jumper with the means and they would undoubtedly embrace it. Right now, they deal with what is available to them, yet some continue to go farther, higher, faster, and in new and different ways. In the world of high-risk, adventure sports, you never know what is coming next. For Tom Sanders, it already exists and he, like so many others, simply loves it.

"This is pure, human flight, to body surf across the sky," he explained. "Whether we jump out of an airplane or jump off a cliff, we're in total control and flying our bodies. When it's done, we open a parachute. You've got to know what you're doing, but it's totally doable. It's far more than a half-brained idea to jump off something just to see if the parachutes open."

THE ADVENTURE OF THE EXTREME— CLIMBING

You don't want to fall so you want to be sure of what you're doing. If it's well within my ability level, I shouldn't fall, theoretically. So I guess I downplay it a bit in my mind. There are guys soloing real high-end routes, hard number routes, and they'll say the same thing, that it's well within their ability level and they should accomplish it. But we all know that anything above fifty feet is called the coffin zone.

—Craig DeMartino, climber

PERHAPS in climbing, more than any other high-risk endeavor, there is a credo that all too often rings true. *You fall, you die.* It is a sobering fact that every climber takes to the mountain or vertical rock face each time out. Whether the objective is a towering peak in the Himalayas or a group of boulders on a hillside in New York, climbers are courting possible danger as they pursue a sport they love. Types of climbing vary greatly. Some climbers prefer one style while others, called generalists, love to do it all. Whenever you meet any climber, however, you'll always find some mesmerizing stories that come with them.

Alpine and Expedition Climbing

Alpine and expedition climbing are terms generally applied to the big mountains. You start at the bottom and climb to the top, whether it's the 14,000 plus feet of Mount Rainier in Seattle, or the 29,000-plus feet it takes to reach the summit of Mount Everest in the Himalayas. A group of climbers setting out to climb one of the world's top mountains expedition-style may spend two months or more on the various slopes, slowly working their way up, setting camps, setting ropes, carrying supplies, all the while acclimating their bodies to the increasing altitude in preparation for the final surge to the summit. It's a long, difficult, and debilitating journey, one which can be planned for carefully, then sabotaged by any number of X-factors along the way. With expedition climbing there are no certainties, and even the world's best mountaineers never know whether they will make the summit or return alive.

"Alpine is where you put your pack on and go," said Canadian Sharon Wood, one of the world's best mountaineers and the first North American woman to reach the summit of Mount Everest. "However, the only way you could climb Everest alpine style is if you were already acclimated [to the altitude]. To do this, you would have to climb other mountains, spend some time at 24,000 or 25,000 feet, getting up there into the death zone, then come down and rest. Then you go for Everest. If someone flew you to the top of Everest and dropped you off, you would die pretty quickly. That's why you must acclimate. With alpine style there are no preplaced camps, no preplaced ropes. Essentially you have to make it from the bottom to the top in one shot.

"You know from the get go that the odds of you personally getting to the summit are pretty low," she said. "One time we started with eleven good climbers, all pretty strong and with a lot of individual experience. Yet it's still a crap shoot. In the end what determines who goes [for the summit] is who happens to be in the right place at the right time and who's left. Of the eleven climbers, there were four of us left who were still strong enough to try and who weren't completely depleted. Two of us made it."

What happens to the human body when it is exposed to altitudes near and at the peaks of the world's highest mountains? Anyone who even remotely thinks about climbing some of the major peaks should be well aware that even if the weather is perfect, the body may revolt.

"Very few people can stay indefinitely at altitudes above 18,000 feet and thrive," said Robert Schoene, a high-altitude physiologist at the University of Washington. The problem is simple. There just isn't enough oxygen to feed the body. The earth's atmosphere contains twenty-one percent oxygen, but the higher a climber goes, the less oxygen enters the lungs with each breath. Mountaineers can easily fall victim to this lack of oxygen, which in the medical profession is called *hypoxia*. Climbers getting up into the thinner air, and who have not given their bodies a chance to acclimate, will begin to breathe harder, even hyperventilate as the lungs

The power wave known as "Jaws" breaking off the Hawaiian island of Maui. A favorite of big wave surfers, the tube of the wave is big enough to hold a bus. *(Courtesy of David Pu'u)*

Alpine mountain climber Sharon Wood takes a short break during one of her many climbs. Wood was the first North American woman to reach the summit of Mount Everest. *(Courtesy of Sharon Wood)*

Veteran sky diver Jim McCormick. *(Courtesy of Jim McCormick)*

With his cameras mounted on his helmet and chute still billowing in the wind, aerial photographer and sky diver Tom Sanders has just completed another shoot in midair, returning safely to the ground. *(Courtesy of Tom Sanders)*

Aerial photographer Tom Sanders flies through the air in a sitting position as he photographs his subject, a sky surfer (sky diving on a surfboard) ready to do his aerial acrobatics. *(Courtesy of Tom Sanders)*

A BASE jumper falls through the air with a photographic trail of red smoke coming from his shoes. After a short free fall, the jumper deploys a parachute to complete the journey to the ground below. *(Courtesy of Red Bull/Bernhard Spottel)*

This multiple exposure photo shows a BASE jumper leaving the side of a cliff and doing a back flip in the air before pulling his chute for a safe landing. *(Courtesy of Red Bull/Ulrich Grill)*

A solitary BASE jumper plummets toward the ground just before deploying his parachute. Part of the skill needed for this thrilling sport is the ability to control the chute so it won't pull the jumper back into the vertical wall of rock that he has jumped from. *(Courtesy of Red Bull/Bernhard Spottel)*

Using bolts and ropes, rock climber Craig DeMartino gets ready to send gear up to his partner perched above as they work their way up a vertical rock face. *(Courtesy of Craig DeMartino)*

A rock climber soloing on a vertical cliff with no ropes is always in danger. The views, however, once he reaches the top are often magnificent. *(Courtesy of Craig DeMartino)*

A vertical wall sometimes doesn't give the climber much. A combination of narrow cracks and well-placed bolts make it possible for the climber to inch his way up the wall. *(Courtesy of Craig DeMartino)*

Rock climber Emma Williams negotiates a tough section of a climb at Yosemite National Park. *(Courtesy Rob Gracie)*

Rock climbers will tackle almost any kind of rock formation. Here a climber begins to repel downward using a rope after climbing a beautiful cut of rock that nature has carved out of the earth. *(Courtesy of Red Bull/ Ulrich Grill)*

Climbing a sheet of solid ice can be difficult enough. This climber is about to move onto an inverted portion of the wall using just a pair of ice axes and foot crampons to stay in contact with the ice. *(Courtesy of Red Bull/ Ulrich Grill)*

It's amazing how rock climbers can scale vertical walls with seemingly no place to hang on. If they can't get a grip, they'll place bolts and use ropes to make it to the top. *(Courtesy of Craig DeMartino)*

Radical Skier Kristen Ulmer.
(Courtesy of Joni Kabana)

Skier Seth Morrison is airborne while skiing a difficult line in Colorado. Extreme skiers often choose the tougher runs so they can showcase all their skills. *(Courtesy of Rob Gracie)*

Snowboarder Elliott Olson goes airborne at Villa-Rica Pucon in Chile. The mountain in the background is the live Llima volcano. *(Courtesy of Shawn Frederick)*

Skier Jason Slaver gets set to jump over a group of exposed rocks as he comes down a difficult slope in Colorado. *(Courtesy of Rob Gracie)*

Shane McConkey skis down a nearly vertical slope as he kicks up a wave of white powder. Skiers high in the mountains must constantly watch the snow behind them, which can break into small sloughs that sometimes grow into a full-fledged avalanche. *(Courtesy of Red Bull/ Christian Pondella)*

Snowboarder Josh Schoenfeld makes his final move before jumping a cliff in the High Atlas Range in Morocco. *(Courtesy of Shawn Frederick)*

Snowboarders practice their jumping skills before doing the real thing on the mountains. The snow ramp is set up to simulate mountain conditions at the Palmer Glacier on Mount Hood in Oregon. *(Courtesy of Shawn Frederick)*

Grant Minor takes his snowboard off a 30-foot cliff at Villa-Rica Pucon in Chile. Minor takes time to grab his board as he does a midair trick before landing some sixty or seventy feet from the jump point. *(Courtesy of Shawn Frederick)*

Freestyle motocross star Mike Metzger.
(Courtesy of Shawn Frederick)

It's hard to believe the bikes go so high and the riders can do these kinds of tricks in freestyle motocross. Mike Metzger, however, looks completely at ease as he watches the camera during an exhibition of his talent. *(Courtesy of Shawn Frederick)*

Mike Metzger practices for an upcoming freestyle motocross competition by flying through the air at his home in Menifee, California. As he hangs on to his bike with one hand, you can get an idea of just how dangerous this sport can be. *(Courtesy of Shawn Frederick)*

Big wave surfer Mike Parsons.
(Photo Courtesy of David Pu'u)

A kayak waterfall jump takes great skill and timing. Here Paul Tefft goes off a thirty-five-foot fall in "The Grottos" at Aspen, Colorado. *(Courtesy of Rob Gracie)*

A surfer rides inside the tube, or barrel, of a wave at the famous Bonzai Pipeline on the north shore of the island of Oahu in Hawaii. A second photographer is swimming inside the wave to also get a shot. *(Courtesy of Shawn Frederick)*

Hawaiian native and big wave, tow-in surfer Archie Kalepa. *(Courtesy of David Pu'u)*

Tandem surfer Bobby Friedman. *(Courtesy of Shawn Frederick)*

Tandem surfers Bobby Friedman and Tiare Thomas are perhaps the only team in the world who can ride a huge wave like this one at the Backdoor Pipeline on Oahu in Hawaii. *(Courtesy of Sylvain Cazenave)*

Big wave surfer Archie Kalepa rides down the face of "Jaws." Notice the two men in the jet ski in the foreground. They are always on hand if the surfer gets in trouble.

Mike Parsons completes a ride down "Jaws." The power of the wall of water behind him shows just how dangerous this sport can be. *(Photos Courtesy of David Pu'u)*

look for more oxygen. Schoene calls this the first of several "struggle responses" by the body to the thinning air.

The hyperventilation causes the heart to beat faster and pump more blood, as the body attempts to protect itself from hypoxia. However, this will be effective only to a point. The deficiency in oxygen often will additionally cause climbers to suffer from acute mountain sickness (AMS), the result of the body, with lesser amounts of oxygen, trying to circulate more blood and oxygen to the brain. This extra blood can actually cause the brain to swell, resulting in headaches, nausea, weakness, and increased shortness of breath. Drinking a great deal of water combined with rest can help alleviate AMS. The problem, however, is that most mountaineers, even the amateurs, usually have the desire to push on. In a kind of cruel bit of mountain irony, hypoxia and AMS often leave the participant unable to make the best decisions. Hence, a downward spiral can begin and easily continue.

The higher a climber goes, the greater the chance of an even more serious form of mountain sickness—high-altitude cerebral edema (HACE), caused by a severe swelling of the brain that is more acute than that found with AMS. The climber suffering from HACE will have trouble walking and using his hands. He may even begin to hallucinate, not a good situation when quick movements and snap decisions may be required to save a partner's life or even your own. HACE may also lead to an accumulation of fluid in the lungs, a condition called high-altitude pulmonary edema (HAPE), which can cause a person to "drown."

Can a climber avoid the dangers of HACE and HAPE by preparing correctly for a climb? Perhaps somewhat. The experts advise climbers, especially those without a great deal of experience, to climb slowly, allowing the body to acclimate to the thinning air. They should ascend no more than 1,000 to 2,000 feet per day. Above 24,000 feet, bottled oxygen should be used. No matter how you view it, there is no shortcut to dealing with altitude. High-altitude physiologist Robert Schoene states frankly that the best way to prepare for mountains such as Everest or K2 is to spend maybe ten or fifteen years dealing with peaks that approach dangerous altitudes. "People who climb even 14,000-foot peaks or hike up the

Rockies have no real experience in surviving the brutal weather or high altitudes of the Himalayas," Schoene said.

An interesting sidelight to the dangers of altitude sickness is that there is one group of people who seem rather immune to it. They are the native Himalayan people called Sherpas. They often serve as guides, porters, and sometimes fellow climbers and rarely suffer any altitude-related illness. Scientists still aren't sure why this is so. It could possibly be a lifetime of acclimating and essentially living in the mountains, but some experts feel it's more likely that these people carry a gene that somehow allows them to use oxygen more efficiently.

If suffering from different degrees of altitude sickness isn't enough, alpine and expedition climbers face a variety of additional dangers. The price for spending a few seconds atop Everest can be exacting. Winds at the top of these ultrahigh mountains can reach 100 miles per hour or more, with windchills stretching downward to as much as 96 degrees below zero. Those daring to enter this hostile and unforgiving realm can also encounter frostbite from the severe cold, sunburn from the rays of a high sun, and snow-blindness from its glare on the white snow. Breathing the extremely cold air can cause violent coughing, the kind that has been known to crack ribs as if they were toothpicks. Then bring in a violent storm and all bets are off.

Even with relatively good weather, the climber can fall victim to a number of natural occurrences, such as shifting ice, crevasses that can break and swallow up a climber in a split second, and perhaps the most fear-inspiring and powerful catastrophe in the mountains—the avalanche. Roaring like a tornado and racing down the mountain at breathtaking speed, pulling more snow, rocks, and maybe trees with it, an avalanche can sweep away the best and strongest climbers in the world, treating them as if they were insignificant blips on a radar screen.

With a balance sheet leaning so heavily to one side—the side which lists all the things that can go wrong—why do people continue to look up at the mountains and envision themselves standing on the summit? Deaths in the mountains have been numerous. Pioneer families died in the Sierra Nevadas back in the nineteenth century just trying to find new homes in California and Oregon. George Mallory and Sandy Irvine disappeared on Everest back in 1924. The list goes on and on. It has been estimated in recent years that one out of every thirty persons who tries to scale Everest won't return. If one out of thirty persons going to football games all over the nation every weekend in the fall didn't return home that evening, how many would continue to attend?

The answer to why people continue alpine and expedition climbing is best explained by those who have years of experience, which means they have continued to return in the face of very real danger, triumphs, and tragedies. Two such people are Sharon Wood and Carlos Buhler, who came from very different backgrounds to become friends, climbing allies, and who are individually recognized by the climbing community as two of the finest. Wood was born in Halifax, Nova Scotia, in 1957, while Buhler came from Harrison, New York, a suburb of New York City, where he was born in 1954.

Wood discovered an adventurous spirit early. Like many climbers, she found she enjoyed individual sports more than team sports and loved going out on long bicycle trips, which she called adventures because she never knew quite where they would lead. Once she began climbing, there was no turning back. "I first had a rope tied around me when I was twelve," she recalled, "hiking with my dad. We were on a guided climb and it was probably the highlight of my life up to that point. Right away I sensed an affinity with the mountains. I just felt at home there, especially above the tree line. Then when I was seventeen, I went to work a summer job in Jasper, Alberta, in the Canadian Rockies. I sought out a mountain guide to take a bunch of friends and myself out and give us an introduction to rock climbing. There was no looking back after that.

"I went immediately to a mountain equipment catalog and ordered myself ropes and pitons. After that, I would drag anybody I could out. Most of us were inexperienced, but I just set about trying to learn how to climb. Soon after, I went to the climbing Outward Bound program in British Columbia, where I met a climbing instructor named Lauri Skreslet. I was so hungry to learn and he saw that. I remember him taking me and one other person wall climbing for a couple of days. His encouragement and attention really kept me going. Soon I was among people who were making their living from the mountains, teaching climbing and guiding. I related very well to them and soon wanted to be one of them as well.

"I found the people to be . . . well, in a sense they were all deviants, all weirdos, just like me. I never really felt I could fit into the social norm in school. In fact, I didn't do well in school at all. I hated it because I never felt as if I fit in. But then when I came across this whole community of climbers working at the Outward Bound, it was almost immediate recognition. Something just told me, this is where I belong and this is where I want to be."

Buhler, on the other hand, spent the first ten years of his life as a typical suburban kid and may well have stayed there if his father hadn't died of a heart attack that summer. Four years later, after his mother had remarried, he moved to Stamford, Connecticut, where he attended a private school beginning in the ninth grade.

"I played football, wrestled, and played lacrosse," he said, "but I didn't take to the everyday tie and jacket routine very well. The only change in my lifestyle came in the summers when I would go out to New Mexico and spend time on my grandfather's cattle ranch. It was the place my mother had grown up and I began hiking into canyons while I was there and loving the outdoor life. But I think my real transformation came between my tenth and eleventh grade years when I joined a five-week wilderness expedition into the Wind River Mountain Range in Wyoming. We were in the mountains for thirty-five days and had all kinds of training from readings maps, to creating meals and cooking over a fire, as well as learning all sorts of expedition tactics."

In 1972, just months after graduating high school in Putney, Vermont, Buhler joined a group of students on a trip to the Italian Alps. The leader of the group was a man named Peter Schreiber, an accomplished mountaineer. "That summer was an absolutely amazing transformation for me. I was just seventeen, and this man [Schreiber] was willing to give me the ability to kill myself. I met him on June twenty-fifth and by the middle of August we were doing things where you could get killed . . . and he wasn't even along [at all times]. In other words, he was telling me that, 'Not only am I going to teach you, Carlos, but I trust you.' This guy gave me the leeway to make decisions in the mountains and that was an enormous gift. I didn't get killed, but we could have. By the time I went to Spain, where I had been before to further my language skills, I was so turned on by mountaineering that I immediately joined a Spanish mountaineering club in Barcelona."

At the age of sixteen, Carlos Buhler knew he was embarking on a journey that could result in his death. Sharon Wood also knew the consequences of continuing to climb mountains. Yet both seemed to find, at an early age, the reasons that they were falling in love with a high-risk sport. "I think among climbers—and I'm being quite bold to say this—there is a certain degree of superiority," Wood said. "It may be because they've been able to escape, have defied the status quo, and have gone beyond. They have dedicated their lives to things other than what most people do. Most people go into a career or into some kind of academic pursuit. Whereas climbers devote a huge amount of time, passion, and energy, their heart and soul, to this seemingly pointless pursuit. So I think they have to spend a lot of time justifying that to themselves and among themselves. And they make a lot of sacrifices, often disappoint the expectations of their loved ones and their parents by making this choice. I'm talking about only the more serious climber.

"I also think that by the nature of the sport, by how close you are to the edge so often, that there is a lot of existential angst among climbers. They spend quite a bit of time talking about the meaning of life. From that, you get a group of people who are perhaps a little different. What makes these people even more extraordinary is that they do see death, and they live through their own epics (defined by mountain climbers to be tantamount to near total disasters). You see a little more of yourself when you're really pressed to the wall like that. You see a lot of human nature come through. Even at the beginning you immediately start out risking. I liked the feeling. As soon as I was there, that externally imposed commitment forces you to dig deep and find a strength you never knew you had. That's what I liked about it. I liked what it did to me. As my skills developed and I became more experienced, I wanted to be a little closer to the edge. I wanted more challenges."

Carlos Buhler was driven by similar thoughts as life in the mountains and the inherent danger that went with it took a firm hold on his entire being. "I never excelled at sports in high school," he said. "I changed a lot, tried skiing and played soccer, but had never gotten good at anything. Then I found a very good feeling about the people who were climbers. One of the most attractive aspects of the sport was the family of climbers. It was kind of the whole scenario, the parties and get-togethers the climbers had, the motivation they had to get up and catch a train at five in the morning to get to the mountains, the idea of dreaming about what you were going to do on weekends, then meeting up with people and doing it. That was so exciting for me.

"The act of climbing itself was just brilliant. There was something special about the combination of using your physical skills along with your mental skills that really grabbed me. With many of the sports I had played, I relied mostly on my body, like wrestling, and then there were all the academic programs where I relied on my brain. Then when I began climbing, someone said to me that I would have to get used to applying both my body and my brain to as high a level as I possibly could. That really caught me. I had to figure out how to protect my climbing and make the climb safe, how to get around in the mountains."

That summer of 1972, climbing on the Eiger in the Alps, Buhler had a harrowing experience. He and another climber were caught in a blizzard during their descent, and at one point, Buhler felt as if he had been hit by lightning and blacked out for a second. He thinks now that it was some kind of static electricity, but the experience at the time was absolutely frightening. "I started screaming, 'Oh, my God, we're gonna die,'" he recalled. "My partner had no clue what had happened. I had been hit and was terrified, scared out of my mind. I was on a ridge and it was snowing hard and we were reduced to a very slow pace."

They finally made it back that night to a hut where they were staying along with some other climbers. The next morning one of the other climbers who had seen Carlos and his friend come in, looking drenched and exhausted, looked at him and asked a strange question. "Does your mother know where you are?" he queried. "I looked at him and said, 'I don't think she does,' Buhler reported. "Then later that day, we went down into the valley and something had changed in me. That experience was so powerful, that I had been given enough autonomy to do a climb like that, serious mountaineering with possible serious repercussions resulting from my decisions. I knew something special had happened. It sparked a kind of enthusiasm for an inner exploration. What could I be capable of? And the feeling of being alive was so strong and so powerful . . . it was just a very, very interesting reaction."

As with many extreme sports, there is almost always an event, a spark, that brings an athlete more fully into the sport and then keeps him there. The reasons aren't always the same, sometimes not even similar, but the conclusion begins to have a familiar ring of sameness. The word *love* and the phrase *being alive* are mentioned repeatedly. Surviving in the face of possible serious injury and death seems to give them a special feeling for life, a way to more fully appreciate the basic fact of being alive. To get this feeling, many pay an extreme price.

Alex Lowe was one of the most admired and skilled mountaineers in recent times. A number of people have evoked the same analogy when speaking of Lowe in almost reverent tones. They called him the Michael Jordan of climbing. Jordan, of course, is universally acknowledged as the best basketball player there ever was, a superstar nonpareil. That's how Lowe was viewed. He was a climber who seemed to represent the absolute best in his sport. Friends remember him climbing a difficult stone buttress high above Montana's Gallatin River several years ago. After making the climb look smooth and easy, he reached the top and yelled out: "What a day! God, I love this!"

He was a man absolutely in love with his sport. Knowing full well the risk and having a wife and three sons at home, Lowe continued to climb because he hoped to fully share his feelings and experiences with his children. He didn't seek fame or fortune, yet his climbing often kept him away from his family for long periods of time, something he wasn't always happy about, though he continued to climb as often as he could. His climbs, unlike some others, often took him to out-of-the-way places. As one of his close friends said, "Alex could be much more famous if he'd spend more time climbing Everest or K2, but he'd rather spend his time climbing this unbelievable stuff out there."

Like many climbers, Lowe went where he felt the next challenge was, the place where he could improve his skills as a mountaineer. It didn't matter whether it was some virtually unknown peak or wall where there were no reporters, photographers, or television cameras. Alex Lowe climbed because he loved it, because he had to climb. There were stories of ice climbs in Montana and Wyoming that no one has ever been able to duplicate, his ability to go up routes "on sight" that locals had been trying to solve for years, his physical prowess that enabled him to do at least 400 pull-ups a day.

Growing up in Missoula, Montana, he was extremely active as a youngster. Lowe's mother, Dottie, remembered that "he always had trouble sitting still, was always the first one down the trail, always [the one] who climbed the highest." Like Carlos Buhler, he began learning the basics of climbing at the age of sixteen, and when he finished high school in 1976, he would tell anyone who asked about his vision of the future, "All I knew was that I wanted to climb some more."

After his marriage, Lowe took an engineering job in an aborted try at living a so-called *normal* life. It lasted barely a year. "It was just work all the time, which was cool," he said. "But then I realized I got only two weeks vacation a year. That wasn't going to work." Not when he loved climbing so much. As with others like him, climbing then became Alex Lowe's life. Everything else had to be worked in around it. The legend of Lowe really began in 1993 when he entered the Khan Tengri International Speed Climbing Competition, an annual race that is held on Kyrgyzstan's 22,950-foot mountain called Khan Tengri. Lowe and a friend were the first Westerners to compete in the contest, in which thirty climbers start at the 13,000-foot base camp, each with a numbered padlock. To prove they have reached the summit, they lock their padlock to a tripod placed there, then race back to the base camp.

The first one back to camp wins. Simple as that. But as Lowe said, "People die doing this thing."

Though he hadn't really been acclimated to altitude and was unfamiliar with the route, Lowe just burst into the lead. In the past, the finishers in the race were usually separated by just minutes. Alex Lowe finished the competition in ten hours and eight minutes, winning easily and breaking the previous Khan Tengri record by more than four hours. It was an incredible performance known to only those hard-core climbers who would take an interest in such an obscure competition. A few years later, there was almost a plaintive tone when Lowe told a reporter, "I've definitely got lists of things I'd love to accomplish as a climber, but let's face it, the world is full of climbers, and the realm of unexplored, unclimbed peaks is shrinking rapidly."

It was almost if he had a special joy for the unexplored, the untamed, the unclimbed. Like others, Lowe was fully aware of the dangers, especially in alpine climbing. When asked about it in a 1997 interview, he talked about dealing with the risk and danger in his sport. "There's no doubt that climbing is a sport—or a hobby—that occurs in a potentially risky area," he said. "I mean, that's part of the appeal. It's what's kept me interested in doing it all these years. But personally, I—and I think most of the people that I grew up climbing with—don't see it as a risk sport. That's not what I'm looking for in the sport. I'm looking for a very simplistic good time in the hills with good friends. There's a fascination and an appeal in doing this in a situation that's potentially risky, but rather than being a risk taker as such, I consider myself and my climbing peers to be risk controllers, and we just enjoy being in this situation and keeping risk at a reasonable level. I think being in a risky environment wakes up some part of my psyche that lies dormant through a lot of the rest of life, the sort of mundane aspects of life. I don't think you necessarily have to go out and put your life on the line to wake up that part of your subconscious or whatever it is. I'm not looking for risky climbing. I'm looking for extremely adventurous climbing. I enjoy the wake-up that gives me, the focus that it allows me to conjure up in myself."

Once again there is a very personal approach, a special kind of feeling that climbing evokes. It isn't like a baseball or football game, where there is a winner and a loser. Rather, it's the adventure of the climb, the various elements that are put into it that provide the attraction. Alex Lowe had superior skills and the instinct to control risk. Yet in alpine climbing, there is always the X-factor, the unknown and unexpected, and it was just such a situation that would cost Alex Lowe his life.

On October 5, 1999, Lowe was part of the six-man team that was attempting to climb, then make the first ski descent of, Shishapangma, a 26,291-foot peak in China. The team planned to summit the mountain from an advanced base camp at 18,000 feet, then immediately descend on skis, coming down the same route they had climbed. At 9:20 A.M., Nepal time, the climbers split into two groups on opposite sides of the glacier to do some reconnaissance of the route they planned to take. That's when the frightening roar arose, a huge avalanche starting above and sliding some 6,000 feet toward the glacier. The five- to eight-foot slide hit the group in which Alex Lowe was traveling. One of the men, Conrad Anker, was thrown 100 feet, injured but alive. Lowe and cameraman Dave Bridges were lost and presumed dead.

The news shocked the climbing world. If anyone was considered immune to disaster, it would be Lowe. But the reality of the mountains is that no one is immune. Anything can happen at any time. It has happened before, and will happen again. Maybe the best tribute to Alex Lowe can be found in his own words, which express not only the special love he had for his sport, but how so many others feel about climbing.

"There are two kinds of climbers," he once said. "Those who climb because their heart sings when they're in the mountains, and all the rest."

While the Alex Lowe story remains one of mountaineering's great tragedies, it wasn't the first and undoubtedly won't be the last. Some four years earlier, in August 1995, the alpine community lost another of its growing legends. Alison Hargreaves, a native of Scotland, was making a name for herself as the best female climber in the world. In May of the same year, the thirty-three-year-old had become the first woman to climb Mount Everest alone and without supplemental oxygen, an achievement of monumental proportions. She had also soloed the six classic north faces of the Alps—the Matterhorn, the Grandes Jorasses, the Cima Grande, the Piz Badile, the Drus, and the Eiger.

With all these triumphs already under her belt, and well on her way to becoming a living legend, Alison Hargreaves wasn't ready to quit. She had a husband and two children at home and, by all accounts, loved them dearly. Upon reaching the summit of Everest, she immediately sent a radio message to her children. "I am on the top of the world," she told them, "and I love you dearly." After Everest, Hargreaves set her sights on a similar accomplishment on two other great peaks, K2 (also called Godwin Austen) in Kashmir and then Kanchenjunga in India. She wanted to do all three in the same year and in August set out for K2, a very steep mountain known for its sudden storms and a mountain considered far more difficult to climb than Everest.

Like Alex Lowe, Alison Hargreaves always felt she could manage the risks. She had begun climbing at eighteen and by 1995 had people asking her often why she continued to court danger with two young children and a husband at home. "If I thought it was desperately dangerous, I wouldn't do it," was the answer she gave quite often. She also had a favorite saying that she would sometimes repeat when asked the question of *why* once too often. "It is better to have lived one day as a tiger than a thousand days as a sheep," she would say.

There were three separate expeditions on K2 on the afternoon of August 13, from the United States, New Zealand, and Spain. All three were near the summit when heavy winds began to blow. Peter Hillary, the son of Sir Edmund Hillary, the first man to summit Everest, was the leader of the New Zealand group. As soon as the winds began, he made the decision to turn back and reached his base camp safely. Two other New Zealand climbers were separated from Hillary and continued upward. They soon met up with

Hargreaves and Rob Slater, an American who had invited Hargreaves to join his group. Despite the increasing winds, the group made it to the summit, then immediately started down.

Some 600 meters into their descent the avalanche came, the great equalizer that has taken so many. It roared down the mountain with frightening power, sweeping away Hargreaves, her three companions, and three Spanish climbers who were nearby. Peter Hillary later reported that climbers had seen Hargreaves's body hanging from a remote ledge near the 8,000-meter mark. A recovery attempt was out of the question, and like so many others, she was left on the mountain for eternity. Hearing about what had happened from his son, Sir Edmund Hillary talked to some members of the media, his words once again echoing the thought that no mountaineer, no matter how skilled, is ever completely safe.

"Peter said the weather and the wind on the mountain were appalling," Hillary stated. "These things can happen on any big mountain."

Luck. That is an element all climbers must have. If luck is with you, there is a chance of success. If it runs out, disaster is usually not far behind. Despite losing his wife and the mother of his children, Hargreaves's husband, Jim Ballard, was philosophical. His words show that he fully understood his wife's passion for climbing and the drive (some might say demons) that continued to propel her upward and to new challenges and adventures. "[Alison] was actually where she wanted to be," Ballard said. "She was on her way down. At least inside she would have had the happiness of reaching the summit."

Alpine-style climbers are a very special breed. They are attempting to climb huge mountains knowing full well that the higher they go, the more obstacles they'll encounter, the higher the risk becomes, and the odds of making it begin dropping rapidly. Perhaps the biggest decision they must make sometime is when to call it quits, when to look up at the summit and say no, not today.

"Whether to continue or to stop can put you in enormously uncomfortable situations," Carlos Buhler explained. "Often times you are struggling to find a balance. Your body or mind is saying, *I'm tired, this is too much, it's too dangerous, it's time to turn around and live to climb another day.* Those thoughts are fighting with your desire to finish the job, the part of you that is saying, *I can do this, I can get this job done successfully, and pull this off.* Your body is telling you one thing and your mind another. But you have to find the ability to make a rational decision. Everybody knows that climbers have to turn around a lot to have a nice, long climbing career. But in order to get that done, you also have to have a certain amount of willingness to push beyond what other people might consider a reasonable point to turn around. There are times when you make what might seem like an unreasonable decision to press on. But as you get more involved, and when you tackle the bigger mountains, you begin to see the repercussions of the stakes.

"When you first start going to the Himalayas, you realize that one out of five or six trips there is going to be successful, where success is defined by reaching the summit. Of course, that also includes getting back down again alive. Then you have to stop holding out for the summit, because if you don't, you'll be so discouraged after three or four failures. Climbing is all about the process, and very little about the product. It's all about knowing when you turn around how you will come back again in a year or two, or even ten years later, and try it again. The summit itself becomes the symbol, but it doesn't become necessarily the end-all. It just has to be a symbol of why you started on the journey in the first place."

So the rational philosophy is in place. But typical of most top climbers—and most top athletes—Carlos Buhler is a competitor. That instinct was tested on Makalu, the world's fifth highest peak at 27,824 feet, during an expedition to the Himalayas in 1984. Sharon Wood was part of that team, as was Dwayne Congdon, who would also climb Everest with Wood. This was an expedition that lasted more than two months, finally reaching a point where the climbers were in place for the final push and the decision was made for Buhler and Congdon to be the ones to try for the summit. The two were climbing without oxygen, and as they made their way toward the summit, the snow began blowing harder. Soon, the moment of truth was at hand and the two climbers began thinking about the problems getting down the mountain in the worsening conditions. Within 300 yards of the summit, they made the decision to turn back.

"It was a feeling of emptiness," Buhler said later. "We just missed it . . . I'm really glad that we had the sense to turn around. It was the right decision and I didn't struggle with it at the time."

Judging by his previous statements, Buhler must have known he made the right decision intellectually. For some reason, however, the failure to reach the summit of Makalu continued to bother him. Two years later, he made a special trip to see a man named Fritz Weisner, who had turned back very close to the summit of K2 way back in 1938, nearly a half-century earlier. Buhler knew exactly why he felt the trip was necessary. "I wanted to ask Fritz, who was elderly when I talked to him, about his experience on K2 back in '38," Buhler said. "I was so upset after not being able to make those last few hundred feet on Makalu, especially after sixty-eight days on the peak. And I asked him, 'Do you ever forgive yourself? Does it ever go away?' So here I am, the guy who's always saying it's all about the process and not the product, and I'm beating myself up because I didn't come home with the product. When I asked Fritz about his experience, he just looked at me and said, 'No, it never goes away.' "

It may not be easy for someone who has never tried to climb a mountain, let alone one of the highest peaks in the world, to know why such a journey can have this tremendous emotional effect on the climbers. Unlike many other sports of much shorter duration, it seems to be the time and struggle, as well as the danger, that leave an alpine expedition climber so exhausted, both physically and mentally, even when they return safely. "Makalu was a whole experience of life, birth, growing up, maturing, living, and dying, all in one sixty-eight-day period," Buhler said. The dying was a reference to the remains of a climber that Buhler came upon during his summit try, a man who had died back in 1976. He continued, "Every one of these trips is like that. But Makalu was an intense experience for all of us. It was such an intense experience that I always stay in touch with the people from that trip. We're bonded by it."

It was on another expedition to K2 in 1996 that Carlos Buhler found a strange way to put his sport into another kind of perspective. He and his team were on the mountain during the summer Olympics that year. "We were there from June to the beginning of September," he said. "We had been working, working, and working, usually in rotating teams of four, setting camps and hauling our gear higher and higher. Each time we would go up on the mountain spending four to six days, and we would work until we were exhausted, then come down and the next team would be right behind us. I remember lying in my tent after a month of that. I was exhausted emotionally. I'd lost about twenty-five pounds and we weren't even close to the summit yet, not even close. It was still miles above us. With two more weeks of the same thing still facing us, I was run down, depressed, disappointed, every emotion churning inside me as if I had thousands of pounds on my shoulders. And I remember listening to the shortwave radio I had, listening to the Olympics, and these athletes were doing the 100-meter dash, which was over in 9.8 seconds. And I remember thinking, 'Wow, why didn't I pick a sport like that.' "

Nearly all alpine climbers look upon their sport as a learning process, a kind of evolution. They often choose peaks and routes that will help them strengthen a perceived or real weakness in their climbing abilities. Thus they learn from their mistakes. When Sharon Wood became the first North American woman to reach the summit of Mount Everest in 1986, her partner was Dwayne Congdon, the same man who had turned back on Makalu with Carlos Buhler just two years earlier. His experience there would prove vital to their final assault on the summit. Wood had thought about climbing Everest for some time, the desire fueled when she was part of Buhler's team on Makalu. During most of the climb she could see Everest looming in the distance some thirty miles away.

The team arrived at the base camp in April 1986. They would climb expedition or siege style, slowly setting camps higher and higher on the mountain, acclimating to the altitude and preparing for a final one-day bid for the summit from the sixth camp. Only they never set the sixth camp. Time and waning strength made it necessary to go for the summit earlier than planned. "Dwayne Congdon and I were selected as the summit bid team," Wood relates. "We were two of four people left who might be healthy and strong enough to attempt it. After six weeks of hard work we started out on what would be the most difficult leg."

They began from the second camp, established at 19,000 feet, with two other members coming for support. It took two days to reach the fifth camp. On the third day they carried about seventy pounds of equipment each to set up the sixth camp in the bid for the summit. Wood remembered vividly. "It took all we had to just maintain our balance from one move to the next," Wood wrote of her experience. "At these altitudes of 25,000 to 27,000 feet you are inhaling four times faster than normal and still aren't getting enough oxygen. To conserve oxygen your brain puts the brakes on some muscle activity, turning you into a klutz. The ground became increasingly steeper, more difficult and dangerous as the day progressed. I did not think it was possible to continue much further given these difficulties and our extreme fatigue. This was one of the two most difficult days of my life. We would never have made it to camp six if the rest of our team hadn't been cheering us on from below through the walkie-talkie radio I was carrying. It meant so much to them that we were trying so hard to complete what they had all invested so much in, giving their best to help get us to this point."

The camp was set up at 27,000 feet. Both Wood and Congdon knew there would be only one try for the summit. If they didn't make it the first time, they were done. They started the final climb late the next morning, struggling for several hours until they came to the *crux*, the most technical and difficult section of the climb. "This would have been another point where I would have turned around if it hadn't been for the surge of resolve my partner showed by encouraging me to start leading through it," Wood said. "The thing that got me over this hurdle was to imagine turning back then and being plagued with the question, 'Could I have done it?' for the rest of my life. I think I asked myself a question I often ask when I am teetering on the brink of taking a risk. 'What is the worst thing that can happen to me by trying this?' I reasoned that I could make three or four moves upward and still get back down. By then I would know if it was too difficult to continue. I followed through with this and Dwayne and I climbed on, piggy backing off of one another's waning and surging resolve. Much, much later at nine P.M. we set foot on the highest point on earth."

Once there, another problem suddenly arose. How would they get back down? The sun was setting and night was almost upon them. That's when Dwayne Congdon called upon a lesson he had learned with Carlos Buhler on Makalu, when they had turned around just short of the summit. Wood relates what happened next. "One reason Carlos and Dwayne had turned around on Makalu was that it was getting dark and they were concerned about being that high on the mountain overnight," Wood said. "They were caught by the night and climbed down in the darkness anyway. We reached the summit of Everest at nine P.M. and knew we would have to climb down in the dark. But Dwayne's previous experience on Makalu told him he could do it. Had he not climbed in the dark on Makalu and had that experience, we might not have made it to the top."

Ironically, getting to the summit of Mount Everest or any of the other high peaks doesn't call for an immediate celebration. That has to come later. It's difficult enough getting there. Once on top, a climber knows he can't stay. The air is too thin and getting down might be a problem. So it's up . . . and off. "There was very little glory in the moment [on the summit] as all we were concerned about was that there was no more up," Wood said. "We were also preoccupied with the fact that we were on the highest point on earth and the sun was setting. All you're saying to each other is let's take the top and get the hell out of here. There's nothing romantic about it. By the time we fell into our tent back down at camp six at three A.M., we had been going for eighteen straight hours."

The climb down was treacherous and harrowing, something Sharon Wood will never forget. In fact, it was so intense an experience that it became the catalyst for her to slowly pull back from big mountain climbing. Perhaps she knew she had dodged a bullet. "We hadn't really eaten for days and were spent," she recalls. "We had been at altitude for two months. All you want to do is sit down and rest. But if you sit down at that altitude, you die. At best you come away with frozen hands and feet, and if you freeze your hands and feet on that kind of technical route where we had a lot of down climbing and accuracy is really important, you don't make it down. So you're fighting this very intense fatigue, this intense desire to sit down and get a little sleep. You're hypoxic, don't have enough oxygen, and everything is coming slowly. Your judgment is impaired and you know that every step counts, and if you stumble, you're gone. [The entire experience] definitely cooled my heels."

When Carlos Buhler stood atop Everest in 1983, he had a similar reaction. His final trek had taken some 10½ hours. "It was a kind of dreamish day. I thought of all the others who had stood there. When I reached the top, I sort of realized a few hazy thoughts about all those things, but it was two thirty-five [in the afternoon] and mostly all I could think about was taking the necessary photos and going on with the descent. I didn't look around much at the view and just had to get photos . . . my moment to be the highest soul standing on earth."

Close calls. All surviving alpine climbers have had them, including Buhler and Wood. For Sharon Wood, a soloing experience in the mountains of Peru might well have turned into a disaster. She was actually in Peru with Carlos Buhler, who was guiding a client at the time. One of the things Wood had never done up to that time was to solo a major peak, which involves climbing alone without ropes or a fellow climber for support. On this day in 1985 she says that they were walking in a valley when the idea just came upon her suddenly and rather unexpectedly.

"I just rounded a corner in the valley and saw this beautiful mountain in front of me," she recalled. "Suddenly, it dawned on me that I would go up this mountain. I think the purpose of my climbing it was to prove myself to myself, check out my degree of commitment on a mountain that looked as if it was within my ability. It had a technical ice face, a fairly steep ice face with possibly some rock climbing. There were questions for sure, whether I could get through the crux, but I felt if I couldn't get through, I could back off. You always look carefully at a route or a mountain before you climb it. You look at where you'll be climbing, try to anticipate the most difficult section with the idea of calculating what you'll need to climb it.

"After we set up a base camp, I just put my pack on and walked up to the valley, sleeping at the base of the route, at the top of the glacier, with the idea of getting up very early the next morning to climb the face. I think I wanted to know what it would feel like. It was a curiosity, and to this point something that I hadn't done. So it felt like a limitation, and I didn't want to be hemmed in by limitations. In a real sense, I was exploring my boundaries. Without a partner you gain a whole bunch of other things. There's a tremendous intensity. It's intense, very intense, because you are just there with your own thoughts, your own chatter, your own voices. Questions are coming to you all along the route and you keep wondering what conditions ahead of you will be like. The questions never stop.

"In addition to that, if you're somehow injured, there's no one there. You have no radio, nothing. It's just you and the mountain, and the idea of soloing is to find perfection. Every step you take, every move you make, has to be well thought out and perfectly executed, because you can't fall. It almost gives you a feeling of omnipotence. The level of commitment imposes a much, much greater level of performance. You're very focused and can't allow distractions at all."

At first the climb went well. It was when she neared the summit ridge that Wood came upon a crisis. "I was actually able to get through the crux very well since it wasn't as difficult as I had anticipated. The summit ridge was a very, very nice edge, a sharp ridge where I had one foot on the south face and one foot on the east face. It was quite vertical, about thirty-five degrees. Then the snow on the right face fractured and avalanched, which really increased my heart rate a lot. It sent me into a panic because it happened right under my foot. So I quickly moved that foot over to the left side. It was one of the most fearful moments for me in a long time. I rushed over the next fifty meters to reach the top. When I finally got there, I had a real sense of relief."

It wasn't over yet, however. At the top, Wood found she had another major decision facing her, one where a wrong choice could lead to disaster. She had seen a group of climbers on the mountain the day before and had assumed they had done the entire route, meaning they had made the summit, then descended by an easier route on the other side, opposite the route she had climbed. The only problem was that the easier route had some potential pitfalls. It contained a lot of crevasses, which are, in effect, snow bridges. So you have to be sure that the crevasses will support your weight.

"I figured if this other group had gone down that way, then the snow bridges were safe, that they had supported the weight of several people. I didn't think the temperatures had changed significantly enough to alter the conditions. What I wanted to see was the tracks of the other party. If they had made the summit, surely their tracks would have still been visible and I could have followed them down. Once I got there, however, I didn't see any tracks, which meant they hadn't made it to the summit. They had turned around and descended by the same route I was climbing. They hadn't gone down the other side. Now I have to think. In this situation it isn't about your ability anymore, it's about guessing whether the snow bridges are strong enough to hold your weight. I decided it would be too dangerous to take the route which was considered the *easy* one. It simply wasn't an option for me.

"The crevasses weren't the only reason. When I looked more closely, I could see that the slopes were at a lower angle, they were below the angle of repose, which means the snow wouldn't slough, or break away, naturally because it was too steep. So the snow just lies there and the avalanche conditions were quite bad. The thought of downclimbing a technically difficult route that I had just climbed up was something I had never done before on my own and without ropes, but going down the other way was just too risky. So I decided to downclimb my original route and it ended up going well. I just had to go slowly and methodically, but I made it."

Because she was soloing, Wood was leery of descending via the same route she had climbed. It's more difficult to see your footings when downclimbing, and without a partner and ropes, you can fall. In addition, she hadn't soloed a great deal and thus had not downclimbed under those conditions. She also explained that the experienced climber has to be able to *read* the snow to some degree, be able to judge how the snow will react when it is disturbed by a climber moving across. It is another way to hopefully avoid a catastrophe, but it isn't always easy. "There is a lot of gray area when you try to read the snow," Wood said. "Nothing is for certain, nothing is for sure. There are so many variables. I guess it's part science; part guesswork. For me, the conditions are very strange in South America. Snow sticks to angles that defy physics. In the Canadian Rockies that same snow would have been long gone. But in Peru there is snow on near vertical inclines."

Fortunately, Sharon Wood had the experience to make the crucial call. There are also times when all the experience in the world cannot help. Carlos Buhler faced just that situation in 1990. That year he led a four-man international expedition to Nepal, where they would attempt to climb Dhaulagiri, the world's seventh highest peak. Three of the climbers, Buhler, a Lithuanian named Dainius Makauskas, and a Sherpa named Nuru Jiri all made the summit of the 26,810-foot peak. Outwardly, it appeared to be a momentous achievement for Buhler, for he became the first North American to have climbed four of the world's fourteen peaks over 26,250 feet. The expedition still haunts him, however, for he feels that a bad decision led to disaster and tragedy.

"Something happened two years before my trip to Dhaulagiri that should have served as a warning," he explained. "I was driven by the fact that no American had yet climbed Kanchenjunga (the world's third highest peak) and didn't make a call to turn around. I wanted it for personal and competitive reasons. We made it [to the summit], but nearly paid for it with our lives. In retrospect, it was a horrendous decision to go on. When I went to the summit of Dhaulagiri, I had a feeling that we were in a very difficult situation. I knew my partner, Dainius, was very competent, a total expert. I felt I was still able to do it, but I had to be sure the others could continue as well. There's no way above 26,000 feet that I have the capacity to care for my partner. Therefore, if he is not able to take care of himself, he will die. In the end, there were three of us who reached the summit, but only two of us made it down alive.

"That was one of the biggest mistakes of my life. What I should have done was turn around and say, 'I may be in control, but I'm not sure my partner is able.' He was fifty years old, older than I was and had been climbing all his life. We're not talking about a beginner here, but when it was over, I was in the hospital for two months with frostbite. My Napali partner ended up losing all ten toes on both feet. I lost the big toe on my left foot and Dainius never made it down. I had to try to explain that to his father and mother.

"We had reached the summit together on an extremely cold day. It was minus forty-nine degrees Fahrenheit without wind chill, and there was about a forty-knot wind blowing. It was also October thirty-first, very late to be on the mountain. We had an enormously difficult day reaching the summit, but we pressed on and that was a mistake. Indicators are always telling you to turn around. Your mind might be saying hey, I'm not getting enough oxygen. I'm dying. You're losing brain cells. Your body is saying my toes are frozen, I'm getting frostbite, and you're going to be up shit's creek here. Get down now! At the same time, the other side of your mind is saying, I can still put one foot in front of the other, I can still put one hand above my head and pull up on this hold. I can still make this traverse. I can still do it. I can still do it. You go through this the entire day, locked in your own little world, a truly intense experience. At the same time there are two other people out there locked into their own little worlds just thirty, forty, or fifty yards from you. And everybody is moving slowly toward the summit as your body's core temperature is dropping. It's a tough, tough call."

There was no jubilation in reaching the summit. All three men knew that getting back down would be exceedingly difficult.

"It was extremely cold and we were working our way down some very difficult terrain," Buhler said. "It's all exposed. One false move and you're gone. That's what happened. Nuru and I were going down a ridge with Dainius behind us. We stopped to wait for him to catch up and he never did. I didn't see him disappear. We didn't know whether he stopped to rest, or had fallen, we just didn't know. We had to keep going because we were freezing. We would stop and call for him at different points, but he just wasn't there. Nobody ever saw Dainius again."

Even today, Carlos Buhler has a handkerchief belonging to Dainius Makauskas on his desk. It's a constant reminder and it certainly makes the alpine climber think about the life he has chosen to follow. "I sometimes look out the window and say no, the price is too high. It's time to stop. There's too much in life that could all be snuffed out. The tragedy of losing Dainius was so great, the pain inflicted on his kids, his parents, his wife, was so intense, why would you ever want to go into a situation where that could be repeated? There was no justification for the price we had to pay. The summit was not significant, and the price was Dainius's death as well as the disruption of Nuru's life as a person who lost all the digits on his feet.

"You go on, but you go on differently. You continue to climb, taking the knowledge that has made you a new person and hope that it will factor into every decision you have to make again. You hope you'll be a better person for it, a better climber for it. And you move forward."

All climbers must maintain a high level of fitness. If they aren't climbing, they are doing other things that will keep them ready for that next trip up a tough cliff and maybe into high altitudes. Carlos Buhler cross-country skis, skis hard on slopes, and does some local ice climbs when he's home in Bozeman, Montana. He also does aerobic training at a local gym, and alternates that with some strength training with weights. "It's a constant process," Buhler said. "I always try to get out and do something. If I can climb, great. If not, I do something else, a gym workout, a pool workout. In the summers I do a lot of trail running and hiking. I'll even go to a climbing gym and do an upper-body workout on the wall."

For Carlos Buhler, a life of climbing has meant a lot more than just struggling to make it to the top of the next mountain. He also discusses some of the life lessons he has learned from alpine climbing. "I was climbing with a young man recently, only twenty years old and really into climbing," he said. "I said to him at one point, 'Just remember, it isn't going to feel very good if for the next ten years you do amazing things, have all kinds of success, get on the covers of all the important magazines, get accolades, and maybe make a fortune . . . and then when you're thirty-two, you have a fatal accident and get killed. That's pretty young.'

"It was a tough decision for me to turn around two hundred feet from the summit on Makalu after so many days on the mountain. But I've had more than fifteen years to climb after that. So every time I beat myself up about not reaching the summit, I say hey, you've had a good twenty-five years or more as a climber, and you've also been able to do all the other things you want to do— eating fine meals, making love to beautiful ladies, all the things in life that give you pleasure. You have to weigh that out against your friends who die at twenty-eight. That's the end of the trail.

"So it's a tough, tough gauntlet to run. And to have long career in climbing, well, I wouldn't recommend it to anyone. It's got to be their own choice."

Ice, Rock, and Big Wall Climbing

There are many avid climbers who don't target the world's highest mountains. Many of them prefer mixed climbs, where they are negotiating frozen waterfalls, ice shelves, rock faces, and vertical walls. These types of climbs are of shorter duration than the alpine-style expeditions that reach for the skies. Some are made along prebolted routes, where the climber clips on to metal bolts already placed in the rock. Others involve specialized tools and screws used to make hand and footholds in ice. Most use ropes for help in climbing and as safety valves. Yet all follow that same familiar and final principle—*You fall, you die.*

It seems that any kind of projection that reaches upward is fair game for the climber. Put an obstacle in front of a group of people, and someone will want to climb it. Ice has become a popular medium, albeit not an easy one. The ice climber has to have several specialized pieces of equipment to negotiate vertical ice safely, and also must be adept at using them, as well as trying to read the ice in the best possible way. Ice climbers wear rigid, mono- or dual-point, step-in crampons (shoes with special cleats) which enable them to set their feet in the ice. Then there is the ice axe, sometimes called the climber's "ultimate weapon." The axe is used to grab the ice, chop a ledge, dig for solid ice, start holes for ice screws, or sometimes stop the climber from slipping and maybe falling. A climber can carry one or two of them, depending on the type of climb.

Kim Csizmazia, often called the best woman ice climber in the world, has traversed many difficult routes in both the United States and Canada. She is the first ever Ice Climbing World Cup Champion and has won three gold medals at the ESPN X Games in ice-climbing competitions. Csizmazia does all kinds of climbing, though many now associate her with the ice because of her accomplishments. "With my climbing, I just like to see what happens next," she said. "For instance, I never thought I'd be an ice climber when I started. I was always a skier and thought winter should be reserved for skiing. Then, pictures of ice climbing began to intrigue me. Now, climbing on a frozen waterfall is one of the coolest things you can do in the natural world. It's really cool, super beautiful. That's basically what attracted me to get into ice climbing in the first place."

For those without real strong skills and the ability to use the tools, Csizmazia said that ice climbing can be an exhausting ordeal, as well as very dangerous. "The most taxing thing is getting the screw in the ice," she said. "Not everyone has the natural ability or know-how when it comes to swinging the tool. For example, if you're a carpenter, you usually have no problem being an ice climber. So there's swinging the tool in the ice, and a little bit of reading the ice so you know where to swing. For beginners, ice climbing can be very intimidating, very scary, and they tend to hold on really right. Until they learn to relax, they're going to find it a completely exhausting ordeal. Just the hanging on can be exhausting, not even counting pulling yourself up. But once you relax when you're holding, and get the knack of getting the tools in the ice, you're beginning to win the battle."

Though people sometimes tend to criticize the X Games as a made-for-television event that likes to exploit the *extreme* in extreme sports, Kim Csizmazia has enjoyed the ice-climbing competition and feels it has helped advance the sport. "I've always had a great deal of fun at the X Games," she said. "I like to compete, but I actually enjoy the X Games more than the World Cup competition. The X Games are a bit different in the way they're set up. The ice is manmade, the climbers wear harnesses, and there is more money to be won. I think people training for the ice-climbing competition in the X Games also learned a great deal about the technical aspect of the sport, using their crampons and ice axes. Competition really made people think about what they were doing and it helped give the sport a big push."

Climbers are judged on how high they can get before falling off, which is similar to the judging in World Cup competitions. There is also a speed-climbing competition. As Csizmazia said, "Ice is ice," but the conditions are pretty much controlled. Ice climbing for sport in natural conditions can be more of an adventure and certainly more dangerous. Ice climbers should always wear a helmet and because a natural ice formation in winter is often surrounded by snow-covered slopes, some of the same dangers, such as avalanche and falling ice, that alpine climbers face can also present a problem for ice climbers.

"Make no mistake," veteran ice climber Craig Luebben said. "Ice climbing is riskier than rock climbing. The elements are harsher, the medium less stable, and falling is more treacherous."

It's suggested that ice climbers carry avalanche rescue equipment such as beacons and a shovel, as well as receiving training in winter survival, self-rescue, and first-aid. They should know how to ski well. It's sometimes easier to ski off a mountain once the climb is finished, rather than climbing down. In essence, ice climbing is a rather specialized skill, one that is usually just a small part of a climber's activities. Most ice climbers also rock climb, alpine climb, or climb big walls as well. Free ice climbers use just their tools and crampons, not relying on harnesses or ropes. It takes a great deal of skill and confidence to climb in this manner and it's definitely not for the novice. Many an ice climber has had to face deteriorating conditions during a climb, where a change in temperature or weather can cause the ice to soften and break. Alpine climbers, by the way, must also be proficient on ice because they never know what kind of conditions they will find at altitude, where the temperatures are below freezing and the snow is always present.

In addition to ice, there are various kinds of rock climbing, climbs of varying durations, and degrees of difficulty. Traditional sport climbing is generally done using ropes, putting in protections, such as bolts, or climbing routes where the bolts are preplaced. Some prefer high vertical walls, which they will scale slowly, either in a full day or over several days. Climbing without ropes is called free soloing, the climber using his hands and feet, and his head. Bouldering is free climbing on ten-, fifteen-, or twenty-foot boulders, again with no ropes. This is a recently developed type of climbing which young climbers are taking higher and higher, moving into what Craig DeMartino calls the *coffin zone*.

Many of the best rock climbers are really generalists, who have tried almost every type of climbing, including alpine, and then have settled on a favorite or two. Some prefer mixed climbs, where the terrain may go from rock to ice and back again. All have one thing in common—a love of the sport and a desire to be the best climber they can be. While Kim Csizmazia, for example, has been called one of the best female ice climbers in the world, by no means does she only travel in cold country looking for that perfect ice slope or frozen waterfall.

Born in Vancouver, British Colombia, in 1967, Kim Csizmazia began alpine skiing after her family moved to Whistler Mountain in the Pemberton area, north of Vancouver. When she was thirteen, her family moved to the Sun Valley area of Idaho, where she continued skiing and eventually Nordic ski raced during her high school and college years. Once she began climbing, it became her number one priority almost immediately. When asked why she has been so drawn to the sport, Csizmazia struggled a bit to find a singular answer. "No, I can't come up with any one answer," she said. "There is something akin to addiction, perhaps. There is also escapism, which is close to addiction, I would think. Or I can say that it's just part of me, something that is part of who I am and how I relate to the world."

Unlike many climbers who like to be the first to do a route, or conquer a mountain, or break a speed record, Csizmazia looks at her sport differently. She would rather pick out difficult rock and ice routes and work hard at climbing them more efficiently. "First ascents are a really big thing in climbing," she said, "something many climbers feel are the end-all and be-all, the cutting edge of the sport. It's in the new, the unexplored, and that's usually what gets the most attention, trying something for the first time. I've never been much of a first ascensionist type. I just don't buy into that whole thing. I've done a fair number of first ascents, but I don't find it any more satisfying than repeating a route. I'd much rather repeat a classic route that's a great route than do a crappy new route for the first time.

"I think my favorite thing is to cover a lot of terrain in one day, whether that means linking up numerous routes, and being a good enough climber where I can cover a lot of territory. In other words, I like to go all day long, and not just do one route, but maybe three routes. Another time, perhaps, I'll do a route that traditionally has been done in a full day and maybe do it in a couple of hours. Perhaps my background in ski racing has something to do with it. It's breaking something down, refining it, making it quicker and more efficient. In addition to ice, I really like to wall climb and aid climb (with preplaced bolts)."

Chris McNamara, a twenty-four-year-old native Californian, got hooked on climbing when he went to a climbing gym with a group of friends during a birthday celebration. He was fourteen at the time and says he soon lost interest in conventional sports and began gravitating to individual sports. "From the gyms you naturally want to go outdoors," he said. "I started on smaller types of rock climbing, using a rope. Back then bouldering was just beginning and I did some of that because there are almost no rocks in the San Francisco area. Basically, everything here is about Yosemite, which is a four-hour drive."

The adventures began coming early. When he was still fourteen, McNamara climbed the north tower of the Golden Gate Bridge. He admits it wasn't legal, but an adventurous climb nevertheless. Soon he was traveling to Yosemite and, when he was fifteen, climbed El Capitan for the first time. He continued to return, going on climbs that averaged between 1,800 and 2,900 feet. McNamara explains the different types of climbing he was able to do.

"Most of the really good routes at El Cap have bolts," McNamara said. "But it really has it all. Climbing there doesn't fit into one category. A good portion of it is just using the natural cracks, which is called trad or traditional climbing. Generally, when you climb using a whole bunch of preplaced bolts, it's called sport climbing. On El Cap, it's a combination. Much of it is trad climbing, but when you get to a section where the cracks run out, there are the preplaced bolts, which you use to pull yourself over the blank section, or just to protect yourself. There is an important distinction between free climbing and aid climbing. In free climbing, contrary to what most people think, you have a rope, but the rope is there just for safety. Whereas in aid climbing, you go up there with rope and gear, and use the gear to pull yourself up, because the climbing is so hard you can't do it any other way. You use a wide assortment of metal devices that go into the cracks and don't use the rope that often.

"The most dangerous type of rock climbing is free soloing, without a doubt. But then again, the people who do that really are the most skilled. The whole thing with free soloing is to do it when it really feels right. You can't do it if you have to think about every move, or that you might fall and get splattered all over the ground. You've got to feel real confident and really have fun. I've never felt that it was all that much fun because it began getting difficult for me."

With the preplaced bolts, the climber uses nylon webbed ladders that are clipped into the bolts. Once they are clipped, the climber goes up the ladder and gains about three feet. Then he reaches up and places another piece of gear, moves the ladder up, and does it again. Of all the types of rock climbing, this may be the safest, though nothing is completely safe when you're that high off the ground. For Chris McNamara, this kind of climbing became too slow. His favorite type of climbing, something not done by a lot of people, is speed climbing. In other words, he wants to get on

and off the rock face a lot faster than most people and has become
so proficient at it that he holds nine major speed-climbing records
on big walls.

"Unlike most types of climbing, you have to deal with a lot of
gear when doing big walls," McNamara explained. "The gear can
weigh 70 to 150 pounds. Most people take three to five days to
climb El Cap, for example. Part of the reason they take so long is
that they are hauling up a whole bunch of food and supplies, as if
they are camping out, vertical style. There's food, water, bedding,
and porta-ledges for sleeping on the rock face. If you are climbing
with a partner, you have two ropes—a climbing rope and a haul
rope. You then climb in pitches. Starting from the ground, you
climb up maybe 150 feet, then stay at what we call a belay station,
a place to hook in, rest, and set up so you can haul the gear up on
pulleys. Now your partner has to come up, following the pitch to
where you are. Then you do it again, breaking the climb up into
100- to 200-foot sections or pitches. It's a slow process.

"In speed climbing, you can leave all of that behind, travel real
light. Then you don't have to stop as frequently and can go thirty
or forty, or even a hundred feet between protection pieces, the bolts.
The longer the distance between protection pieces, however, the
more the risk of a big fall. The way it works, basically, is this: If I
start on the ground and climb up ten feet, then let go, I'm going to
crash back to the ground. But if I climb up ten feet, put in a protection piece and clip a rope, if I fall I'm not going to go anywhere
because the rope will catch me. If I climb 5 feet above that, I can
only take a ten-foot fall. I don't think I've fallen more than fifteen
feet, but I know some climbers who have taken hundred-foot falls.
Usually the injuries come from hitting something on the way
down, like a ledge that sticks out, before the rope stops you. Yosemite, however, has pretty clean rocks and the rope is elastic, so
you don't get jolted too badly."

So Chris McNamara tries to go from the bottom to the top as
quickly as he can. But it's not a race. In most cases, he's not even
being timed. "A lot of it is just doing it in a day, wanting to deal
with the climb in under twenty-four hours instead of five days," he
said. "Without all the gear, all that food and water, you have a

much different sensation when climbing. You feel more naked and more free on the rock face. You're moving over the terrain much faster, which is the draw of it."

For McNamara, there is a whole world of climbing just on El Capitan. "I'm going up amazing routes. There are eighty to a hundred different routes and variations. Each one is a different difficulty. The routes that have the most big cracks are generally easier. Some of those I've done in three to three-and-a-half hours. The ones that have the really small cracks take much more time, much more equipment. On those, the record will be something like 36 hours continuously. There are even some routes that are so difficult that no one will try to do it nonstop."

Therein lies one inherent danger. Fatigue. To be climbing for nearly a day and a half, nonstop, not only tests a climber's endurance, but his ability to survive and prevail. "I've been up there for as long as thirty-eight hours with little or no rest," said McNamara. "That's exhausting. You're in a whole other state of mind. Generally, you try to keep it under fifteen hours, in the daylight. If it gets dark, you climb with a headlamp, like a miner. As you get more tired, you may begin going a little slower, but you're always aware of what is going on around you."

Though he has traveled to places such as Baffin Island and Norway to rock climb, McNamara prefers to stick to Yosemite and the Eastern Sierras. He also has said he has no interest in climbing a Mount Everest or any of the other huge peaks in the world. His personal challenge is simply moving up a rock wall as quickly as he can. He even feels that his style of climbing—at least for him—is relatively safe.

"The real risk in climbing is when you deal with snow," he said. "That's when you deal with objective dangers you can't control, like avalanche and horrendous storms. Rock climbing is done with nice temperatures, no real danger of a rock fall because you are generally on good rock. On an alpine snow face, even without an avalanche there is danger. You slip once and it can be over. Ice climbing also has more dangers," he added, confirming what others had said. "On ice you're often doing steeper stuff and are more careful and tuned into the dangers."

Like some of the others who have accumulated a good deal of climbing experience, Chris McNamara feels the greater danger in the sport is often found by young and inexperienced climbers. "Everyone takes risks when they are younger," he explained. "There are people now who take some pretty huge risks, but it's often hard to know exactly what they are doing. They may not even know what they're doing. There are a lot of sports where you don't realize how much trouble you're in until it's too late. With rock climbing you are aware of it. If you're free soloing and get above even twenty feet, you're aware that if you let go you're gonna crash to the ground."

Craig DeMartino is a climber who has free soloed, going up rock faces that are sometimes 800 to 1,000 feet high. He enjoys it because it's a very free and quick climb, though it certainly can be dangerous.

"The most difficult route I free soloed was semivertical," De-Martino said. "At the very top there were some overhangs, but they were pretty much featured, so there was a lot to grab. I had done the route before and it was a really good day for me. So I just went out and did it. When you don't have a rope on, you can cover ground very quickly, so the climb is very fast. That climb was in New York at New Paltz, but I soloed once in El Dorado Canyon near Boulder, and I was a little sketchy about it because the rock was loose in places. The only difference was that I rehearsed a few moves several times before I made them. I was going through this tight little constriction in the rock where you kind of had to wiggle through. I just did that twice to make sure it felt right, then committed to it and did it.

"By rehearsing in this case, I climbed up twice and looked at the constriction. Then I downclimbed to a ledge and rested a bit. All the while you're evaluating, just making sure you know exactly what you have to do to get through. This particular spot was about two hundred feet high and without a rope you don't want to be falling from there. So you want to be sure of what you're doing."

Like many other climbers, the Pennsylvania-born DeMartino played football and baseball as a kid, but soon found he wasn't a big team sport player, and would rather do things with just a single partner. He fell in love with rock climbing the first time he tried it at age twenty-four, and eight years ago moved to Colorado so he could pursue his climbing with more intensity. The 5-foot-10, 148-pounder makes keeping in shape for climbing a family affair, since his wife, Cyndy, is also a climber and joins him on some of his outings.

"We built a climbing wall inside our garage," he said. "As soon as it gets too cold to boulder outside, I do it in there. I climb in there for probably an hour at a time three times a week. We also have a finger board or hang board and I'll just hang on different-sized ledges. The only time I've done any weight training was after I had some bad tendinitis in my elbow and had to build up the other muscles, instead of those I use for climbing. That's the only time I use weight. Weight training can put bulk on you, and as a climber, that's the last thing I want. All climbers are lean and gangly. I don't know one who's heavy. I've seen a couple of wall climbers who are big guys, but wall climbing is a little different. You're standing on your placements. They're stronger guys, usually."

Bouldering, wall climbing, and ice climbing are the disciplines that DeMartino usually pursues. He has climbed over much of the Eastern United States, including Virginia and West Virginia, and has also found places to challenge in California, Colorado, and Utah, as well as going bouldering in Texas. Of all the types of climbing he does, he feels that ice poses the most danger simply because the ice can break. He's also rock climbed in the Black Canyon of the Gunnison in northwest Colorado, a 2,000-foot-deep natural formation where he says the rock is also unstable and can break. When he climbs there, DeMartino takes extra pieces of gear for safety. Like most climbers, he is acutely aware of what can happen if he falls.

"Rock climbing is probably the most physically demanding," he said. "I'll push the level of difficulty a lot higher there than I will on ice. On ice, I just won't hedge my bets. I don't want to fall there. Screws can pull out if you put force on them. On rock, if you fall, the gear will stop you. Plus with most known rock routes, there are books that tell you where you're supposed to be, and you follow the natural weakness in the rock. It might be a crack, or a system of edges. In ice climbing, you pretty much go where you think you're gonna get through."

Again, it's what the individual climber wants to do. Carlos Buhler and Sharon Wood always felt the call of the big mountains, the challenge of getting up into altitude and trying to prevail. Like Craig McNamara, Craig DeMartino has no desire to tackle Mount Everest or anything like it. "I have friends who do the alpine stuff," he said, "and I've done a little, but it's just not what I really enjoy doing. To me, it's a lot of walking and slogging, and that's not my thing. I like to do harder, technical climbing rather than going out and walking up a mountain. So I don't have the desire to do Everest or K2."

DeMartino, a photojournalist by profession, spends most of his time away from work with other climbers. He has found, however, that over a period of time, climbers sometimes tend to come and go. Only the real hard-core ones stay around. "I've noticed with climbers that when they first get into the sport, they go through this thing where all they want to do is climb," DeMartino said. "There's a complete immersion into it and they climb constantly. You do get real addicted to that focus you get from climbing, so that's what causes them to go full boat at first. But you don't run into a lot of climbers who climb for a long period of time. By that, I mean more than five years. A lot of people will climb for a couple of years and then stop. I'm not sure why that is. Maybe they either get hung up with a job or have a family and feel they shouldn't do it anymore. I've always been lucky in that I'm able to climb, do my job, and spend time with my family.

"I still get the same enjoyment from climbing as I did the first two years I climbed. As I get older—I'm thirty-six now—there are certain things I won't do. I wouldn't go soloing today because of my family situation and I don't want something to happen. But I wouldn't say, oh gosh, I can't climb anymore."

DeMartino also feels that the new climbers coming into the sport today are pushing it to new levels. "A lot of the young climbers learned to climb in a gym," he explained. "You're graded there on how hard you climb and it's very hard to get hurt in a gym, what with the use of harnesses. But many of these climbers are taking the gymnastic moves they learned inside and bringing that whole mentality outdoors, and when they began going outside, they just tore it up. There are kids half my age bouldering today who are just incredible. They're very strong and willing to boulder stuff that is very high, well over fifty feet. That's very difficult because of the chance of falling, but they're willing to do that.

"The youth culture—the MTV generation—is geared toward pushing a lot harder and being better. Not the best, but just being better, being yourself. A lot of the climbing kids I see—and there's a definite difference between kids who climb in the gym and those who climb outside—are not afraid to fall. They just push through things. I think their mentality is that they aren't going to get hurt. I remember one guy telling me there are bold climbers and there are old climbers. But there are no bold, old climbers. There's a lot of truth in that. You have to know where the edge is and where the line is. You can go up to it and you can stick your head over it, but you have to know when to pull back. It's something you learn through trial and error."

Abby Watkins is a climber who enjoys it all and especially loves mixed climbs that often combine rock, ice, and even alpine. Born in Australia in 1969, then spending an incredibly athletic childhood that saw her become a world-class gymnast, Watkins was introduced to climbing after she went to the University of California at Berkeley on a gymnastics scholarship. Once she started, there was no thought of stopping.

"All the different types of climbing have their draw and their enjoyment. In bolted sport climbing, you really become internal, focusing on overcoming personal, physical, and mental barriers. There is also very much a gymnastics side of it as well, so that appeals to me on that level. Yet I think if I only sport climbed, I would not be satisfied. The next level would be traditional rock climbing, where you are placing your own protection. There's more art to that, because you have to have a greater understanding of how to put the pitch together and set your bolts, especially if it hasn't been put together for you by the first ascensionist. So there's more art to know how much gear to take, where to place it, how much to keep for later. You have to understand the entire dynamic of the climb and how to put it together.

"Then you can add ice or snow or altitude, or even the length of the climb. Adding more complications makes it more interesting to me. I live in Canada now, in the Canadian Rockies, and the alpine climbing here is some of the best of the world. It's very enjoyable because not only do you have to understand how to put the climb together, but you have to understand the changing conditions, when it's safe and when it's not safe. That's what really appeals to me, how to put a whole climb together from crossing the glacier, climbing the ice face, climbing the rock where you might have to place petons and route finds. Then watching the weather becomes important, understanding it, knowing what to make of the clouds in the morning, the temperature, feeling the texture of the snow, predicting what is going to happen and how the conditions will be, and how all of that is going to affect your climb and keep you safe. The true mountain sense, the true sense of that word, can't be gained overnight or by reading a book. It's a kind of pilgrimage, an art form, a craft perhaps."

With more women becoming involved in climbing, Abby Watkins might be something of a role model because of her skills and the climbs she has done. It's not surprising, then, that she has also worked to encourage more women to become involved with the sport. "I think as more women fulfill their potential, there will be more role models and women will just take it for granted that climbing is something they can do. So yes, I think women in climbing is still quite young as far as the development is concerned, where women in the sport are going. It's not that women should, it's that they can. Climbing is very enjoyable and women can find a lot of enjoyment, success, and satisfaction in it. However, I think there is still some sexism in the sport of climbing and some attitudes that need to change on both sides.

"It used to be that if men and women were climbing together, the assumption was that the guy was leading everything. But that's not true anymore. I climb a lot with my husband, Rich Marshall, and he and I are great partners. In some aspects of climbing, he's stronger, and in other aspects, I'm stronger. And in still other aspects we're fairly equal. Either of us can take the lead."

Kim Csizmazia, who is a frequent climbing partner of Watkins, has some of the same feelings about prevailing attitudes thrown at women climbers. She gives her take on the same subject. "I think the attitude that women can't do certain things within the climbing community is still pretty much there, but the belief that you can't do that because you are a women is now held mostly by the women themselves," Csizmazia said. "Whether they have been told that by a man, another woman, or society, it doesn't really matter. Not if they believe it. I've put a lot of thought into it when I'm conducting clinics or climbing with a lot of different female partners. I did this climb just recently with a man and I thought gosh, I've done this route now and I guess I don't have to come back. But then I realized that the route still hasn't been done by two women together. I mentioned it to my partner and he asked if it mattered, acknowledging that we were equal partners and we had done it. I said yes, it does matter because everybody looks at it differently. You can say okay, Kim went and did this with Raphael yesterday, or Kim went and did it with Abby yesterday, and it gets looked at differently and considered differently.

"I think it's looked at that way by most climbers. There is always this underlying kind of thing that Raphael got me up the route to some degree. It isn't really true and Raphael knows that, but that's how people look at it. So it's important to us, as women—to most of us as women—to go out and do certain kinds of climbs together. I'm not trying to make this huge statement about men and women, but in this particular instance in climbing, it's significant to me that the route, which is an all-time classic here in the Rockies, hasn't had two women doing it. Maybe there just haven't been enough women to actually climb that hard, to even go up there and do that route. It's a significant thing to me as a female climber. It doesn't have to matter to anyone else, but it matters to me."

Are climbers like Abby Watkins and Kim Csizmazia going at their sport harder because they feel they have something to prove as women? Perhaps. Women have traditionally followed men in nearly all sports, even the so-called traditional ones. There have been pioneers, women who have broken new ground in nearly all of them. In the adventure sports, however, women take the same risks as men, and there have certainly been too many fatalities. Witness the story of alpine climber Alison Hargreaves, which was discussed earlier. Yet women like Abby Watkins and Kim Csizmazia continue to climb. They may not be known for feats such as soloing Mount Everest, but they go up the same walls, rock faces, and ice slopes as the men. There will always be those who say women don't do it as well as their male counterparts, but the validity of that statement may not be true and, perhaps, isn't really important.

There is one other phenomenon in big wall climbing that doesn't exist in any other sport. To those who haven't experienced it, even the mere thought will send shivers racing up their spines. Think about where you sleep. For most people, the answer is a comfortable bed. People have sometimes been known to sleep in their cars, in Pullman cars on trains, on airplanes, or perhaps in a tent or sleeping bag while camping. Homeless people are sometimes reduced to sleeping on a bench or in a cardboard box, a rather sobering thought for many of us. Comfortable, semicomfortable, or downright uncomfortable, all these various modes of sleeping quarters have something in common: They are pretty much sitting firmly on the ground.

No such luck for big wall climbers who know they have to spend three or five days on a wall to complete their climb. They sleep in something called a porta-ledge, which is bolted to the side of the rock face and can be 1,500 or 2,000 feet above the ground. It's the bedroom, living room, and bathroom all rolled into one, and a place where you don't dare roll out of bed. What is it like for a climber to sleep in one of these porta-ledges? Can they relax, rest, and even sleep, knowing that if by some crazy chance the bolts come out, they will have a long dark fall to the ground?

"I've done maybe half a dozen big walls," said Craig Demartino, "the longest one being six days on El Cap, the shortest about two or three days' duration. I've got to admit that the first time I *bivied,* spent the night on a porta-ledge, I was completely freaked out. It was in Zion, Utah, and I was scared. I was on a porta-ledge for the first time and the whole night I was laying there thinking the anchor was going to rip out and we were just going to plummet. You're sleeping on a hammock, basically, so you can't roll off. You still wear your harness and you're in a whole separate anchor for that. So even if the porta-ledge collapsed, you wouldn't fall, though it would probably scare the hell out of you. You'd be left hanging. But now that I've done it enough, I find it very peaceful. Once the ledge is set up, it's a soft place to sit. You can relax. You can read. You can watch the sunset. It's just a great place to be and I sleep like a rock."

Abby Watkins also finds the porta-ledge a nice place to be. "It's the most comfortable thing you could ever imagine," she said, "and that canned food is delicious." Kim Csizmazia also says the first time is the toughest. "It crosses your mind that the bolts might come out," she said, "but now I'm very comfortable up there. The reality is that there's no way it's going to come out while you're sleeping. So you let that thought go, just relax and enjoy yourself. The vertical world like that is an incredible place to spend time."

Craig DeMartino volunteered the answer to a question he is asked very often. "People who know what I do always ask me if I carry something to use for a bathroom," he said. "It depends where you're climbing. In Yosemite and Zion now, you have to carry what they call poop tubes, which is a PVC pipe that has lime in it. It's sealed at both ends. So you go to the bathroom in a bag, then drop it into the tube. That way, you bring everything out. As bad as this sounds, when I first started wall climbing, you could throw it off the ledge. Then you were supposed to go back at the end of your climb and clean up the base of the cliff. What happened was that people weren't doing that, so the National Park Service made a rule that whatever you take in, you also take out. It's actually cleaned up a lot of climbing areas, which is good."

To many, this probably sounds like the good, the bad, and the ugly of big wall climbing, but to those who find scaling a big wall irresistible, you enjoy the climbing process and do whatever is necessary to complete the task at hand. Look at it this way: Sleeping on a porta-ledge makes you immune to someone ringing the doorbell, driving past with music blaring or a horn blowing, or hearing someone blasting a television in the next room. There was a time when the telephone wouldn't ring either, but with the advent of cell phones, that part has changed in many places. That notwithstanding, DeMartino maintained, "I think the neatest thing is when you go to bed at night, you can't see anything. But when you wake up and roll over to look over the side of the bed, it's really cool to be looking down at the side of the cliff."

There are those who still say that climbing is not a natural function of man, at least not climbing 3,000-foot vertical walls or mountains that stretch more than 25,000 feet into the sky. They are the naysayers, the ones who will usually state, *Those people are crazy.* It isn't easy for someone who has never done it to understand climbing, or any of the other extreme, or adventure sports, Those who climb, however, are skilled and devoted, and absolutely love what they do.

5

THE ADVENTURE OF
THE EXTREME—RIDING

Injuries are part of the game, something to be expected. I have a friend who always says screw it if I get injured, because everybody gets hurt. But it's still a bummer. It's actually a worse experience for us than normal people because normal people can lead their normal lives with an injury. Our lives go on hold, so it's actually more devastating.

—Kristen Ulmer, radical skier

SOME jump, some climb, and others ride. That, in perhaps its simplest form, defines the sports that are considered dangerous and extreme. Jumpers and climbers notwithstanding, those who ride tend to push the envelope just as hard, making trips to the edge with their own brand of daring-do. While the average person associates riding with bicycles, cars, maybe even horses, these riders use skis, snowboards, surfboards, kayaks, and motorcycles to perform maneuvers that were once thought next to impossible. Like the other athletes, they know the risks they take can lead to serious injury or death, but that is just part of the game, a dreaded by-product that still visits the extreme a little bit too often.

These sports are not all as closely related as are jumping and climbing sports described earlier, except that it also takes a great deal of time and skill to perfect them. Free-riding skiers and snowboarders often perform on the same kinds of mountains that alpine climbers love to scale. Coming down steep slopes, jumping off rock faces, and sometimes trying to outrun small snow slides call sloughs, which are created by the action of their skis or snowboards and which can easily build into avalanches, these snow riders are seeking freedom of expression and new forms of creativity, while often earning a living at the same time. Increasing numbers of these skiers and boarders are opting for the more extreme forms of their sports while leaving behind traditional ski racing—slalom, giant slalom, and downhill.

Surfing was long a sport associated with a relaxing day at the beach. Sunbathers and swimmers enjoy watching the surfers launch their boards and paddle out to catch a wave, then jump up and ride the wave back into shore. Of course, there are waves, and then there are waves, but there are only a few places where there are *big waves*. Still a relatively small and exclusive fraternity, just a special few surfers now practice the highly dangerous and thrilling sport known as big wave surfing. These waves are so huge that a surfer simply cannot paddle out to catch them, the longtime traditional way to grab a wave. Big wave surfers have to be towed into the wave at a special angle by a jet ski, something that takes a great deal of practice and timing. Once in, the ride on one of these huge, breaking waves can be the thrill of a lifetime. Make a mistake, however, and the consequences can be lethal.

Kayaking is another sport often associated with a leisurely day of paddling on streams and lakes. But there are a few hearty souls who have decided it would be fun to launch a kayak off a waterfall and fly through the air before landing in the pool below. With no parachute or elastic rope to break their fall, these kayak jumpers depend on their skills and the ability to *read* the water below, judging the amount of aeration and depth in the landing area, then must angle their craft perfectly if they are to avoid a potentially serious injury.

At first glance, those who ride motorcycles might seem a bit out of place. While auto and motocross racing are certainly dangerous sports, well organized and very popular, they are not really considered extreme and thus are not among those being discussed here. However, there are growing forms of motorcycle riding that allow the riders to showcase a variety of talents while taking even bigger risks than the racers take. Freestyle motocross consists of contests in which the rider launches his bike off a ramp, and while in the air does a variety of gymnastic-type maneuvers before getting back on the seat and hopefully landing safely. Because the tricks are becoming more technical and increasingly dangerous, the sport is seeing more of its share of injuries and, in some cases, fatalities.

Other motorcyclists enjoy the type of stunt riding similar to that made famous by Evel Knievel. Though it isn't quite the same, and might be considered a bit on the periphery of the type of sports being examined, these riders, nevertheless, often risk life and limb in much the same way that others do. When they aren't doing stunts commercially, they often go off on their own and try to set records for jumping and flying on their bikes.

Skiing and Snowboarding

Skiing is an old sport, snowboarding a relatively new one. In fact, history tells us that perhaps as much as 400 years separates the two. Remnants of skis found in Norway and Sweden have been estimated to go back to about the sixteenth century. The sport evolved into its modern form in the middle of the nineteenth century, was introduced to the United States by Norwegian immigrants around 1850, and became an Olympic sport in 1924. For nearly a century, the most celebrated skiers in the world were those who brought Olympic medals to their homelands. Ski racing through a gated course, as well as the speedy downhill race, competing in the World Cup and the Olympics, was what all young skiers aspired to achieve.

Snowboarding, on the other hand, evolved more from skateboarding than from skiing. The first rudimentary board, something called the *Snurfer,* wasn't created until 1965. The sport didn't begin taking off until the late 1970s and into the 1980s. Soon, recreational snowboarders began sharing the slopes with skiers, though the two didn't always mix since skiers tend to go straight ahead, while snowboarders usually *carve* down a hillside, going side to side. That often made for inadvertent collisions on the slopes. But the snowboarders had another discipline as well. It was called the *half pipe,* and consisted of two rounded ramps of snow, set opposite each other that actually resembled half a large pipe. Snowboarders would go from side to side, catching air at the top of the pipe on each side, whirling around and doing some quick gymnastic-type tricks before landing, swinging over to the other side, and doing it again.

Snowboarders also began going out of bounds, riding their boards over fallen tree trunks, jumping off rocks and snow ledges, and generally emulating the street-style skateboarding that had also become a newfound craze among young teens. Then, in the 1990s, the snowboarding and skiing began to merge, both evolving into new forms that were faster, more exciting, more dangerous, and more attractive to extreme athletes.

New Hampshire–born Kristen Ulmer has a reputation as one of the best of the high-risk, radical skiers on the planet. Largely self-taught as a kid, she nevertheless fell in love with the sport and then set about achieving the same goal as so many others—making the United States Ski Team that would go to the Olympic Games. "I was naive," she said. "I skied in jeans until I was twenty, never read a ski magazine until I was twenty-one, yet by the time I was twenty-three, I made the U.S. Ski Team. So I was clueless, and all my peers in skiing were living, breathing, dreaming through skiing. You could say I took an unusual route."

Ulmer's improvement was fast and dramatic. She became a top mogul skier on the U.S. Ski Team, and also began running out-of-bounds courses—courses with natural obstacles such as trees, rocks, and no cut trails—on larger mountains. The magazines took note and it wasn't long before she was considered one of the best extreme skiers in the world. It was a knee injury, as well as the prevailing economic climate of the time, that precipitated her decision to stick with the high-risk skiing. "I was still nursing the injury and mogul skiing (going over a series of successive mounds while doing tricks) is a constant jarring of your body. Big jumps you encounter while free skiing down the course of your choice give you a bigger jar, but you do it much less frequently. I also found I could earn a living. With the U.S. Ski Team, I had to pay all my living and traveling expenses, and I just didn't have that kind of money. Since I was beginning to have so much more success as an extreme skier, I quit the ski team after one year."

Soon, Ulmer was being recognized as a skier who was willing to take almost any risk and ski nearly impossible routes. "I found I really liked the danger," she said. "I really liked putting my neck out there and somehow surviving. As I became a better skier, I began taking bigger and bigger risks. I don't think I consciously decided to get into a dangerous sport. Skiing in New Hampshire, for example, avalanches aren't even part of the equation, but now I have to face them all the time, and they're terrifying. Unfortunately, that's the natural progression of getting better and better."

Since becoming a full-time professional extreme skier in 1991, Ulmer has been in nearly two dozen ski movies, has been known for her cliff jumps and other dangerous stunts, and has been all over the world, all by the age of thirty-three. The last several years she has been focusing on ski mountaineering, first climbing steep mountains, then skiing down them. That's just another example of an extreme athlete—very skilled in one sport, then combining that skill with yet another, high-risk discipline. "The extreme sports world I live in is quite demented," Ulmer said, tongue slightly in cheek. "Those athletes who hang their necks out the farthest and still manage to come home alive or uninjured day after day get the most sponsorship money, film jobs, and publicity. It's a completely gender-free game. Women play hard, too, although the numbers are lacking. In skiing and snowboarding, for every thirty guys willing to ski steep, you-fall-you-die descents, or jump fifty-foot cliffs daily, there's only one woman. The international snow scene has perhaps a dozen truly significant female athletes. I'm one of them and I ski with men. I've struggled my whole life to execute flips or tear through steep trees at breakneck speed, because that's what it took to ski like a man, to satiate my own internal drive, and to be taken seriously."

For a long time, Ulmer's philosophy was that for a woman to make her mark in an athletic career, she should try to emulate the best. To do this, however, can be very difficult since Ulmer feels that 9.99 times out of 10, the best is a man, or men. However, in recent years, she has backed off that stated desire to be as good as the men, at least on a regular basis. "There was a time when I felt I was at the same level as the male skiers in this country," Ulmer said, "but I don't think I am anymore. Mostly because it's exhausting to be that competitive, especially being in a sport that has a lot of injuries. It's scary. And to stay at that level all the time is totally exhausting. Now I know I don't have to go out and take that many risks. It's not necessary in order to be a professional athlete."

She does take risks, however, especially since she began combining climbing with skiing. The kind of skiing she does can be absolutely incredible and a totally frightening experience to those watching for the first time. Coming down almost vertical slopes, setting off sloughs or miniavalanches in her wake, skidding at top speed over bare rocks that have poked out from the snow, taking forty- and fifty-foot jumps that beckon ominously, making sharp turns that resemble a slalom, and attaining the speeds of a downhill racer, Kristen Ulmer does it all. But Ulmer has never been one to duck a challenge. Back in 1997, she wanted to be the first woman to ski the Grand Teton, a 13,000-foot-plus mountain in Wyoming. It was a mountaineering ski trip. First climb up, then ski down.

It would seem more logical when challenging a new and dangerous mountain to simply let a helicopter fly you to the top. Then you just have to worry about the ski descent. If you climb, not only are you encountering potential dangers on the climb, but you can exhaust yourself before the ski part, when you need all your energy and focus. "Sure, I would always prefer to take the helicopter, but they're expensive and sometimes it's just fun to go out and hike and climb," she said. "I'm really an avid climber, so to combine my two favorite sports increases the challenge. It's true, though, that climbing can definitely exhaust you. In fact, the first time I tried to ski the Grand Teton, we were so exhausted before we ever reached the top that I thought there's no way I'm going to have the strength to focus and ski."

One of Ulmer's partners on that first attempt was the legendary climber Alex Lowe. Even with his considerable presence, the climb was extremely difficult. The group took what is called the Ford/Stettner route, and as Ulmer said, they "had to climb seven thousand vertical feet and still have the strength to make solid turns down a forty-five–fifty-five degree slope on what is typically very bad snow." The climbing included rock and ice faces, a mixed climb with a lot of falling ice, rocks, and water from the slopes above. The temperatures were a bit too warm and the danger of avalanche too great. Some 1,300 feet from the top they quit. The avalanche risk was the deciding factor.

"It's a heavy thought to realize if you fall, you die," Ulmer said. "But it's even heavier to realize if you fall, you kill the world's best climber and a father of three [Lowe] and your best friend and a father of two."

Ulmer, however, couldn't get the Grand Teton out of her head. A short time later she tried again. Lowe wasn't there this time, but conditions were a bit better so Ulmer and her partners made it to the top. It was June 8, 1997, when Kristen Ulmer became the first woman to ski down the mountain. "According to [my partners], on my third turn I knocked down the mother of all snow slides," she said. "I remember jumping on the slope really hard and feeling the snow wash away, then start to accelerate. In fact, it accelerated like nothing I've ever seen, seventy miles per hour, hit a rock wall, and exploded into the air. The avalanche could be heard crashing down the mountain for at least a minute. As I skied down, every turn set off another major slough. The technique was take one turn, stop, wait for the slide to accelerate, then turn again, stop, and wait again."

Halfway down, one of her partners took the lead. "The terrain was five feet deep and pure ice on a fifty-five degree slope," she said. "His full body weight rested on the tips and tails of his skis, threatening to bend them in half. On my turn I'd never felt more alert in my life. Will the skis hold? Is that an avalanche coming? We finished the ski descent in under an hour."

Looking back, Ulmer admits the risks on the Grand Teton were probably a little too much. "Yeah, I think we went a little overboard," she said. "But I was absolutely determined to ski the Grand Teton. Once I get my mind set on something I want to do, I do it. The pressure to do it came from myself, and on the practical side, I knew it would be huge for my career." Yet in spite of all the risks, Ulmer still says she has no trouble walking away if something doesn't seem right. "We stand at the top and look at it like a risk-and-reward analysis. If the risk is greater than the reward, I have no problem walking away. I won't lose sleep over it. But at the same time, I know how happy I'll be after I accomplish it."

The closest Ulmer has ever come to death? It was on a mountain in Canada when she was caught in one of the five avalanches that could have killed her. This one was especially bad because it knocked her over and threatened to sweep her over a forty-foot cliff that was at a forty-five-degree angle and comprised of sharp, dangerous rocks. "Even though I was traveling at a high speed," she recalled, "my instinct was to right myself and I managed to get up on one ski. At the last instant, at the very edge of the rocks, I pushed with everything I had and did a swan dive away from the rocks so I wouldn't be grinded to bits on them. When you're falling, you want to go limp except for when you have to make a quick move. Somehow, in the middle of tumbling, I was able to do it."

Ulmer was literally being swept down the hill by the avalanche and being pushed directly toward a group of sharp rocks that could have injured her severely. Because of her ability to stay calm and her great skiing instincts, she was able to make a last-second move that took her away from the rocks and got her out of the avalanche, and that, in a nutshell, is Kristen Ulmer, radical skier supreme.

Like many other adventuresome athletes, Shane McConkey pursues more than one sport. He's a sky diver, a BASE jumper, and a freestyle skier. In Chapter 3, McConkey talked about his early fascination with catching air. That's what would lead to his later sky-diving and BASE-jumping exploits. He loves being airborne. The thirty-three-year-old grew up ski racing, however, but soon gave it up after his first taste of the extreme. "Skiing is a sport all about freedom," he said, "the wind in your face, speed, and air. I just sort of progressed to wanting to go faster and catch more air. I really tried all aspects of it and now enjoy freeskiing, filming ski segments, and freeriding competitions. In competitions you have a starting gate at the top of the mountain, no boundaries, and a finish line. So you do pretty much whatever you want, express your own creativity, take jumps, do some tricks, whatever strikes you. It's really about going out and showing off."

McConkey explains that the skiers plan their own programs, take cliff jumps, do flips, ski a really tight line through the rocks, then pick up speed and jump over things. With this type of skiing, some of the danger is removed because the competitors have a chance to check out the mountain, plan their route, and even cruise over it at a slower pace, but it can still showcase some pretty radical stuff. The sport has grown to the point where there is now a World Tour in freeskiing in both North America and Europe, with some thirty or forty events around the world each year. There are also five major events which have about a hundred participants each.

Though his freeskiing activities are organized and planned, McConkey says that the dangers are still real. "When you're skiing steep terrain and with certain types of snow, you have to be care of your sloughs," he said. "You also have to watch for rocks when you're landing a jump and of falling in no-fall zones where there's a likelihood of tumbling or star-fishing over rocks." Pretty much all the competitions are in venues that are steep and dangerous. They are judged by (1) degree of difficulty, (2) aggressiveness, (3) control, (4) technique, and (5) fluidity. These are the kinds of contests that were not held a few years ago, but with more skiers opting for the more dangerous freeskiing, something had to be created for them. It's one example of how high-risk sports have come into the mainstream.

McConkey divides his time between skiing and BASE jumping, and says that most high-risk athletes pursue more than one sport. "Many of the skiers and snowboarders also snowmobile," he said, "usually freestyle snowmobiling. Or they skateboard. One of the reasons I do these things is because it's such a cool feeling to be just reacting, rather than having to think. To me, it's one of the most fascinating and enjoyable things in life, when you're doing your sport and it's all reaction, all happening, and you're not thinking about anything else except what's right in front of you. That's a pretty cool thing."

Circe Wallace fell in love with snowboarding immediately, after ten years of modern and jazz dance. She also skateboarded, but found something special gliding over the snow. "I think I really went for the free-flowing movement in snowboarding," she said. "I felt it opened up a whole new arena of self-expression. You do bigger, wider, more graceful turns, and it just came naturally to me. Snowboarding felt more like what I was doing in dance. I felt a lot more graceful on a snowboard. I felt less restricted than on a skateboard. Because my feet were attached, I felt I could push it a little harder."

Soon Wallace was competing in half-pipe contests, as well as racing. But with more and more videos being filmed, she gradually began going up on the bigger mountains to make freeriding videos. Many times she had to reach her starting point by heli-copter. "You can pick your own line when you're in the copter," she explained. "You'll be flying over the mountain and decide this is where you want to ride. You have a kind of freedom to be ex-pressive on the mountain and this is something I always loved. Doing the film work, I was able to pick up sponsors, and that made it easier to keep doing what I loved."

Though she always loved being on her board, Wallace found the mountains to be intimidating, especially when dropped off by helicopter. "When you go up in this helicopter in the middle of nowhere and get dropped off on a mountaintop, you're putting your life in the hands of mother nature," she said. "It's a really rad-ical, awesome experience. I've had a few close calls with some good-sized sloughs or small avalanches. It's important to be really educated and tuned in to others, as well as picking a top-notch film and support crew to work with you. I wanted the people with me to have a really good knowledge of the snow, how it appears to be packed, and what it might do as I ride it, so I would know what to expect. Sometimes snow that you think is mellow can be a sleeping giant, and you have to be very careful of the low-angle snow that can build up to more substantial slides, because the steeper snow more naturally sloughs. It's also about temperature. You've got to watch that carefully. The sport is definitely very intimidating, es-pecially when you're alone, the only rider up there, as is usually the case in Alaska."

Radical snowboarding runs, such as Wallace described, can last from thirty seconds to four minutes, depending on the elevation and how much vertical slope there is. Like some others, however, Circe Wallace feels the best is yet to come where freestyle snow-boarding is concerned. As with some of the other sports, she feels it is the younger generation that will show the way.

"We're starting to see a technical progression moving over to big mountain riding," she said, "where people are doing more technical tricks off cliffs. Everyone is always pushing it to the absolute maximum all the time. We're seeing huge strides and progression every year, especially from the younger riders. Young and dumb. They don't know fear and it works to their advantage and for the sport. There are also more people getting into snowboarding at an early age. When I was a kid, no one was doing it," the thirty-two-year-old Wallace added. "A lot of the kids now have been doing it since they were eight or nine, so they're starting with some better fundamental skills. We were first-generation pros. Now they're doing things younger."

Snowboarder Rob DaFoe has jumped off a great many cliffs on his board, as well spending time at big mountain riding. He has seen jumps up to 140 feet off a 60-foot cliff, but riders doing that kind of high-risk maneuver must have a great deal of experience to avoid injury. "You need the perfect drop and the perfect landing," he said, "and that's not easy. If you don't jump a certain way from path to landing, you can break your legs every time. Scouting the location and checking out the landing area very carefully are extremely important for a successful jump. You can't go into this area of the sport in a haphazard way. You have to know the rules before you can break them, and know the parameters before you decide to stretch them.

"There are always challenges. Every year I go to a mountain in Chile. The snow is always different and jumping there becomes a fight with yourself, with your own mind. It's all about having to push yourself. When you're with your friends, it's still something like a dare . . . that I can do something you can't. If your friend does one trick off a jump, you want to do a harder one. There's an unspoken competition between riders, even when they aren't doing it for the money."

DaFoe says that riding the big mountains, top to bottom, isn't difficult if you pick an easy line with few difficult obstacles. Riders, however, tend to challenge themselves again, usually choosing the hardest line to come down. He also agrees with Circe Wallace that young riders are doing crazier things. "The equipment is better," he said, "but I think it comes down to the kids wanting fame, wanting it fast, and knowing they have to push hard and go further out to the edge to get it."

Kevin Quinn has been all over the extreme scoreboard. He has been a professional hockey player, has bungee jumped and sky dived, has done white water kayaking, rope freeflying, freestyle skiing, and has also been a big game hunting guide. Quite a résumé.

"I started with ski racing, slalom, downhill, giant slalom," said the thirty-three-year-old Quinn, "even went to the Junior Olympics when I was thirteen. But skiing has changed so much from then to now. It's all about freedom, especially with people skiing these big mountains. I think racing is becoming more a thing of the past. It's still popular, but you're seeing more and more big mountain freeskiers, extreme skiers, being able to go where they want. Now we call the slalom racers 'stick chasers.' It's great for skill development, but it's boring. Being able to go fast and being prepared for whatever comes next has a far greater attraction, that overall freedom to explore the mountain."

Forty-year-old Tom Day currently rides his skies as a high-risk cinematographer who films radical skiers in some of the most out-of-the-way locations on the planet. All that can lead to an extreme adventure that rivals any in the high-risk sports world. As a youngster, Day remembers watching the annual Warren Miller Cold Fusion videos that showed skiers in more adventurous locations, such as high up in the Alps. It was a change from the traditional ski racing that still dominated the sport.

"It was more of an adventure than an extreme thing," Day said, "and it certainly wasn't hyped as extreme back then. I grew up in Vermont around a small ski area and used to read magazines about other places. Aspen, Colorado, was the big area at the time, way out West where the snow was deep. Yet you still always had this vision that somewhere else the skiing was even better. I never made major plans about the future, but did go out West and finally began skiing in some movies. Since I also had an interest in photography, skiing in movies sparked another interest in cinematography."

As a skier, Tom Day was always intrigued by the unknown elements found in the snow that made it virtually impossible to predict what a day on the slopes or on a mountaintop would be like. "That's the main thing that kept me going with skiing," he said, "the things you cannot just predict. Every day is different. It may seem as if you're doing the same thing every day, but the feelings you get from it are different from day to day, run to run. If they were the same, I probably would have given it up a long time ago. I'm getting ready to go skiing as we speak and I can't tell you what will happen. Maybe it will just be an average, blasé day, or maybe I'll come across something that's just cool. It's a feeling from the snow that goes from your feet to your head."

During Day's skiing career, he found there were always different types of challenges, some that happened very quickly and demanded instant reaction, and others that unfolded slowly, with the danger ever present. "The ones that happen really fast are usually the result of you skiing very fast," he explained. "At that point, you're focused solely on what you are doing, such as when you've picked a line that has a straight shot to a cliff jump. You can't really think, you just have to do it. But if you're on a big, big, steep exposed face with all kinds of dangers around you, then there's more time. You might be in that predicament for twenty minutes to a half hour. Then you often have way too much time to think about where you are. It can be a bit daunting."

In Day's role as a cinematographer, the dangers haven't really lessened. At the time he was interviewed, he had just returned from a rather perilous journey to the island of South Georgia, which is located in the middle of the south Atlantic Ocean east of the Falkland Islands and just north of Antarctica. The island is just 100 miles long and 20 miles wide. He was part of a six-person film group, including four skiers, all there to film a shoot for Warren Miller's latest Cold Fusion video, the same video series Day watched as a youngster.

"This was slated to be a five-and-a-half-week trip," Day said. "Even getting there was adventurous because we had to get a sailboat in the Falkland Islands and sail for four days, twenty-four hours a day, with nothing but ocean and an occasional iceberg. There were already fears because the seas can be extremely rough in that part of the ocean. Fortunately, we were blessed with good oceans, but boats have been known to disappear down there, so the whole mental game going into the shoot was quite challenging."

Day explained that the island of South Georgia has some rather extreme history. It was the place that Ernest Shackleton, the explorer who tried to make an Antarctic crossing in the early 1900s, had to find to save the lives of his men. Their ship, the *Endurance*, had become stuck in Antarctica when the ocean froze during winter and it took him and his men two years to return to civilization. The *Endurance* had been badly damaged by the ice and was no longer seaworthy. Once the ice melted, Shackleton and his men set out in their small rescue boat, leaving the peninsula of Antarctic and striking out for the island, which was then the last refueling and supply stop. At that time, there were a couple of whaling stations located there. They finally made it to the island, an incredible navigational feat back then. That made the trip even more intriguing for Day.

"It was a chance to see a remote part of the world that had some historical significance," he said, "as well as giving me a film project that would be challenging physically, mentally, and professionally. So it was a personal challenge for all of us. The athletes have to face the challenge of these remote, frozen mountains and decide if they can do it. As a cinematographer, I have the challenge of documenting it. But I'm out there with them and know full well that if conditions deteriorate, I have to try to survive as well, and I've got my camera and equipment with me, which doesn't make it any easier."

Once on the island, the group began to experience something they hadn't expected—incredibly high, gusty winds, which were potential killers. "I've never experienced winds like this before. I was literally blown off my feet several times," Day said. "It wasn't that cold, but it was powerful and it jeopardized our safety. We lost three tents in one gust while we were sitting in them. At one point

I decided to try filming in it because it looked cool the way the wind was blowing everything. Once more I was literally blown off my feet, actually picked up off the ground and blown over a snow wall, landing upside-down on a tent. It was like when a wave catches you and throws you up on the beach. I had never experienced that before, never even realized it could happen. Because we lost our tents, we had to retreat back to the boat, which now became our base camp for the rest of the trip. The wind also made us think about the mountains we had to climb to do the shoot, and how long we would be exposed. You couldn't predict the weather because the wind storms just seemed to come out of nowhere. If you were up on an exposed mountain face and the winds started up, you could literally be blown off the mountain."

Working in such treacherous conditions, Day says the most important thing was communication between group members. "You talk as a group constantly," he explained, "and you're always talking about the *what-if* factor. What if weather comes in? What if there's an avalanche? What if these crevasses open up? Everyone knows where we are. We are a long way from help if someone gets hurt. You talk about these things because constant communication is necessary. In addition, you look to the group leaders and the people who have the most experience, and constantly bounce ideas off of them. When you have a feeling or a good decision for the group, you voice it. If they follow, great, but if they don't, at least it was said and someone may have a counter to it, something better."

The group was on South Georgia Island for 3½ weeks, completing their shoot under dangerous conditions. Fortunately, everyone returned safely, but it was certainly a trip where no one could really relax and lose the focus of what they were trying to do. "Most people get hurt when they let their guard down," Day said. "With a lot of this so-called extreme stuff, if you do get hurt, it tends to be bad. A lot of athletes will tell you they get hurt when they feel they're in a controllable situation and become lackadaisical. You've got to keep a high level of concentration and never let your guard down, not even for a short period of time."

Like so many high-risk athletes, Tom Day has had his share of close calls. Working in mountainous snow conditions, he has met with the same frightening occurrence that has sealed the fate of so many others—the avalanche. "I was on a trip to the Wrangell Saint Elias Range in Alaska," he related. "Sometimes when you film, you're filming from one mountain across to the other, where the skiers are. So you usually put the skiers on the good snow, and I end up going down the bad snow. This time I set off a pretty good avalanche. I knew it was going to slide, but I didn't know it was going to slide the way it did. I was lucky I didn't go down in that one. I was right on top of it. I did a ski cut knowing it would probably avalanche. I thought it was going to be what you call a point release, which starts off almost like a snowball at one point and goes down as a pyramid. But it ended up being a slab fracture, which is one that just rips all the way across and goes down as a huge face. Luckily, I was at the crown and didn't go down with it. It was one of those things that went a lot bigger than I thought. After you do something like that, you ask yourself why you did it, but you never can totally predict how the snow will react, even when you think you can."

Skiing with his filming equipment can also be a handicap when it comes to dealing with hazardous conditions, almost making his job as a cinematographer more dangerous than if he were just a skier. "I have to look at things differently because of the weight I'm carrying," Day said. "The pack weight can be fifty to fifty-five pounds, depending on the scenario and the amount of food I'm carrying if I'm going to be out a long time. So I have to be constantly making the decision as to whether I should ski down a certain line with the pack. A lot of times when you're skiing normally and have to deal with an avalanche or some ice terrain, you have to be spontaneous. With the heavy pack, I lose that spontaneity. My reactions are a lot slower and I can't always do the same things to escape a dangerous situation. Sometimes you have to outrun the snow, ski really fast on a straight line to a safe point. I don't always have that ability with a camera. It's a major handicap which sets my skiing ability back a few notches. That's why I have to decide even before I go out whether I think I can deal with the conditions."

❖   ❖   ❖

There are people skiing and snowboarding all over the world, on commercial slopes and out of bounds, on high mountaintops and sometimes on remote cold-weather islands. Even on the trails of commercial ski resorts tragic accidents can happen, however—witness the deaths of Sonny Bono and Michael Kennedy. They weren't even being extreme. High-risk athletes, of course, have more skills, but then go out and test them to the limits. High-risk riders, whether on two skis or a single snowboard, are constantly taking their sport to new places, pitting their skills against the natural elements in the mountains. They have to deal not only with rocks and cliffs, and blinding speeds, but also with the vagaries of weather and of the snow itself. It is a world that is at once beautiful and dangerous, and often potentially deadly.

Big Wave and Tandem Surfing

Tom Sanders, the aerial photographer, sky diver, and BASE jumper, knows firsthand what can happen if something goes wrong, having seen his wife killed in a BASE-jumping accident. Yet when talking about his sports, Sanders casually made the observation that sky diving was an easier sport than surfing. Then he took it one step further . . . out to the extreme.

"In my personal opinion," he said with finality, "the most radical sport on this planet is big wave surfing. It's kind of like walking into a volcano. Those guys are going into a moving mountain."

For many, it's probably difficult even to envision surfing as an extreme sport. The prevailing images may still be of *The Endless Summer*, a bunch of guys hustling from beach to beach with their surfboards in search of the perfect wave. Maybe it's a couple of quick scenes from *Baywatch,* where a novice surfer gets in trouble only to be rescued by one of the hero lifeguards. In big wave surfing, however, it may be nearly impossible to rescue a surfer who gets in trouble. That's because the waves are simply too big and they aren't flowing straight in to the beach. Rather, they're offshore, rolling over reefs that are perhaps a half-mile out at sea. Just a single statement, this one from Bobby Friedman, a tandem surfer also familiar with big waves, will tell you just how extreme this sport is.

"These kinds of waves take lives all the time," Friedman said. "People get caught in the reefs. There are holes in the sand by the reefs that can be two and a half to three feet deep, and the wave can pound you to the bottom. You get knocked out, and if you're in a hole, they never find you. Last year, a surfer flew in [to Hawaii] from California, found a perfect wave, went in, and they just never found him. Never. He was sucked into a hole and covered with sand. The holes can be as big as a Volkswagon. You can be pinned by the tide to the side of the hole, and the sand will eventually just cover up the dead body."

That the ocean can be a deadly and unrelenting force is not something new. However, danger and potential tragedy at sea are mostly associated with weather—storms, hurricanes—and sometimes with natural predators such as sharks. But a sport such as surfing? The usual associations are the sun, warm weather, tanned athletes, and sometimes macho behavior. All true. Yet when it comes to big wave surfing, all bets are off. This sport is different—so different, in fact, that only a handful of the very best watermen dare challenge it.

"You can't lay on your board and paddle into the really big waves," explained big wave surfer Mike Parsons. "Those giant waves are moving too fast and you simply physically can't catch them. With certain breaks, you might have a chance of catching one, but there is too much playing field, and if you paddle in, sit there, and get caught inside, you are now in the middle of the biggest danger in surfing, getting caught inside by a set." Using the language of surfing, Parsons is explaining how a wave breaks outside of the surfer and then rolls over him. "So you're being hit by it while you're paddling in. You're caught inside the break. Waves like that come in sets, five, six, or seven in a row, real big ones. The danger is that they hold you down and you drown."

Instead of paddling in, the big waves surfers are towed in by a jet ski, a way for them to catch the wave, then try to ride it. The skill and timing between driver and surfer must be perfect. That's why the surfers also drive the jet skis, and the jet ski drivers are also big wave surfers. Like most other top surfers, Mike Parsons has spent pretty much a lifetime surfing, learning about the ocean, and building up to catching the big waves. The thirty-six-year-old Parsons was born in California and began surfing at the age of six. He played several team sports as a kid, but by the time he was in high school, he dropped both volleyball and basketball in order to surf. In the early days, his idea of surfing was the same as many others.

"Surfing was just fun, being with your friends, and going in the ocean," Parsons said. "I started going to Hawaii when I was sixteen, going out to Sunset Beach to surf eight- to ten-foot waves. I loved it. It was unbelievable to me and it just kind of snowballed from there. I soon found I liked the side of surfing that had some adventure attached to it, going to places where I had to draw on my experience. I went to places where you jump off rocks in between sets, paddle out in tricky currents and tides. To me, that was what surfing really was, to be out there and survive. I guess the big waves were a natural progression."

Archie Kalepa took a slightly different route. He is a native of Hawaii and grew up in the tradition of the Hawaiian waterman. "We live on an island surrounded by water so surfing is like second nature to the kids here," Kalepa said. "I started surfing when I was about seven, and also spent time doing other sports such as dirt bike racing, para gliding, deep water diving, and canoe surfing. When I was nineteen, I really began getting into surfing in a more serious way."

Tow surfing as a way to ride the huge waves that break out over the reefs offshore didn't evolve until the mid-1990s. At first glance, the surfers might look like water skiers, being pulled by a 30-to-35-foot-long water ski tow rope. The jet ski will tow the surfer onto the wave, then angle off the top and whip the surfer into it. As the surfer begins riding the wave, the jet ski goes behind it so that it is safely out of the way. The timing must be perfect for it all to work.

"This kind of surfing is so much different because it's no longer one guy," Archie Kalepa said. "Whereas traditional surfing is just you and the wave, tow surfing is you, your partner [driving the jet ski], and the wave. You can be the world's best surfer, but if your partner doesn't know how to get you in there, he can be setting you up for disaster. Communication then becomes the key ingredient. You can't communicate verbally because of the noise, so there is eye contact, a whistle, a hand signal. It can take years of practice to get it right. The more time you spend with a partner, the more it starts to jell. You develop a system and then you become comfortable and know what the other is thinking. The driver has to imagine himself at the end of the ski rope, because that's where you want to put your partner who you are whipping into a wave. So you have to drive and physically be in one place, but mentally you are thirty feet behind with your partner so you can figure out where you are going to whip him into the wave so that he can let go."

"The tow has really lifted the standard," Mike Parsons added. "You can paddle up to a certain size, but you can tow surf up to any size."

Because conditions for big wave surfing occur so infrequently, the surfers are always looking for a place where the waves will rise. In 2000, Mike Parsons traveled to the Cortez Banks, 105 miles out in the middle of the Pacific off San Diego. There is volcanic matter under the water that sometimes rises to within four feet of the surface. When the water crosses it, it has no choice but to rise up and break. The waves are huge. "That's where I caught the biggest wave of my life and won the Double XL Award for biggest wave of the year, " Parsons said. "It was sixty-six feet high. To qualify for the award, you have to successfully make the drop of the wave. In other words, the wave could hit you and knock you off, but you qualify if you are still on it as it breaks."

Archie Kalepa has also been on the 60-foot waves and feels that someday a 100-foot wave will be possible. Because a surfer may go out to the really big waves only two, three, or four times a year, they often ride to exhaustion. "You go out as many times as your body can physically handle," Kalepa said. "You can ride twenty waves in an hour. After more, your legs begin shaking. Sometimes we'll take a break, have lunch, then go back out for another session."

Unlike traditional surfing, the tow-in boards have footstraps.

The boards are streamlined now, narrow, small, but heavy. "You're up as long as you can stay on the wave," Kalepa said. "Today guys are pulling into tubes that can fit three busses, that's how big they are. It's really insane because you're also traveling at speeds up to thirty miles per hour, really hauling butt. You have to know where to be on the wave, not going too far down at its bottom. It's important to stay in the safest part of the wave because you can be killed by a wave carrying that kind of pressure from the water. It's an enormous amount of energy coming down on you."

All surfers know that sooner or later they're going to fall and be pulled under by a wave. While they also know that even the best can drown if the circumstances are right, they work hard to make up the odds of their survival.

"Part of it is about how strong your lungs are and how well you can hold your breath," Mike Parsons said, "and about how well you can swim. We do a lot of swimming and other exercises to strengthen the lungs. I don't work out in a gym, but swim, ride a mountain bike, and do a lot of cardiovascular fitness training. Much of it involves holding your breath and getting your heart rate to slow down. That's important, because when you're caught under water, the tendency is for your heart rate to go up, because you're frightened. It's a matter of keeping yourself relaxed and slowing down your heart rate so you can hold your breath longer. You also know that you can't ever panic, because if you do, you'll lose your breath much quicker. And you can't struggle. When one of the waves hits you, you've got to go into a completely relaxed mode. The two worst scenarios are being caught inside and falling on the front face of the wave. If you fall at the bottom, the wave will then take you up and, as we call it, over the falls. Then you go down deep, come up, but you still have to be alert because the next wave can get you. When you finish a wave, you tend to be out of breath anyway. So you've always got to try to be calm and relaxed, have your heart rate slowed down. That's the best advice and the best thing you can have going for you in these situations."

Both Parsons and Kalepa feel that big wave surfing cannot be taken lightly, that it is a discipline for only the experienced, not for the young and foolhardy. The sport is simply too dangerous. "I'm thirty-eight now," Kalepa said, "and probably in the best shape of my life, more controlled, focused, aware. That comes with age. When you're young, you just kind of go out and do it foolishly. Now it's all analyzing and preparing. The biggest risk in this sport is definitely death. Beyond reason, beyond doubt, that wave will kill you."

Mike Parsons has seen young surfers coming along and, as in other sports, begin to push the envelope a bit. "I'm all for the sport being pushed," he said, "but I do caution against the motivations of some people. Some are doing it for the wrong reasons and I would caution against that because of the dangers involved. It's high risk. If you want to be good at this sport, you've got to be cautious and respectful, especially in the ocean because you had better realize you're dealing with something you can't control. Even in a twenty-foot surf there are no guarantees. Depending on the conditions, it's the ocean that's going to dictate what happens, not you."

Yet Parsons is optimistic. He feels the next generation of big wave riders will literally take the sport to new heights. "The future of the sport will see guys riding bigger and bigger waves," he said. "I personally think it's possible that the face of a wave—measured from top to bottom just before it breaks—could be a hundred feet and you could ride it. I think whatever's out there with the equipment, and the tow-in capabilities, and the knowledge we have, that given the right day and the right conditions, we can ride whatever the ocean will throw at us."

Another amazing surfing story being written today is in the little-known sport of tandem surfing, where a man and a woman ride a board together. Until recently, it wasn't really a high-risk sport . . . that is, until Bobby Friedman took it there. In fact, Friedman might be one of the unlikeliest extreme athletes for the simple reason that he came to his sport later in life and learned very quickly. Friedman grew up in California, having been born there forty years ago. His father always told him he could do anything he set his mind to do, advice he has never forgotten. Before long, he embarked on a sports odyssey, a successful one, but not one that could be considered extreme.

"When I was seventeen, I really began to take skateboarding seriously," he said. "I traveled all over Europe as a professional skateboarder, but when I returned to California, I didn't want to do it anymore. The funny part was that I gave it up just as it was becoming big and all these guys began making a lot of money. Then I turned my attention to racquetball, moved to Texas, and played professionally. I made it all the way to number seven in the world. From there it was beach volleyball. I teamed up with my brother and we played on the circuit for a couple of years. My brother had been an Olympic player and I knew I was holding him back since I was just five-foot-eleven. So I told him to get himself a new partner."

The need to earn a living led Friedman to the construction business, then to open his own retail store. For a while, he exercised very rarely. It was as if his athletic career was over. Then his store went out of business. "I was depressed," he admitted. "I had become a suit, and sports was on the back burner. I went back into construction and had more time on my hands. One day I walked into a surfing store and saw some pictures of tandem surfing on the wall. It was like something hit me on the head. I stared at these pictures and said, 'That doesn't look so hard. Looks like fun, too.' The guy in the store was a smart salesman. He was working me and the next thing you know I'm buying an eleven-hundred-dollar board. So I brought this girl in that I was starting to date as my first partner. I didn't even know how to surf and we're coming into the store every day and practicing lifts."

Suddenly, Bobby Friedman discovered something inside him that had long been dormant. It was a drive, an ambition, a desire to excel as he never had before. He wanted to be the very best at something, and tandem surfing would be the vehicle that gave him his chance. "This was finally my dream," he said. "I decided I wanted to be the best at something in my life. I considered seventh in the world in racquetball a failure. I considered not being the best at skateboarding a failure. So I began surfing every day. The first time I took the board to water, I was horrible, getting thrown and tossed. We kept crashing, the two of us taking hits, and the board is flying in the air. But it didn't take long for the whole thing to become an obsession."

That was just seven years ago. In a relatively short time, Bobby Friedman and his current partner, Tiare Thomas, have become the best tandem surf duo in the world, taking the sport to places it had never been before. "Tandem surfing was a nondangerous sport," Friedman explained. "From my skateboarding experience, I felt I could do something on the board with a partner that other people hadn't done. When I saw all the publicity the big wave surfers were getting, I changed the direction I was heading. I decided to become extreme."

Tandem surfing in Hawaii was more of a tradition than a sport. It started as a courtship. Hawaiian kings would court girls by taking them out on a surfboard and holding them in a cradle in their arms. So it began as a ritual. From there tandem became, as Friedman says, a beachboy thing. They would take girls out for surfboard rides to make money. After that, tandem couples began doing acrobatic-type lifts on rather mild waves. Friedman wanted more. "We'd do lifts, too, on some of the bigger waves," he said. "But you're limited in the lifts you can do because you have to have more points of contact. You have to stay on the board. My partner and I surfed a fifteen-foot wave last week, which is a thirty-foot face. We're the only ones in the world who can do that. For years they measured waves from the back, but the ocean drops in front of them and now they measure the front face. This year or next I think we'll do forty feet. We use an oversized board and we paddle in."

Friedman's first partners weren't up to joining him in pushing for more. His first lasted four years, the second three. "It's ninety percent mental," he said. "You can train all year long, but when you're looking over the ledge of the wave, it's breaking through the clear water and you have to mentally know you're gonna make it. My last partner had ability, but to be a champion you have to have everything. She didn't have the discipline and it finally came down to her looking over the ledge of the wave and fear drowning. She just didn't train enough."

Tiare Thomas was just nineteen and already a professional surfer when she approached Friedman about working with him. He said he knew early that she was going to be different from his other partners. "She had the same desire I had," he said. "I could see that she had the same look in her eye." Friedman explained that tandem surfers always paddle into the wave with the man on the back, the girl in front. "Her legs are kind of around my hips, kind of straddled," he said. "My chest is on her butt. With ninety-nine percent of the tandem teams, the guy helps the girl up at the bottom of the wave. I taught Tiare early that as soon as my chest comes off her butt that she had to get up fast. That way, I don't have to bend down to help her up. She gets up with me. We really do it differently. We can get up so fast together that you can't tell if I got up first.

"I probably count on my partner tenfold more than most people. We have a fifty-fifty partnership and we have to be in synch. If not, we're gonna crash. We communicate through hand signals. I'll grab her hips as she's getting up. She takes my wrist. Then she takes the weight and pushes down to make me heavier and her lighter, so there is very little weight on the front of the board as we make the drop. We're just inches apart. I pull her very tight to my body. The way she pushes down on my wrist, the board doesn't know I have a passenger. It reacts as if I'm a 300-pound guy."

Friedman and Thomas have developed their own techniques on the big waves to get the board on its edge and turn it as they make the drop. "On a steep wave, a twelve-foot board can't go straight down. It will nose under," Friedman said. It's a difficult technique and that's why most tandem surfers don't do it. Yet the two now surf the Bonzai Pipeline in Hawaii, which has the largest waves tandem surfers have ever tried.

"These kinds of waves take lives all the time," Friedman said. "With us, though, the biggest danger isn't the reef. It's our board. It's so big and so thick. If you fall with a normal longboard where you maybe go over the falls and land on it, the board will snap in two. Our board is not going to break. It weighs forty pounds and it will break you. It's made out of fiberglass, foam, and a big half-inch piece of wood going through the middle. I was knocked cold by

the board in 1998. My partner then grabbed me and started helping me back up. She kind of had me halfway onto the board when
I came to. So there is a real danger from the board if you fall."

In many of the high-risk sports, the athlete is concerned with
his own survival. He is aware of the dangers, and as so many have
said, as long as no one else gets hurt, the risk is all mine. Not so
with tandem. Bobby Friedman feels responsible not only for himself, but for his partner as well. "It's one thing to put yourself in
danger," he said. "But if something happens to my partner, they'll
always point the finger at me, and I know that. In regular tandem
surfing I don't have to worry about that. But when the waves get
bigger, I'm always concerned for my partner. She's in my hands.
I'm steering the board and she's listening to my signals. We know
we're pushing the limits and we know what we're doing is dangerous. There's a fine line between dangerous and the extreme."

Even though he is forty years old, Bobby Friedman still considered himself a newcomer to his sport, since he's been at it for only
seven years. "I don't feel as if I've peaked yet," he said. "I'm still
not sure where I can ultimately go with this. A few people have
talked to me about trying a tandem tow in on even bigger waves. It
hasn't been done. We could go out with a jet ski tomorrow and be
towed into a large wave and be the first. But you don't want to do
it just to have done it. You want to be towed into a real wave that is
too big to paddle."

As with the other sports, the limits in tandem surfing have not
yet been reached. Will Bobby Friedman be the one to approach
those limits? Perhaps. Right now he is the only one with a logical
chance. "I'll always push myself to get to the next level until I
reach a point where I feel my body can't keep up with my brain . . .
or can't keep up with my dreams. That's when I'll begin looking seriously for a student to teach everything I have learned."

The world of the extreme is known for taking a sport previously
considered rather mild, changing it, reshaping it, and eventually
bringing it to a place where few people want to go. For years,
kayaking was good exercise and recreational fun. Its most danger-

ous use might have been in the frozen North, where the natives of that area used kayaks for hunting and fishing. Then someone began turning a leisurely afternoon of paddling into something more, going into more rapid water, and finally into white water rapids. That not only increased the danger, but also attracted more people to the sport. However, there is one aspect of kayaking that definitely fits the mold here, because it's right on the edge. It is the sport of kayak waterfall jumping.

Corran Addison, a kayak designer and regular waterfall jumper, described the essence of waterfall jumping when he said, "With waterfalls, once you're airborne, your trajectory is set. If you make a mistake, you can't correct it on the way down. If you land completely flat, you'll turn your back into chalk dust. Either your plunge is dead on, or you get seriously hurt."

Addison speaks from experience. He once broke his back trying to jump a seventy-five-foot waterfall in North Carolina. You don't even have to go up that high to suffer an injury. So much depends on the jump and the kind of water at the bottom of the fall. Canadian Scott Feindel has been canoeing and kayaking since he was a youngster in Winnepeg, Manitoba. He began canoeing at summer camp and loved paddling from the start. His résumé includes a lot of white water, and when you are paddling on a certain kind of creek, you're bound to find waterfalls.

"Kayakers will usually freestyle on a river, do tricks, find a wave or a hole and play in it," Feindel explained. "Creeking is when the rivers tend to be a little smaller and the gradient, or slope, is a lot sharper. It tends to put waterfalls in there. The more I paddled, the more waterfalls there were. It became another challenge. People are now doing tricks over waterfalls, but not over the really hard waterfalls. We call them falls, but not jumps.

"There are two different ways to run waterfalls. Sometimes you can do what's called a *boof*, and that would look more like a jump. It's when you fire your boat straight out. The other way is to *pencil*. That means maintaining the same angle as the water, basically going in perpendicular to the ground. There are also angles in between. The problem is the potential to be seriously injured."

A pretty bold statement, and a pretty big risk every time a kayak rider goes off a substantial waterfall. Not surprisingly, Feindel says that there is no substitute for experience. This is not a sport someone can go into cold and just begin jumping. His first jump was just ten feet, and as he increased, he had to learn about his own abilities and the water in which he was jumping. "There's no one way to do this," he said. "There are hundreds of little tricks and you have to know which applies to each jump. Eventually, you have to push yourself. Some people will never run big waterfalls because they will always take that step back. They're not at the edge of their ability and will never get there, or even close to it."

Scott Feindel has jumped waterfalls up to sixty feet, with many drops between forty and fifty, and a number between fifty and sixty. While there certainly is a bigger danger level in the higher drops because of the potential impact, he said that smaller drops can be extremely dangerous as well, because of the nature of the water in the landing area. "Some waterfalls have massive pools to land in, big and foamy, with lots of foam," he explained. "That's the safest. Others might have a tiny little slot that you have to land in, and if you miss, you might hit a rock. A good general rule is if you can't see the bottom while you're in the boat, you should be getting out and looking."

Besides being able to control the angle of the kayak in the air, the key to making successful jumps is the water in the landing area. Most people simply aren't aware what a difference a little air in the water can make. "If you misread the water or don't do what you had planned, and you land pretty close to level, then all the impact goes into your spine," Feindel said. "By the same token, you can go off a thirty-foot waterfall and land flat but in white, foamy water, and you won't hurt yourself. Or you can go off a fifteen-foot fall and land in green water, which is basically still with no foam in it, and break your back. There's no set rule, like once you're over twenty feet, you can't boof. It all depends on the degree of aeration in the water. Aerated water is like a cushion—it compresses when you land on it. With still green water, you have total surface tension.

"Even with aerated water, once you get over forty feet, you pretty much want to start penciling, landing more down than flat.

Do it that way and the whole boat might go underwater. You just disappear for a few seconds, but because the boat has so much air in it, you come back to the surface pretty quickly. You've also got to know the depth of the water. If you pencil in to just a few feet of water, you're going to get hurt."

Feindel described the kayaks today as being about eight feet long, made of all plastic. Depending on the manufacturer, they either have a foam block in the middle of the bow, or plastic and foam to make them stronger. The cockpit is oval and has become bigger over the years to allow the rider to get out quickly if the need arises. It also has a skirt that the rider wraps around the outside and pulls tight to keep the water out. As he said earlier, there are people riding creeks who will come upon a waterfall and jump it, but now others specifically seek out waterfalls. They'll drive up to the spot where the fall is, put their kayak in the water, jump the fall, and then take it out again. The name given to that is to *park and huck*.

"There are now some people taking chances by running stuff they aren't sure of and can't see," Feindel added. "It's yet another aspect of the sport called expedition kayaking, but I think it shows bad judgment. It's like a guy jumping off the garage roof and not knowing what's below."

While there are sponsorships from boat manufacturers, not too many athletes make a living from jumping waterfalls. There are other types of kayak competitions, but they don't approach the extreme that is the waterfall jump. Shoulder injuries are the most common for all-around paddlers like Feindel, but it's definitely the back that takes the hardest pounding from waterfall jumping. His jumping has resulted in some stitches in his chin and a black eye, nothing worse. Thus far he's been lucky.

Freestyle Motocross and Motorcycle Jumping

Motorcycles have been part of American culture for many years, having been used for transportation since the beginning of the twentieth century. Hollywood has also taken the two-wheel

machines to heart, with many films either centered around motorcycles or with a memorable motorcycle chase scene. And they
have featured some famous actors, such as Marlon Brando in *The
Wild One* and Steve McQueen in *The Great Escape*. So-called
biker movies have been a genre that has been around now for several decades. Even former pro football star Joe Namath once
starred in one called *C.C. and Company.*

Then along came Evel Knievel. He made his motorcycle the
vehicle that brought him fame, fortune, and a slew of broken
bones as America's most well-known stuntman. Knievel made a
career of doing a variety of wild and sometimes outrageous stunts
on a motorcycle, spawning a bunch of wannabe stunt drivers who
never quite attained his status. At the same time, various types of
motorcycle races were becoming more popular in both America
and Europe. Yet there was one type of motorcycle race that would
come much later, and it would evolve from an unlikely source—
BMX bicycle racing.

Kids were beginning to race their BMX bikes over courses with
all kinds of bumps, dips, and jumps. At the same time they were
doing tricks on the small but sturdy bikes, being creative and in-
ventive, and increasing their risks. Because the bikes could only go
so fast and jump so high, the risks weren't huge. Soon, however,
young motorcyclists began to wonder how it would feel to do some
of the same types of racing and tricks as the BMXers. First, motocross and supercross racing were born—with riders going around
irregularly shaped tracks with the same kinds of bumps and jumps
that BMX racing featured—sports that would increase in popularity throughout the 1990s and at the turn of the new century. As
with so many sports before it, there were riders looking to do new,
more exciting, and ultimately dangerous things. Then, following
the direction being taken by sports in the 1990s, riders began creating the sport of freestyle motocross.

Unlike most high-risk, extreme sports, freestyle motocross usually takes place indoors, in an arena. The premise of the sport is
quite simple. A rider goes off a ramp at twenty to twenty-five miles
per hour, reaches a height of twenty-five to thirty feet, then performs one or more tricks in midair as the bike sails some seventy

feet across the arena before hitting a second ramp and, hopefully, a safe landing. Competitors are judged on how they do their tricks, their originality, and degree of difficulty. The first-ever freestyle event was held in Las Vegas in 1998. So the sport is still in its infancy, yet the competitors are doing more dangerous and high-risk tricks every year.

"Jumping a motorcycle, period, is pretty high risk," said Mike Metzger, one of the "old men" of the freestyle world at age twenty-six. "But it's something I've done since I was a young kid."

Better take Metzger at his word, because the native of Huntington Beach, California, went for his first motorcycle ride when he was still in diapers. Both his father, Ted, and grandfather, Fritz, were riders. In fact, it was a broken back that ended his father's motocross racing career and led him into the construction business. But he was determined to get his son on a bike and wasted no time. "I started riding the smallest cycles, KR50 Suzukis, by myself when I was three years old," Mike Metzger related. "When I was six, I started racing motocross at Corona Raceway in Corona, California. I was already jumping my bicycle right in the driveway at that time. My dad would make ramps that were pretty steep. All the while I continued racing motocross, moving up to bigger bikes as I got older. I already had a total love of riding and did a lot of everything. I hung out with BMX racers, did BMX freestyle, rode mountain bikes downhill, trained on mountain bikes, and rode trails on motorcycles.

"Freestyle motocross was something that just happened, copying my friends' BMX tricks on my dirt bike. All the while I was doing that, I continued to race motorcycles. We actually began doing freestyle on our own about 1991, years before it became an organized sport."

The midair maneuvers can be quite complex, but must be done quickly and with style, since the bike is only high in the air for a matter of seconds. The names of the tricks are similar to those in skateboarding and BMX freestyle competitions. For example, the *can-can* is accomplished by the rider taking his right or left leg and swinging it over to the opposite side of the bike, in midair, then pointing it outward. Both legs are on the same side of the bike, only one on the peg, or footrest, with the other foot pointing up in the air. The *double-can* is like sitting side-saddle in the air with both legs pointing upward. The *knack-knack* is done by swinging one leg to the opposite side of the bike with the rider standing, with one foot on the peg. The *double-knack* puts the rider on one side of the bike, but supporting himself only with the handlebars, no feet on the pegs. And at the next level, the rider takes his hands off the handlebars.

The tricks were becoming more complex and difficult. When they were done on natural dirt ramps in the desert, no two were the same and the riders could be hurt easily. Metzger says that organized competitions have one advantage. "They started making ramps specifically designed to do tricks. That makes it a little easier. Once you start to jump the ramp and get the feel of it, it becomes very consistent. So when you hit the ramp, it's always the same. The kids today who are learning freestyle are pretty much just jumping off ramps and practicing every day. We jumped off dirt and practiced whenever we felt like it."

Even with standard ramps and jumps, however, inexperienced riders sometimes don't realize that this is an extreme sport where injuries can be severe. Shortly before being interviewed, Mike Metzger had set up his own freestyle demonstration event called the Metzger Freestyle Frenzy. The day before, some young riders were practicing.

"There was a sixteen-year-old named David House who was just getting into freestyle. We have a basic seventy-foot jump set up and he was working on it. He took off, but angled the bike too high. The front end was pointed upward and he decided to dismount in midair. He fell straight down from thirty feet and landed flat, impaling his legs into the ground. I was told he crushed the top of his tibia and fibula and lower femur together, causing compressions. Before surgery, he had to have his knees opened on both sides to relieve pressure. It was the first time he had ever been hurt on a motorcycle, and unfortunately, it was a very serious injury. He was talking about never riding again. I've been through it all in my career—the broken arms, broken backs, broken legs.

You try your hardest not to have that happen, but in this sport it does."

Freestyle motocross is now part of both the Gravity Games and the X Games, where it is called the Big Air. There, you have three jumps at three different ramp takeoffs. Conditions are usually controlled to minimize the risk as much as possible. But controlled or not, it seems as if the young freestyle motocross riders keep pushing the envelope. At the Gravity Games, a rider named Carey Hart became the first to do a complete backflip in a freestyle competition.

"Guys were talking about a backflip for some time because it seems they do it with ease in BMX freestyling," Metzger said. "Carey stepped up to the plate first and went for it. Problem is that after he did it, there was more pressure to do it again, so he tried it once more at the X Games. Only he was coming back from a collarbone injury and had surgery four weeks earlier. He shouldn't have tried it because he was weak in his upper body, and when he hit the jump, he just couldn't hold on to the pressure and force of a 220-pound motorcycle. He broke his tailbone, had a compound fracture of the right ankle, and some other injuries. Falling out of the sky from thirty feet isn't fun."

At twenty-six, Metzger isn't the oldest guy on the circuit. "Mike Jones, a buddy of ours, is ten years older than me. He's an iron man. Just recently, though, he broke his back. He was hurt freestyling at a contest because of one of his signature moves, a no-handed lander. You jump in the air, let go with your hands, and land without holding on to the handlebars. I don't know if he thinks he has to do it, but I don't think he enjoys it. Every time he lands, he seems to jar his back a lot."

It seems as if all freestyle stories end with an injury. Although Mike Metzger has had his share of injuries, he has a signature trick, called the *McMetz,* that he can perform perfectly. He actually created it by accident. "In 1999, at the Dans Triple Crown in San Diego, I was going for a bar hop," he explained. "Back then, the courses were small and in a two-minute run you had to get sixteen tricks off. So I went for the bar hop, which is basically a jump up over the handlebars where you stick your feet out as far as you can, then swing back through the handlebars and land on your pegs. When I went to do the trick, I felt I wouldn't get my legs back over the handlebars, that I would catch the back of my boots on the handlebars and crash. So I just let go of the bars with both hands, swung my legs around the handlebars, grabbed them again, and landed perfectly. Now I've got to do it every time I'm out there. It's still the gnarliest trick for me. There's a few other kids who can do it now, but I still try to start my routine with the McMetz because if I stick it, I'll feel pretty good about the rest of my routine."

Ironically, Mike Metzger says he doesn't take freestyle moto-cross seriously. His racing career has always been number one. Freestyle, for him, started when he was just fooling around with his friends, using their own ramps to see what they could do in the air. Now, combined with racing, it enables him to ride full time. The price is often exacting, however, and the youngsters coming into an increasingly dangerous sport will probably also be feeling the pain of broken bones for years to come.

Seth Enslow, a twenty-six-year-old from upstate New York, grew up jumping over things, including a bunch of his friends when he was a kid. He would have them lie on the ground along-side one another, then make a ramp and jump his BMX bike over them. Not surprisingly, his dream from as far back as he can re-member was to have his own motorcycle. He finally got it when he was sixteen, a 125 cc bike, which he began racing almost immedi-ately. When he graduated high school at age eighteen, he already knew what he wanted to do.

"Everyone was writing about how they wanted to go on to col-lege," Enslow said. "I wrote that I wanted to go to California and pursue a career as a motorcycle stuntman." It wasn't that Enslow wanted to be the next Evel Knievel; he just wanted to be a good rider who entertained people and was also able to make a good liv-ing from it. "I looked up to the top pros because they were such good riders and I could learn by watching them," he said. "And some were making a couple of hundred grand a year just for riding their dirt bikes. I thought it would be great to be paid to do something I truly loved, but as for role models, I really didn't have any one person I wanted to copy."

Enslow continued to race as all phases of motorcycling became bigger and more commercial during the 1990s. Then in the latter part of the decade he began doing the things he really wanted to do. "I do big jumps off ramps in front of crowds, jumping over cars and trucks, things like that. We often set up in parking lots. I tried some freestyle motocross for a while, but didn't really like it. I'd rather do bigger jumps outside because the indoor arenas were so small. So I began going higher, staying in the air longer, and going long distances. I borrowed a ramp from an old stunt rider named Johnny Airtime, a real good takeoff ramp for big distances, and I began doing jumps like he used to do, and also making videos. We often go out to the sand dunes, the natural rolling hills in California, looking for two humps we can clear, using one for takeoff and one for landing. I've also done some motorcycle stunts for movies."

Some of Enslow's jumps have been in the 200-foot range, and he has jumped over twenty cars or so. He knows there is risk because something can suddenly go wrong with the bike or the wind can gust and become a dangerous factor, but when he uses the same bike and ramp, he says he can usually judge speed and distance to do the jump successfully. One of his film stunts was made in Luxemborg, where he was part of a biker movie and had to speed through an intersection, knocking down some other bikes and weaving his way through automobiles.

In a sport where injuries are commonplace, Enslow has also had his share. Like the others, he doesn't want it to happen, but knows it's part of the game, and in a way, the potential for a wipeout has contributed to his popularity. "Part of the mystique of my career is that I've had a lot of big crashes doing some of the big jumps. So I have that Evel Knievel thing working for me where people come to see me because there's a chance I might not make it. It's not like I pull it off successfully every time and make it look easy. Sometimes I do, but I've also crashed hard a number of times. If people feel this guy is gonna put on a show one way or another, they figure it's worth going to see him. I think the anticipation of a possible crash does play a role with a lot of people, but most don't want to admit it. It's the same as in auto racing, though our sport is less controlled and done in the open with no protection, which makes it easier to get hurt. Knowing there are people like that out there, you have more pride and confidence and want to pull it off just to show them."

As for injuries, Enslow says he's been pretty lucky. But his idea of *lucky* would probably made the rest of us cringe at the thought. "I've blown out ligaments and tendons, separated shoulders, dislocated my wrist, suffered a broken collarbone, fractured my ribs," he said matter-of-factly. "The only time I've ever needed surgery and had metal put in me was when I hit my head on the handlebars going for the all-time distance record. I crushed my sinus bone and they had to pull my face off, put titanium in my forehead, and staple me back together. But this is pretty much the job I created for myself and I have to keep doing it unless I want to quit altogether. Then I would have to go back to doing construction work, something I've already done for many years."

The distance record is something Seth Enslow would love to achieve. The record at the time of our interview was 253 feet. "I've done 230 a couple of times," he said. "I went 245 the time I hit my head on the handlebars. There was a tailwind and I was working my way up toward the record. I should have gone about 230 on that jump, but the tailwind gave me extra distance and I overshot the ramp, landing flat, got thrown forward and then off the bike at about 70 miles an hour."

Like others, Seth Enslow continues. He has goals (the distance record) and maybe a few more years to keep doing his jumps and stunts to earn the kind of money he wants. When it ends, he says he couldn't hack a desk job. He'll have to find more speed, like car or truck racing, or maybe speed bike racing. "My grandparents and my mom always told me to do something that was less dangerous," he said, "but I wanted it so much that I would laugh and shrug them off. I definitely wasn't too scared to do things growing up. I was always going fast and raising hell, and I always wanted to be a stuntman. Seeing stunts that amazed me growing up always made me want to do them. What I do has become very popular. I made my video debut in 1994 doing a sand dune launch for a film called *Crusty Demons of Dirt*. The launch I did for the video also launched my career. There were more than 100,000 copies sold and pretty much everyone in the motorcycle industry knew me after that."

Whether jumping, flying, climbing, or riding, extreme athletes continue to go forth, loving and living their sports to the hilt. The preceding three chapters have served to introduce and describe both the sports and the athletes, the risk and the dangers the participants court, as well as allowing them to tell the stories of their lives, including some of the adventures they have lived and, for the most part, continue to live. There are, however, other aspects to their high-risk adventures that have yet to be touched upon and which, to a much larger degree, will answer the question as to why these athletes are willing to step out on the edge repeatedly, risking their bodies and their lives for activities that don't always make them rich and famous.

6

COPING WITH AND

OVERCOMING FEAR

Oh, yes, there is always a level of fear. You ask yourself questions. What if there's a hole there? What if this decides to break off? What if I catch an edge? But you have to stay focused on getting to the bottom and not let fear overcome you because you're there because you want to be there. No one is forcing you. Only you can figure out what you have to do.

—Circe Wallace, snowboarder

FEAR. A small, four-letter word that says so much. In fact, that little word controls a great deal in the everyday lives of most people. There probably isn't anyone alive who doesn't have some kind of fear. It can be something not-quite-defined, as a fear of commitment or a fear of change. Or it can be something very real, such as a fear of the neighborhood bully, a fear of flying, a fear of heights. One basic dictionary definition calls fear "a panic or distress caused by a real or impending danger . . ." High-risk athletes may experience both kinds of fear—a general, not-quite-defined fear, and a very real fear that is directly connected to the sport they are pursuing. For a "real or impending danger" is something that extreme athletes face every time they begin to climb a mountain, jump off a cliff, are towed into a big wave, or pick a line to ski down a mountain. How they handle and react to that fear may well determine whether they will be successful or not.

There are several dynamics at work here. Many of the athletes have already talked about taking risks as youngsters, doing things impulsively and not thinking about the possible consequences, which in most cases meant being injured. When sky diver Kevin Quinn reminisced about jumping off his balcony at age seven or eight, he quickly added that he "never even thought about the landing consequences." Motorcycle jumper Seth Enslow was even blunter when he said, "When you are a little younger, you don't let fear bother you. You just say fuck it and go. You don't care if you get hurt."

So there are those who start with no fear and, in a sense, grow into it. Many of the athletes have talked about the youngest people in their sport as being the most fearless. Some of it, they say, comes from ignorance, from not really yet knowing or understanding what can happen and what it can mean. In that sense, then, the athlete's attitude toward fear changes as he or she ages. The demographics tell us that many of the most dangerous sports are practiced by younger people, but that's often because the physical prowess needed to get out to the edge diminishes as athletes age. They may still pursue their sport as they age, but they often have to pull back from some of the more radical activities. In that sense, there doesn't necessarily have to be a relationship between fear and age.

Others actually chose a high-risk sport in order to overcome a perceived or real fear. Once they overcame or at least controlled their fear, these athletes found they enjoyed the sport so much that they simply continued with it. Still others have made a case for the confidence generated by their sport as also helping to give them the confidence to overcome fears in other walks of life.

Fear plays yet another role in high-risk sports. Because an athlete has fear, and is very much aware that the slightest slip in his performance could result in an accident, an injury, or worse, he has learned to let fear become a positive element in his performance, its presence giving him an increased focus and awareness. None of these possibilities applies to all the sports. Sometimes the very nature of the sport can alter the role that fear plays. A sport of short duration, such as BASE jumping, can inspire one kind of fear, while a sport of much longer duration, such as expedition alpine climbing, can inspire another. As with so many other things in life, there are patterns and generalities, but no one set formula. For each athlete is an individual, with his own mind and psyche, and each has his own way of approaching, dealing with, and using fear. But make no mistake, there is not a single athlete who steps out onto the edge who doesn't have to deal with fear. It is an almost constant companion to high-risk adventure sports.

The Jumpers and Flyers

The jumping and flying sports are among the shortest in duration of the high-risk adventures. Sky divers have a relatively short free fall before opening their chutes and floating to earth. For BASE jumpers, the time is even shorter, a matter of seconds or, as they themselves have said, fractions of seconds, in which many things happen before the chute is deployed. For most jumpers, the fears have to do with height and the sensation of falling, at least at the beginning.

Mick Knutson sky dived before he BASE jumped. It wasn't until he decided to try a jump that he remembered a long-standing fear of heights. "I was in the midst of getting instructions for my first jump and it hadn't hit me," Knutson said. "I didn't even recall at that moment of being afraid of heights and not wanting to go up anywhere. I was just twenty at the time. But as soon as I walked onto the plane, I began to think that this wasn't what I thought it was going to be. The plane took off and all of a sudden the ground was going bye-bye. Now I was afraid. Luckily, it was a real quick flight and I jumped from three thousand feet. No free fall, just opened the chute. It turned out that it wasn't as bad as I dreamed it would be, being up high. I figured out that the reason was because the parachute was on my back and I had control of the situation. It wasn't like when your uncle carries you on his shoulders as a little kid. He trips and falls, and you're toast. With the jump, I realized it was all me."

As Knutson got more into sky diving and eventually switched over to BASE jumping, he found that his fear was still there, but he now had a deeper understanding of how it worked. "Yes, I still have fear today," he admitted, "but my fear isn't necessarily of height. My fear is of not being in control of a controllable situation. I was in Las Vegas recently and we were about 250 feet up in one of those glass elevators at a hotel. I put my head to it, looking down, and began thinking that the glass had to be thick because of so many people using the elevator. Because I felt I was safe, I knew I was in control and wasn't afraid at all. Whereas fifteen or

twenty years ago that never would have happened. Now I understand myself more and understand situations better."

Jim McCormick is a veteran sky diver, now forty-five years old,
and a man who also takes great care before special exhibition
jumps and anything out of the ordinary. McCormick has already
said that knowing, in theory, that you can be killed on any single
jump is part of the draw of the sport, but also thinks about fear in
a very analytical manner.

"I don't think fear is positive," he said, flat out. "I think fear's
positive effect is negligible. I think you have to move past fear to
be effective. I've heard people say, and I've thought about it, that
fear is an effective motivator, up to a point. My contention is this:
If you are going to allow fear to be your driver, it's going to absolutely put a cap on how much you succeed and how much you
can accomplish. It's only when you make that transition out of fear
into a really deeply held and reason-based confidence, that you
can progress to the next level. Fear is so powerful that you can't
counteract it. In other words, you can't go head-to-head with fear
and have any possibility of winning. That's how powerful and profound it is.

"Your only hope is to accept that the fear is there, let it wash
over you, let it come in and admit, *Yes, I am really frightened. I
could kill myself. This could really work out poorly and could be
the end of my life.* It's only when you go through this process of really inventorying your fears and what frightens you, that you start
making the transition into overcoming the fears. You have to
openly accept that you're afraid and admit it. At that point, you
may decide it doesn't make sense to go ahead and that's okay. But
if you are going to proceed, you have to consciously identify all the
sources of your fear. Only then do you start to get the handle to
putting yourself on an even keel with the fear."

McCormick is certainly not denying that the fear is there, not
even after more than a decade of jumping. On a routine sky dive,
where he simply opens his chute and relaxes, there is probably
little to no fear, especially after that chute is deployed. But when
he does something new and different, it all comes back and he
must go through the process once again. He alludes to the exhi-

bition jump he made into Candlestick Park in San Francisco before the start of a Giants' baseball game. Though he described in Chapter 3 the way he plans a jump to the smallest detail, he now says that even all his careful planning did not fully alleviate his fears.

"It's definitely there," he said. "The Candlestick jump is a perfect example. The jump was at seven in the evening. By midday, I was truly not capable of putting together a complete sentence. That's how nervous I was. As you can tell by our interview, I'm not at all hesitant to talk, but I honestly could not put together a sentence that afternoon. I was that frightened. At that point I had to sit down with myself and start to go through a list of everything I was frightened about. What could happen, what the risks were, what were the various possible outcomes. It was only by going through that process that I started to find a place where I could function again and return to all the things I had to do to prepare effectively.

"When performance time comes, I definitely go into a zone. I go to a place where I have intense focus on the goal and kind of filter out most of the world. I have intense focus, and until the time when the challenge has been successfully completed, nothing else matters. That generally begins about an hour before the actual jump and at that point the fear is gone."

What Jim McCormick is saying might not be so different from Mick Knutson. Knutson talked about controlling a situation in order to control his fears. McCormick speaks in terms of finding a total confidence before going ahead. Prior to the Candlestick jump, he says all the potential problems came at him at once, and brought with them fear. They made him question whether he could successfully negotiate his jump. He began to question himself, *What the hell am I doing? I can't believe I agreed to do this. This is crazy. Maybe I made a big mistake? Maybe I should try to get out of it?* Once he broke the barrage of problems down, and dealt with them one by one, he settled down, regained his confidence, and dispensed the fear.

Miles Daisher, who has sky dived, has BASE jumped, and did radical free flying rope swings with the late Dan Osman, also talks about controlling fears, though he puts it into a slightly different context. "The only time I don't become afraid of something is when I've gone through it repeatedly, maybe forty times or so," Daisher said. "Then I feel right at home and comfortable with it because I know exactly what to expect. But if I'm going to a place for the first time, something I'm scoping out but still don't know exactly what is out there, then I'm really scared and tentative. I won't jump until I can control my fear, and by controlling my fear I have to know what I'm getting into. I'm always trying to minimize the chance of something going wrong. If I do this and still feel the fear, feel I'm too scared to do it, then I'll back away. Although when that happens, I usually come back again and try to figure it out even more, control the fears, and then do it."

Then Daisher gave yet another take on this sometimes complex element of high-risk sports. "Fear is fun, though," he said. "It's fun to be a little scared, as long as it doesn't overwhelm you. If you panic from fear, then you begin making mistakes, and if you make mistakes doing what we do, you can be seriously injured or killed. When I scope something new out for the first time, I like to do it with someone else, someone I can talk to, analyze with, and who can bounce ideas back and forth with me."

Kevin Quinn, who has pursued a variety of sports, including sky diving and BASE jumping, gives a more graphic portrait of the kind of fear that follows jumpers. "Fear can make you nauseous, can give you gas, and can make you feel as if you gonna shit your pants until you're in the zone," Quinn said. "I think Miles [Daisher] puts it best. We'll be flying in a plane with fifteen people, half of them we don't know, people we just met at the drop zone. When we're going up to altitude, somebody always stinks the plane out and Miles will say, 'Ah, the smell of fear.'

"As far as I'm concerned, sky diving is completely safe, but there is always a fear or nervousness, maybe in anticipation of what you are about to do. I'm an experienced jumper and the guys I sky dive with are some of the best in the world, some of them with thousands of jumps. But if you think about it, it's not normal to jump from a plane at thirteen thousand feet, free fall for sixty seconds before opening a chute. It's not a normal feeling and I'll probably have that nerve gas forever. So if I haven't jumped for a month, for instance, then I'm a little spooked. It's an hour's drive down to the drop zone and I'm nervous the whole way, with the jitters and sweaty palms. Now, once you get there and jump maybe six or seven times in the course of the day, then you don't even think about it."

Skier and BASE jumper Shane McConkey, a friend of both Daisher and Quinn, says he also feels elements of fear before he performs, adding "that's what kind of makes it that much more rewarding." McConkey is equating fear with danger, feeling that danger and risk are what drive him, but trying to make it happen also creates the fear. "When I know there's a line out there I haven't skied before in an interesting area, and I know that I can do what perhaps no one has done before then, yeah, it scares me sometimes. My palms begin sweating and on the way to skiing it I'm scared. But right before I'm about to drop in, that feeling is gone. If I'm still afraid at that point, then I'll ski away. If I'm fully prepared and know exactly what I'm going to do, then the fear is usually gone and I'm settled down a bit."

McConkey seems to be using fear as a barometer. If it's still there in too great a degree right before he starts to ski, then he'll pull back. The fear is telling him he is not fully prepared to perform.

For aerial photographer, sky diver, and BASE jumper Tom Sanders, the fun and enjoyment contained in what he is doing now far outweigh the fear, but in fact, his sky-diving career started with pure fear. "I had no desire to jump out of an airplane," he said. "It petrified me, and it became a challenge because I was supposed to prove to myself that I could do something I firmly believed I couldn't do. I didn't care that much that I was afraid of heights. Most people are content to live with that fear and just avoid situations that might put them up higher than they care to go. I was attracted by the challenge and the sport appealed to me, even though I was afraid.

"The first time I jumped, it was scary, but it was also fun. In fact, I didn't do well on the first few jumps, but I eventually got through it. Now I'm afraid on an occasional BASE jump or sky dive, depending on what we're doing. If I'm jumping from 23,000 feet where the oxygen is a big issue, or doing a real low BASE jump with a movie camera to shoot a Nike commercial, then I'm scared. So there are still a lot of things to be nervous about, but not whether the parachutes are going to open anymore."

For the athletes in these sports, some degree of fear is always there, always present, especially when they are doing something different, something new, or something with an increased risk. However, these athletes have learned to deal with their fears, put them in perspective, and when they take that final step out onto the edge, the fear is gone. If the fear is too strong, then they will walk away, or start their mental process all over again to find control, confront their fears, answer the questions and self-doubts, then go ahead.

Climbing

Unlike the jumping and flying sports, climbing is a process, one that takes time. Rock climbers can be on the open face of a cliff for up to a week before finally reaching the top. Expedition climbers might spend two full months trying to negotiate the peaks of K2 or Makalu, moving up and down the mountain in stages as they work their way to the top. While BASE jumpers move so quickly that they deal with fractions of a seconds, climbers might deal with inches and feet. As Kim Csizmazia put it, "Climbing is sometimes slow motion, sort of strung out . . . It's slow, slow, slow, and then, wham, it could be over."

Does this kind of scenario inspire a different level of fear? After all, it's one thing to fear a jump that might last for only seconds, or minutes. As the athletes said, they work through the fear beforehand, and by the time they are ready to go, that fear is basically gone, pushed into the background, so they can focus on the business at hand. But a climber, spending days, weeks, or months on a single quest, has to deal with elements of danger and potential disaster for nearly the entire length of the climb. Is the fear always there, or can it be somehow tabled or erased while the climber struggles to reach the top?

Carlos Buhler, whose alpine résumé reads like a *Who's Who* of the world's highest peaks, has spent his entire climbing life thinking about and dealing with fear. Like so many high-risk athletes, he believes that fear is not something to be taken lightly, so it has to be analyzed, confronted, and hopefully controlled. But on a long climb does it ever really leave, or does it just take a short hiatus here and there before returning?

"Fear is an interesting thing," Buhler said. "From my perspective there are two types of fear. The first is the fear of falling, your protection pulling out, smashing your leg on a rock, breaking your body up as you hit something on the ground. That's the immediate fear that people deal with when they're climbing. The other kind of fear is when you cross points of commitment, through a project or climb, that leave you more and more distant from the starting point, or in my mind where you left the car at the road head. And that was sort of the last place where you were totally safe.

"Let me give you an example. Suppose you had to hike four hours into a trail and then you began getting into higher elevation and you cross a difficult boulder field. By crossing, it suddenly means that if you had an accident like breaking an ankle, then you wouldn't be able to get back across it very easily. If your partner had an accident, you would be all the more in trouble trying to get him out. Then you might begin an upper climb by crossing a small glacier. There could be crevasses in the glacier, and every time you cross one, you're a little farther from where you began. Again, you're a little more committed. Then, as you get up onto the face itself, you're making more decisions and taking on new levels of commitment, all of which are taking you down a path of fear. And that fear is something going wrong at a point where it would be more difficult to find a way out, a way back.

"That kind of fear builds up over many hours and days, as opposed to that immediate fear of falling off, which you are dealing with all the time. You have fear every time you lead a pitch. When that pitch is finished, the fear dissipates. Then it's your partner's turn to lead the next pitch. So there is a flow and ebb. In addition, there is always that gnawing fear that you exchange with your partner when one of you is leading a particularly difficult pitch. Okay, it's my job now to lead safely and efficiently the next 150 feet, and how am I going to do it. That's the immediate gripping fear. It all builds up over many days in a long climb. What happens if we run out of food? What happens if a storm comes in and we get pinned down for three days? What happens if somebody has an accident? Can we descend? What happens if somebody gets sick?"

With so many fears over a period of days, weeks, and sometimes months, how does the alpine climber deal with them? What makes them able to overcome the fear and continue to climb, especially when they know the fear will increase the higher they go? "You tackle it by taking little, little increases in what you can handle over many years," Buhler continued. "The fear in climbing is a process, at least for me. I was never one to leap into a much higher level of risk or fear than I felt I could handle. After ten years, for example, I realized that I was pretty comfortable in situations that other people were not. It's like a surfer who knows how to navigate the big waves in Hawaii. Someone who has been doing it for ten years has a sense—and he's no less cautious—but he has a sense of what he can do, how he can minimize the risk, and get out of a situation. This comes only after many, many outings.

"There is even a third kind of fear, the anticipatory fear that comes the night before a big climb. I don't enjoy it very much. This is the fear of the unknown, of how you will perform, of whether or not you'll live up to the task, of whether or not something will happen. You find that fear most often when you set a goal that's a little bit too much for your ability. And of course, every climber has an avalanche fear. So there are all these things building up over time. They are enormously uncomfortable situations and often times you find yourself struggling to find a balance."

The fear in alpine climbing seems to reflect the duration of the sport. It builds up, it has a flow and ebb, the nature of it changes during a climb, but it's always there, something climbers have to accept and live with. That's why Buhler and others have described climbing as a process, a learning experience, where some climbers always feel they aren't quite good enough. But they climb anyway.

Sharon Wood says she deals with as much of the fear as she can before she actually begins a climb. "I think every climb you make is a calculated risk and you are measuring a number of factors against one another," she explained. "So I try to take into consideration my ability, whether my ability and experience can meet the difficulty of the climb. There are objective hazards such as avalanche and rock falls pretty much with every climb, although they increase with certain routes. So you have to plan your strategy on every route and try to anticipate what kinds of things can happen. You can deal with a lot of your fear up front by making these calculations.

"But there is still the unexpected and the unpredictable. I think I can best recall real fear during a waterfall ice climb I was doing. The ice was a little more brittle than I'd like and I didn't feel quite as on my game as I would have liked to have been. Then I noticed my tools and crampons were not sharp enough and I was becoming too tired, too soon on a pitch that still had a hundred feet more to climb. I began getting a feeling of nausea in my stomach, because all the blood is going to my vital organs as it does in a crisis. In a situation like that, I really have to talk to myself a lot.

"Ironically, the fear is almost easier to deal with when there isn't an option, when you know you can't get down, that you have to fight through it and get up. In those situations, I find I'm able to somehow pull myself together, take myself in hand, and fight my way through it. I think that's because your perspective narrows, shuts out all the peripheral mind chatter including the fear, and all you're thinking about is the next move you need to make that's going to be perfect enough to keep that space between your feet and the ground. That's how I deal with fear, and in a way, I like going there. I'd say in that kind of situation climbing becomes eighty percent mental.

"When I climbed Everest and we had so much trouble on the descent, it really made me pull back. The following summer I went on a dream climb on Mount Hauscaran in Peru. It was a hard route and very scary, and I was feeling more frightened than excellent. Normally, I become completely absorbed in a climb. Yes, I have fear, but it's all part of the fuel for good performance. But this time fear overwhelmed all other feelings and I realized this was just not my time for this anymore. I wasn't having fun. I did one more climb just to confirm that I had had enough of that kind of climbing."

For alpine climbers, the process is indeed a long one with experience as the teacher and the equalizer. But then there are the odds. If an alpine climber survives a decade or more of climbing at altitude, has some close calls with storms and avalanches, and has friends who are killed in the mountains, it only stands to reason that the fear will surface again. Maybe it's the odds, a when-it-is-going-to-be-my-time kind of thing. Or maybe it's just the years of dealing with the fear, trying to control it and push it into the background. In the long run, too much fear will start to erode the joy and other satisfactions the climber gets. It can eventually do what storms and avalanches can't—cause the climber to back off and consciously begin reducing the risks.

Do climbers who choose not to challenge the Everests and K2s of the world have the same kind of trepidations when they go out? Kim Csizmazia says the nature of her climbs, as well as the conditions she faces, influence the degree of fear she feels. Like all climbers, she also harbors the knowledge that in the mountains or on the sides of cliffs, a tragedy can happen in the blink of an eye.

"I'm definitely not going to feel scared when I know a route," she said. "But by the same token, there are some routes when you might feel scared every time you do it because of its very nature. Conditions also influence fear. If they're very bad, it can be quite frightening. Sometimes I find that fear makes me more focused, yet it's not fun to be really scared. I don't think anyone finds it fun. I imagine there would be more immediate fear in the gravity sports, such as skiing, BASE jumping, big wave surfing, things that move faster. I made a climb just recently, not necessarily a super hard climb, but we were doing it in January when the days are really short and conditions much more harsh. I was pretty nervous thinking about it. It's whether I make the right decisions that makes me the most nervous. Did I make the proper assessment of the conditions? Is it going to avalanche? Is something else going to take me out? It was a long ice climb, almost like an alpine climb because it was so long. It's just a long day out there with a certain amount of objective hazard.

"I think it's the length of time that you're out there that makes it different. Climbing is so much slower, an all-day twelve-hour kind of thing, and at any turn you can make a mistake. On this climb I didn't have any extra clothing and I was barely staying warm. If I twisted an ankle four hours from nowhere, I could be hypothermic within a half-hour. That kind of thing makes me nervous for sure. As the margin for error gets smaller and smaller, you know you can't mess up. That kind of situation can be frightening."

For rock climber Craig DeMartino, the fear usually arrives before the climb. "For me, it's always worse before I climb," he said. "If it's a climb that I know is going to be really difficult, I'll be nervous for days before I go out. But while I'm on the actual climb, it [fear] isn't usually a problem. In fact, it forces you to focus more on the task at hand. So once I get into whatever it is I'm going to be doing, it's much better. I'm very calm.

"What I just described happened big time last year. I did an ice climb in Rocky Mountain National Park, and for the week beforehand, I was a basket case, but once we got there and once I tied in and actually started to climb, I was fine. Why do I react this way? I'm not sure. I don't think my fear is of falling, so I guess it's fear of the unknown. You're not sure what is going to happen; you're not sure what the conditions will be, and you're not sure if you're gonna be tired. Then you begin asking, What if I don't feel good? What if I twist my ankle? What if the ice breaks? What if I fall? A ton of things go through your mind before you start."

DeMartino says he always goes through the worst-case-scenario drama in his mind, a laundry list of things that can go wrong, he calls it. With climbing, as the list indicates, there are so many things that can go wrong that thinking about them almost has to cause varying degrees of fear. Craig DeMartino seems to have found a way to block all that out once he begins climbing, and others have talked of their focus. As Kim Csizmazia said, "Slow, slow, slow, and WHAM!"

The Riders

Freestyle and out-of-bounds skiers and snowboarders, by their very motion on the mountain, create sloughs that can grow into an avalanche. Big wave surfers challenge mountainous waves that can make a surfer disappear. Freestyle motocross riders hurl themselves in the air and then do tricks on a 220-pound bike that can easily crash to the ground. Waterfall-jumping kayakers jar their backs almost every time they land. Are they scared? With the kinds of risks these people take, it stands to reason they must be scared. The trick, as with all extreme sports, is finding a way to handle it.

For Kristen Ulmer, fear is a check. Though she is considered one of the most radical and fearless skiers in the world, Ulmer is fully aware of the possible consequences of her repeated forays onto mountaintops and steep, dangerous ski trails. In her usual no-nonsense style, she confronts fear head on and puts it squarely where she feels it has to be. "If you're feeling fear while you're doing these things, you're dead," she said. "You can't let it affect you. I only feel fear before or after I do something sketchy. I don't mean a second before. If you're feeling fear, for instance, just before you do a big jump, or if you're feeling fear going into it, you're gonna crash, you're gonna hurt yourself. Sure, I'll feel fear, but it will be so far back in my psyche that it won't remotely play a part in the decisions I'm making. I'm not saying fear is bad. Fear is a good thing because it makes you realize that, whoa, this is a dangerous situation. If you had no fear, then you would also be dead, because you would make a stupid decision.

"So fear is a check. But if you let it be in the front of your psyche, and because of it allow yourself to fall apart, then you'll die. The wonderful thing about fear is that people who have it play too big a part in the front of their brains when they're doing something, know enough not to get involved in those situations. Like I said, it's a natural check. If I'm about to do something I know is reasonable and that I can visualize doing successfully, then I just stuff my fear back. Fears can also be irrational at times, and I pride myself in making good decisions, at least as often as I possibly can."

Kristen Ulmer is a very confident athlete, one who has proved her mettle many times over during a spectacular freeskiing career. Her theory about fear obviously works or she probably could not have earned her lofty place in the extreme skiing world. Yet there was also an acid test, Ulmer's near obsession to ski the Grand Teton in Wyoming. That perilous journey was described in Chapter 5. When talking about her fear of the Grand Teton, it sounds as if she had to wage an internal struggle to keep her theory working for her.

"I was terrified three weeks beforehand," she admitted. "The day I was actually up there, I didn't feel fear. No, that's not true. I did feel fear. It's really hard to explain. If I was up there and didn't feel any fear, then I'm an idiot. But you have to look at things and ask, 'Do I have legitimate fears here?' What are the legitimate fears? Is it an avalanche? That's certainly a legitimate fear. If you just turn that off and say no, it's not gonna avalanche, everything's fine, then you're gonna die. But if you go into this thing and say, it could avalanche, but if I take certain steps, it should be safe, then your fears have shown you what the dangers are. On the other hand, if you squash the dangers to the point of being an idiot, you're gonna die. There are very few people who just squash them and those people tend to be very short-lived in this sport. But if you take your fears, learn from what they are telling you, and then decide whether they are rational or irrational, you can learn from them and make a conscious decision whether to go or not. If you're simply quivering with fear and thinking you don't want to go down there, then you shouldn't be up there in the first place. I was scared beforehand because I knew how dangerous the Grand Teton was, and as much as you learn about avalanches, there are still too many objective hazards you have no control over."

Ulmer's description of fear, especially when applied to her experience on the Grand Teton, shows once again how difficult it is to cope with fear in the world of extreme sports, when death can be an unwelcome guest at any given point. The knowledge that danger is imminent and omnipresent makes it extremely difficult to define fears in a singular fashion.

Snowboarder Circe Wallace admits the scariest times of her life have been in the mountains. "You realize how small you are," she said. "You go up in this helicopter in the middle of nowhere and put your life in the hands of mother nature. That's a really radical, awesome experience. You just have to get through it, though. As long as you have done everything you can to prepare, once the helicopter drops you off, you can't get back on. You've got to make it to the bottom. It helps somewhat when there is another rider with you, or a cameraman in the helicopter across the valley. But when you pick a line in Alaska, you're doing it on your own. It's still a solo experience even with people keeping their eyes on you and, yes, there is always a level of fear. You just have to stay focused and not let it overcome you. You've got to remember that you are there because you want to be. No one is forcing you."

Freestyle motocross rider Mike Metzger has had his share of crashes and accidents. He, too, knows that on any given day he can end up in the hospital having a cast put on another part of his body. That has to be daunting. Yet he has been doing it for so long that fear rises up only when he is trying something new or jumping in a place he has never been before.

"There is definitely a fear factor in hitting a ramp jump for the first time," Metzger said, "at a new stadium or a new jump park. You know the jump is going to be seventy-five or eighty feet long, and you know you have to do it in second gear pinned or third gear three-quarter throttle. You know what you have to do, but you haven't jumped that particular jump yet, and that's probably the biggest fear factor I have, knowing I haven't jump there before. I don't want to come up short. I don't want to go too long and land flat down because then I'll take a beating to my ankles, my wrists, and my lower back. But I think the fear makes you safer, especially when you get a little older and don't want to take the beating. You kind of step back and let the younger guys do it first. Then you go from there."

The exhibition jumper and stunt cyclist Seth Enslow would concur with the as-you-get-older-let-the-young-guys-do-it-first theory. While those who challenge the mountains certainly know about the dangers and the numbers of climbers lost, there are still those who, while having some close calls, emerge relatively unscathed. Motorcycle riders, however, are injured periodically— almost steadily—during their careers, and very few get away without breaking a multitude of bones. As the injuries mount, it's not surprising that the fear factor becomes more prominent. Let the young guys do it first. It's part of the natural progression that makes any athlete slow down, pull back, and eventually call it quits. Let's look at how those who battle the water feel about fear, because there is little doubt about the ultimate power of the big waves.

"Sure, there is always fear," said Archie Kalepa. "The minute there is no fear, there's nothing left but danger. To me, fear is like my best friend. It awakens senses that tells you to be careful. It will tell you when something is wrong. Fear is always in the back of my head and it's what keeps me safe. I think the fear always helps remind me of the risk involved, helps me analyze the degree of risk we're dealing with and how I should handle this danger. But once I'm on the wave, I'm focused and concentrating, and confident in whatever decision I make."

Like others in his sport, Kalepa knows that the biggest risk is simply death. "That's how extreme this sport is," he said, "and that's why the fear is always there." On the night he was interviewed and asked about fear, Kalepa laughed. "Right now it looks as if we're going out tomorrow," he said. "And all the while we're talking, my palms are sweating. I'm already thinking about it."

Mike Parsons, another veteran surfer, also knows about the ultimate. He, too, says that anyone can drown at any time while pursuing his sport. That is the main fear, being pulled under and not getting out. "You have to try to be as physically ready for that situation as you can possibly be, but more importantly, you try to avoid that situation," he said. "Most of the breaks have what you call a channel, where the water is deep, and then where it breaks. So you sort of play a game of cat and mouse, between sitting where you can catch a wave and paddling to deep water where you're going to miss them. Making good decisions definitely helps, but the fear is always in the back of your mind. You know you can drown. You're completely aware of what you are playing with. In fact, I would relate it to mountain climbers. They know an avalanche can roll over them and that might be it. They draw on all their knowledge of snow conditions to avoid it and still climb the mountain. We do our best to still catch the waves and not make a fatal mistake."

Tandem surfer Bobby Friedman says his fear has increased as he takes on bigger and bigger waves, but his fear revolves around his partner. Because he considers himself the lead surfer on the team, he feels responsible if something unexpected should happen. "I can honestly say I don't fear the wave," Friedman said. "If it's big, my heart pumps and I say, 'Here we go.' But I don't usually fear it."

In big wave surfing, as with alpine mountain climbing, the biggest fear is obvious. No one wants to die and the athletes work to avoid that possibility while knowing that each high peak or each big wave could be their last. Fear is a check; fear makes you careful; fear allows you to minimize the danger wherever that's possible. It's always there, a constant companion that can be somewhat suppressed, sometimes put on the back burner, somewhat transformed, but never denied. It can help to a degree, and it can rise repeatedly with longer events, such as expedition climbing, but nearly every athlete has to find the ability to put it aside, if only for a short time. Maybe kayak waterfall jumper Scott Feindel said it best:

"You have fear at the top of a waterfall, but if you don't get over it, you're not going to be successful. So you just get over it, make sure you get on your line and focus on what you're doing. Then go and do it. At that point, there simply is no time for fear."

THE ADDICTION OF

THE RUSH

The jump itself is like when you're in grade school and someone is picking on you and you finally reach your boiling point where you want to punch him, even though he's twelve inches taller than you. That's the rush you start getting. That's the rush you get when you're standing on the edge thinking, I'm about to jump off this thing and, okay, how do I do it? And you're pushing yourself, three . . . two . . . one . . .

—Mick Knutson, BASE jumper

WITH so many things in life that can make someone feel good about themselves, why would a person want to engage in an activity that could lead to a serious injury or death? For athletes to shun traditional sports for the likes of big wave surfing, freestyle motocross, mountain climbing, BASE jumping, rope flying, and freestyle skiing and snowboarding, there has to be something waiting for them at the other end. For these athletes, the rewards aren't always financial. Extreme athletes are not operating with the multiyear, multimillion-dollar contracts that most top professional athletes have today. What, then, is the reason they court danger, and sometimes death, on the regular basis?

Obviously, they must get something very special from their sport, something more than the admiration of their peers and a picture in a magazine. Some call it a rush, a high, or even an adrenaline addiction. Whatever it's called, it is a special feeling of satisfaction that they cannot find elsewhere. The other question that must be asked is whether there is something special about the personalities of high-risk athletes that makes them seek out this rush? Is it a need, a desire, or truly an addiction? Because everyone is an individual, there cannot be one set answer or one set formula. Listening to these athletes talk about the satisfactions they get from their sport makes it apparent that they are all doing it for very personal and individual reasons.

Keith Johnsgard, a professor emeritus of psychology at San Jose State University, suggests that those who seek high risk and the satisfactions it brings them might be born that way. A January 1996 article in the journal *Nature Genetics* gave support to the theory by reporting that some people may possess a gene that makes the brain especially responsive to the neurotransmitter dopamine. Johnsgard refers to this as the brain's "feel-good site," adding: "It's the kind of site that gets hit when you take cocaine, have good sex, or jump out of an airplane."

If true, it would mean that people who have the gene may be supersensitive to its pleasure-inducing effects and have a need to maintain high dopamine levels. Looking for these stimuli, such as those found in high-risk, extreme sports, will allegedly keep the levels high.

Another theory, which almost sounds as if it is on the opposite end of the spectrum, says that so-called sensation seekers have a low level of the enzyme monoamine oxidase B (MAO B), which plays a central role in regulating arousal, inhibition, and pleasure. This hypothesis basically states that the low levels of MAO B dampen the impact of stimuli on the brain, leading these people to look for high amounts of stimulation, such as radical sports, to reach a level of satisfaction that an ordinary person might achieve from a seemingly mundane activity such as going out to dinner and taking in a show.

Not surprisingly, most of the athletes are not interested in theories. They don't want to know if they have an extra gene or low levels of an enzyme in their brains. They do what they do for their own reasons, and the satisfactions they get vary as much as the types of dangers and the sports themselves. While many of these athletes showed a propensity for high risk at an early age, a significant number did not, playing conventional sports or engaging in very little sports activity. All came upon their present situations from their own separate directions, taking individual roads and, aside from their pursuit of an extreme sport, often living very different lives. All, however, find a great deal of satisfaction in what they do.

Jumping and Flying

Extreme sports athletes are well aware that the very nature of what they do can cause several chemical changes within their bodies. The late Dan Osman touched upon this when asked why he continued his incredible rope swings and what pleasure he could possibly get out of flossing the sky by jumping nearly 1,000 feet and allowing his body to swing through the air perilously close to the ground. Did he have some kind of addiction to danger, people often wanted to know.

Said Osman, "I'm not an adrenaline junkie. I want an endorphin high. People confuse the rush of adrenaline with endorphins. Endorphins give a feeling of satisfaction, of success, of overcoming fears. It's very empowering."

What, exactly, was Osman talking about? The very fact that he could make a statement like this shows that he had done some homework. Like Osman, most high-risk athletes are quite intelligent and think very deeply about what they do and why they do it. To amplify and understand Osman's statement, adrenaline refers to secretions from part of the adrenal glands, which are situated above the kidneys. Though *adrenaline* is the common name given to the hormone that is released, the medical term is *epinephrine,* which is released from the adrenal medulla. It relates to extreme sports in that it is released as a powerful stimulant in times of fear or arousal and has many physiological effects on the body. These effects include increased breathing, heart, and metabolic rates to provide quick energy, constricting blood vessels, and strengthening muscle contractions. Obviously, if it is released in times of fear or arousal, this hormone (which will be referred to as adrenaline here) plays a huge role when a high-risk athlete is performing. Many will speak about an adrenaline rush or shot of adrenaline when talking about the satisfactions they receive during and after a performance.

Osman, however, rejected the theory of an adrenaline high and spoke about an endorphin high instead. Endorphins are defined by *Barron's Dictionary of Medical Terms* as "any of several naturally occurring chemicals (proteins) in the brain, believed to be involved in reducing or eliminating pain and in enhancing pleasure." According to the medical dictionary, the role of adrenaline is known, while endorphins are "believed" to enhance pleasure. Either way, it appears these bodily reactions play a significant role in the reasons high-risk athletes continue to pursue their sports.

Sky diver Jim McCormick has also given thought to the adrenaline junkie theory. "Yes, I think it's valid, that there are people who become adrenaline junkies and just can't get enough of it," he said. "I think it's a relatively small portion of the athletes, but those who have it continually up the odds. I've been jumping for thirteen-and-a-half years and remember early on having a conversation with a guy who said that I was going to become an adrenaline junkie. That statement concerned me and inspired a lot of thought. I can really only speak about what has happened for me.

"As I became more accomplished in the sport and had the opportunity to jump more places and experience more things, I began to appreciate the beauty of the sport more. In fact, I think I appreciate it more now than in the first eleven years I was sky diving. Obviously, it has been there all along, but now that I've become sufficiently comfortable in the setting, I can take great joy in the fact that there are beautiful clouds in the sky, or beautiful greenery down on the ground. I remember this past spring being touched by the California poppies that were blooming on the ground. As you got down to about a thousand feet, you began to see them. I couldn't help thinking that very few people in the world get to see these things from my perspective. I do a lot of sky diving down by Monterey, California, and it's not uncommon to be up at jump altitude and see Big Sur, the Monterey Peninsula, Pebble Beach, Monterey Bay up to Santa Cruz, then look the other way and see the snow on the Sierra Nevada Mountains. To be able to see that with nothing around you but some goggles or a face shield, that's something nobody experiences except birds that fly."

Yet McCormick has seen sky divers who feel the casual jump is no longer enough. "I think it's frustrating and sad for people like this because they continually have to up the odds and there comes a point where they place a bet they can't win. There are people who do a couple of hundred sky dives and suddenly it's no longer sufficiently exciting for them and they have to go out and do something else. Or they have to do things in such a way that it considerably increases the risks. To me, they are spiraling downward. It's a different personality, a different individual. Because the initial high is never good enough and they keep going, going, going, and going . . . and then they are dead."

McCormick is a longtime performer who has been in his sport for more than a decade. The satisfactions have changed, deepened, and are now fully appreciated and enjoyed. At age forty-five, his perspective is obviously different from an athlete of twenty-five, though he sees what is happening with some of the younger athletes. So does BASE jumper Mick Knutson, who also differentiates between the rush that these athletes are looking for and what they receive.

"There is a stereotype called an adrenaline junkie," Knutson said. "In my opinion, though, an adrenaline junkie is someone with very little knowledge and education. They don't know what they are doing. They're just addicted to riding roller coasters or jumping. They aren't smart people. I love BASE jumping, but I don't consider myself an adrenaline junkie. Yes, I do get a lot of adrenaline out of it and some people may stereotype me. I will say this: Right now it's winter and there isn't much jumping here at Salt Lake City, and I'm thinking, man, I could really use a jump. But that's because it makes me feel so good and I love being outside. I love it because of everything it encompasses—the outdoors, the scenery, the travel, the different people I meet. I'm addicted to that, the whole environment. As far as jumping, there are times I've gone up and made one jump, while other people were making twenty-five. I'm just happy to be there, part of the whole thing, not just the standing on the edge, although that is an important thing. I would say that maybe twenty percent of the people who jump all the time have to have that standing-on-the-edge adrenaline, but they also like the whole experience."

Knutson has also pondered the so-called endorphin high. "I don't really think I get that," he said. "You get an endorphin rush if you have an accident, really hurt yourself, something like that, but that doesn't really come with the jump itself. You're relaxed as soon as you go off, almost on autopilot because you have done it so many times. It's great. Then you get to the ground and about ten seconds later, while you're picking up your parachute, it hits you like a ton of bricks. Oh, my God, I can't believe that jump. The visuals on the cliff were amazing. It just all of a sudden pushes these buttons in you. You train yourself to know that when you jump, the anxiety and adrenaline will catch up to you later. And it does."

Knutson does feel he gets an adrenaline rush, a special kick, from each jump. There are also times, such as the winter of his interview, when the weather prevented him from jumping and he felt he could really use one. That, however, seems far removed from an adrenaline addiction. Like McCormick, however, he has seen jumpers who do seem to have that extra need for the shot of adrenaline.

Skier and BASE jumper Shane McConkey refers to what he does as "dangerous or adrenaline sports." He likes the feeling he has when he skis and especially BASE jumps. The feeling is definitely something he wants to experience again. "It's a feeling you don't get anywhere else," he says. "You definitely feel like you want to do it again. When you work something out and it's gnarly and it scares you, and then you stick it, it's one of the coolest feelings in the world, a really satisfying feeling that makes you want more. These dangerous or adrenaline sports we do, if you can call them that, are just a bunch of levels higher than having a hot tub, for example. A hot tub is cool and fun, and it gives you satisfaction when you're finished, but doing these sports, it's just elevated a million times. If I'm playing soccer and score a goal, it's a really cool feeling; everyone is stoked for you and you're happy. But nothing beats the feeling of jumping off a four-thousand-foot cliff and flying away from the wall and landing perfectly on the ground. When you do these adrenaline sports, they are simply so many levels higher."

Like so many other high-risk athletes, Shane McConkey loves what he does for the rush or satisfaction it provides. Comparing jumping with other pleasures in life seems to be no contest. He comes right out and says gets a feeling from BASE jumping that he finds nowhere else. Whether he will feel the same way in five years, ten years, twenty years, no one can say, not even McConkey. He'll have to wait to find out.

Miles Daisher, who has jumped with McConkey, has similar feelings about his sport. "There's no feeling in the world like

BASE jumping," he said. "There's just a huge exhilaration. You're just stoked to have done it, especially if it's clean and perfect. You're just so fired up that you did it that precisely. You also feel a huge sense of accomplishment that you've done this, especially with the more gnarly things. That's what it's about for me, an accomplishment, that you were able to do something. And yes, you always want to try to do more gnarly things, but you also have to know your limits. If I can't see something happening, and there's too much doubt, I won't do it."

Kevin Quinn, who now runs a heli-skiing business when he isn't skiing, jumping, or guiding big game hunters, believes he'd become bored without the excitement of the rush.

"Yeah, I think I need it," Quinn said when asked the adrenaline junkie question. "You get to the point where you're bored and everything is sort of stagnant. If I'm hunting a bear in Alaska, stalking a big moose or big bear, I get that same adrenaline and feel invigorated. However, if I go stagnant for a long time, and I don't get to go skiing or sky diving, just do the day-to-day office crunch, life just starts to go by a lot faster. When you're taking part in a lot of these sports, time just slows down and you get to experience more of life, as opposed to just going through the motions of day to day. I hope to sky dive forever, ski forever—all of the above. Obviously, we won't always be able to push the boundaries as we do now, but I always want to be an accomplished athlete and very good at what I'm doing."

Dr. Robert Leach, who has been treating all types of athletes for decades, and is a rock climber and sailor as well, does feel that those who push beyond reasonable limits indeed have a need, something akin to an addiction. "It's the person who keeps challenging and challenging that I don't understand," Dr. Leach said. "It isn't a high percentage, but there are some. It seems to me that they must [have an addiction] because they continue to do it, putting themselves at risk beyond which seems excessive."

The pattern that seems to be emerging is that all these athletes, whatever the explanations, get a special kind of satisfaction from pursuing their sports. Adrenaline plays a major role. Are some addicted? It appears they are, to a degree. But that begs the question: Addicted to what? A thrill? Excitement? That big shot of adrenaline? Or perhaps just being active and doing something they enjoy? In most cases, the latter seems the best bet, the most solid overall reason with bits and pieces of the others added to different individual situations. Let's see what some of the others have to say.

Climbing

There's a big difference between much of climbing and the jumping sports. The longer duration of a climb seems to preclude the same kind of rush, or adrenaline shot, that BASE jumpers, some sky divers, and rope swingers feel. Yet there obviously must still be some incredible satisfactions to keep climbers going repeatedly into altitude and the death zone, or camping out on the side of a 3,000-foot rock face, looking into the face of avalanches, cold winds, storms, frostbite, and possibly death.

Despite the absence of that immediate rush of adrenaline, expedition mountaineer Carlos Buhler says, unequivocally, that to him climbing is something of an addiction. "There are many aspects of climbing that are attractive to me," he said, "and yes, there's a bit of a junkie type of reaction. You do become kind of an addict. Intellectually, climbing for me is based around the idea of growth. I think I will continue to climb as long as I feel there is growth. If the risk was there and I was stagnating, then I feel I would leave it. As long as the risk was producing growth and I was getting something back, then I felt the risk was justifiable. The more risk I was taking, the more I needed the growth. I also knew that stagnating in my life was equally as bad as death. I'm not sure if that came from my upbringing, or my own personal desires, but I think that stagnating as a human being didn't make any sense to me. It wasn't something that I thought was worth living for."

Buhler seems to enjoy every aspect of climbing, including the arduous task of putting together all the elements needed for an expeditionary climb, from getting the funds together, raising a team, obtaining the necessary permits and equipment, to finally having it come together at the base of the mountain. Collectively, this process is a large part of what he describes as growth, consistently becoming more efficient in every aspect of his sport, including the climb itself. This would appear to create a long and deep satisfaction, which increases as he becomes a better and more experienced climber.

For Sharon Wood, the greatest satisfaction seems to come from the ability to fight through difficult situations, as well as being part of what she feels is a special kind of fraternity. "Climbers dedicate their lives to things other than what most people do," Wood said. "We tend to spend a great deal of time with other climbers, talking about our desires and dreams. As for immediate satisfaction, I think it's the whole notion of self-mastery. It's like, holy cow, I held it together there, or we held it together here. You know, it's a feeling of defiance. But reaching the top of anything is not what it's all about. It's when you're in the thick of it and you're pushing through it. That's what I'm always looking for, that place, that zone that you go to, to push through and get there. I'm not a very strong person physically, yet I've done some pretty big climbs. That's what the big attraction to climbing is. It's not so much what you have; it's how well you use what you have. I have very little physically compared to some other climbers, and because of that and what I have done, I would say that climbing is about eighty percent mental. That's what makes you feel good."

Abby Watkins's thoughts on the subject seem to be between Buhler's and Wood's. "I don't think [climbing] is an adrenaline rush," she said. "That's fight or flight, and if you're at that point climbing, you're in trouble. No, the satisfaction comes from a lifelong journey of learning and self-discovery. I think climbing gives us the opportunity to be put in situations where the sport asks a lot of us, and our reaction to that, or what we learn from that, is the ultimate satisfaction. It gives us the opportunity to be better than ourselves or better than we think we are. In a sense, it's the whole process from coming up with an idea, then doing the research and the work putting it together, and finally executing it. That's very satisfying."

So the satisfaction is also a personal challenge, for the climber to go to new and different places, both on the mountain and deep within himself, learning from a sport that has a great deal to teach. Again, for Abby Watkins, it's a process, a long, deep, and growing satisfaction rather than a short-term adrenaline rush. For rock climber Craig DeMartino, there is both the challenge and a rush, as well as something rather surprising. Climbing, he says, is a kind of sedative, relaxing him and making him forget some of his everyday problems back on the ground.

"If you're frightened of doing something, especially when you're way up high and fearful of a fall, there's a great feeling of satisfaction to just swallow that, saddle up, and get the job done," DeMartino explained. "Once it's done, you have an almost euphoric feeling, akin to an adrenaline rush. Now, you're up there, but the climb is behind you. At that point, there's a great perspective in your life. Suddenly, the things that you worry about down below are very far from your mind. Did I bounce a check? Does the car need repairs? Things like that are pushed far into the background because you're so focused on what you're doing. In that sense, I find climbing to be actually therapeutic. To be so focused on one task that you can't think about anything else at the moment is a pretty nice thing."

The reasons for climbing vary, as do the reasons for jumping and flying. For climbers, there can be an adrenaline rush at certain times, but there is also the satisfaction of overcoming a challenge, of experiencing a learning process to be treasured over a long period of time, a kind of exploration of self-discovery, as well as a relaxing, therapeutic way to push other problems aside. Similarities and differences. As in all other hobbies, sports, and recreational activities, people have their own reasons for following a star. If it leads them to the top of Mount Everest or over the top edge of El Capitan, they don't do it on a whim. It's too dangerous for that. However, they do it for very specific reasons, willing to risk paying a price for the joy they ultimately find at the end of their chosen rainbow.

The Riders

Once again the sports become fast and furious. Skiers, snowboarders, surfers, motorcyclists all court danger with each run, each event. Whether they are performing for a film, looking to win a contest, or just challenging themselves with another gnarly ride, these athletes go hard and fast, jump long and high, often while risking serious injury or death. When they are nursing their bruises, or resting their tired bodies at the end of the day, how do they feel? What makes them want to do it again? In other words, any adrenaline junkies here?

"No, I don't really look at big wave surfing as an adrenaline addiction," said Mike Parsons. "I'm definitely not that. There's certainly a rush when riding a giant wave, and there are certainly moments when you feel an adrenaline rush. The difference is I'm not one of those people trying to top it every day and I don't always need that feeling. I just like being in the ocean and surfing, and to me riding big waves is the most challenging thing you can do as a surfer. That's why I do it. I'm challenging myself, but I don't try to top what I did the day before, and that's why I'm not an adrenaline junkie.

"There's just the satisfaction of pitting your skills against mother nature and being successful at it. There's nothing like riding a really big wave and making it. It's incredibly satisfying, but something people who haven't done it can't really understand. They can't comprehend the difficulty involved, and how it takes a lifetime to get any good. I've been doing this for thirty years and I've heard people say I'm crazy, that I'm an adrenaline junkie, stuff like that. But this is simply part of my life, something I enjoy doing. It's very well thought out. I can compare it to the best mountain climbers in the world and why they do it. That, to me, is comparable to surfing."

Parsons was very thorough and compelling in his reasoning. He admits to an adrenaline rush, but doesn't have the need to top his performance at every turn. After all, there isn't much difference between a fifty- and a sixty-foot wave. The ever-present danger in any wave around that size is enough to test the skills and mettle of the few surfers who can ride them. No wonder Mike Parsons gets tremendous satisfaction from the ride, and no wonder he continues to do it. Perhaps the operative word here is *love*. He simply loves his sport.

For Archie Kalepa, the native Hawaiian who considers himself part of the long tradition of the waterman, surfing is something he feels almost compelled to do. The satisfaction he receives from being a part of the ocean and going out on his board is almost understood, yet he still admits that "tow surfing is the ultimate rush. Surfers, as they progress, want to ride the bigger waves. As long as [the sport] is guided in the right direction, it's going to go places we never even thought it could."

There's no way a tow-in surfer can ride a big wave, court disaster, go through the tunnel of a wave that is big enough to hold a bus, and listen to the roar of the water all around him, without being pumped sky high. That's why Archie Kalepa's palms sweat the night before he goes out. No matter how it turns out, he knows he's in for the ride of his life.

Skiers and snowboarders, it would seem, should experience similar reactions. After all, both are moving at breakneck speeds on a mountaintop that could avalanche or drop off suddenly into nothingness. It isn't so different from the mammoth waves that surfers battle, where things can change in the blink of an eyelash. In fact, the kind of skiing Kristen Ulmer pursues doesn't give her much time to think about a rush. The performance is one thing; the satisfactions come later.

"I don't have an adrenaline rush while I'm coming down a mountain," she said. "You can't really feel any emotion while you're doing it or you're dead. Emotions will just get in the way. You have to be really focused, so you don't even come down a slope hooting and hollering. We're not a bunch of yahoos going *Wooooooo*. There's too much to focus on when you're skiing these kinds of lines. Afterwards is when you feel it. The sense of accomplishment comes when you're done, especially when you just finished something that's really intense. It's really the kind of satisfaction that says, 'Man, I can do that. I'm special.' But I've never been addicted to adrenaline. I don't even know what adrenaline is. I'm more addicted to excitement. I need that. I continue to do what I do because I'm really good at it and that makes me feel good about myself."

Circe Wallace, who has snowboardeded some incredibly difficult lines, said she is completely focused when making a run. But she quickly added, "Oh, yeah, and your adrenaline is just pumping. You're still on a high when you finish. You feel really alive. In fact, many times I would feel real shaky when I finished. My body was just trembling from excitement. It's kind of an overload because of the difficulty of the line you have just come down. I did it as long as I did because, for me, it was a matter of self-expression, and I always had competitive tendencies. That keeps you going, too."

Tom Day, who was an avid free skier before becoming a cinematographer, described two different types of rushes. "I get two distinct feelings from skiing," he said. "One is the pure enjoyment of it, and that comes in more of a relaxed format, where it's just total fun. Then there's the other side, which is the challenging side, the tough lines where you are dripping, scared, and you don't necessarily enjoy it until it's over. In fact, you simply are not enjoying it at the time because you're so focused and scared, and sometimes wondering what the hell you are even doing there. But then you really enjoy the rush you get from it. It's a huge adrenaline shot and a mental satisfaction as well. You just got over a huge hurdle. You just proved to yourself that yeah, you looked at something, thought you could do it, and you did it. Some highs can last a couple of days."

With a high that lasts a couple of days, it would seem that Tom Day would want to repeat it, get that feeling again. When he was younger, he says he did have the feeling that some people call an adrenaline addiction, that he had to go out and do something a bit more dangerous than the time before. "Yes, for sure," he agreed. "I've experienced that myself and I have seen it in other people. There's definitely a great deal of truth to that. Now that I'm forty years old, I don't feel that need anymore, but I do know some skiers out there in their forties who aren't stopping, who continue to challenge themselves. Age may be a factor, but I also think it's an individual thing. But sure, there are times when you just need that rush again, like you need another cup of coffee."

In freestyle motocross, with its great risk and the need for intense concentration, there is a definite rush that is companion to performance. Mike Metzger feels that the combination of fear and the goal of completing midair maneuvers safely is the reason for the rush.

"I think the fear factor builds the adrenaline and makes you step up and do what you have to do," he said, "and that's the goal at hand. If the goal at hand is clearing an eighty-foot jump, you've got your adrenaline pumping and pumping a little harder when you're thinking about the jump. Once you go up the ramp and you're committed, the adrenaline is pumping but the fear is gone. When you know you're going to make it and land safely, the adrenaline is still pumping and you know you can do it again. The feeling of getting over the jump the first time is great. You think, 'Okay, I'm not hurting. Let's do it again.'"

All of the players on the fields of the extreme are undoubtedly high on their sports, and always feel of special rush or satisfaction from challenging themselves, competing against themselves, pushing their talents to the limits, courting risk and danger, and coming through it with an intense, high-focused performance. They find it incredibly satisfying, albeit in different ways and, in many cases, also feel special, almost as if what they do is a privilege. As for the adrenaline addiction, the term may not be quite accurate, but apparently the need to continue to look for a special feeling, that surge or rush, is very strong.

8

LIFE, INJURY, AND
DEATH

I've probably put myself through hell on earth growing up. Torture I call it. I've broken both my femurs, had rods put in both of them and taken out again. I've had operations on both knees, broke both wrists several times, broke my back three times. I'm already full of arthritis at age twenty-six. But I train harder than at any time in my life and I'm ready to take on the world.

—Mike Metzger, freestyle motocross rider

HIGH-risk athletes are natural optimists. The glass is always half full. They tend to look at their sports and their lives in a very positive way. There's no doubt that they love what they do and, as we just learned, get a very special kind of rush and satisfaction from challenging themselves while courting risk and danger. There is, however, a huge downside to every sport that has been discussed here, the continuing specter of injury and death. Nearly all the athletes who survive know people who have been killed. Many have lost good friends and mentors. Yet they carry on, often espousing a resiliency and a philosophy that not everyone can understand.

Many of us avoid talking about death. Young people, especially, often feel immortal and indestructible. Older people are reluctant to admit that the end is getting near. With extreme, high-risk sports, however, reality can get in the way of so-called normal living. Life can end in an instant. You can be talking, laughing, breaking bread with a friend one day, and preparing for his funeral the next. Yet instead of mourning, most athletes go on, feeling that the one who didn't make it would do the same thing if he were the survivor.

Injuries also take a large toll. A severe injury in this world can almost be as bad as death, because it deprives the athlete of the thing he loves the most—pursuing his sport. On the other hand, injuries that the average person would consider severe are sometimes looked upon as mere scratches to the high-risk athlete. Their powers of recovery and willingness to get right back on the proverbial horse are sometimes nothing short of amazing. How is it that these athletes can look upon injury and death in such a different way from the rest of us?

Carlos Buhler already mentioned finding the frozen body of a climber on Makalu, and knowing immediately that he could be that man within the next ten or twenty hours. Yet he still climbs in spite of having the knowledge that death has claimed so many over the years.

"Early in my career I lost a couple of significant climbing people in my life," Buhler said, "and when it first happened to me, it had an enormous impact. Though I had seen my father die when I was ten, death in my climbing community was relatively rare. Then suddenly, when I was twenty or twenty-one, I began to see the affects of bad luck or misjudgment and it really, really hit me hard. I immediately understood then that this was a very serious game. So, for the first time, I knew I had to find a point to balance my desire to go forward or turn tail and run."

Buhler, of course, decided to go on. That wouldn't be the last of the deaths he would experience, and like others, he had to find ways to deal with it. It wasn't easy then and doesn't get any easier as the years pass. "You begin examining it when you first experience it," he explained. "You hear your friends talk about it, read the literature, the famous books. Then you begin to hear the stories about what happens with frostbite and what happens in avalanches. You read those incredible tales, but when you see it for the first time, maybe see someone bleeding all over the cliff and you hear two days later that he died, or that someone you actually know gets killed in an avalanche, yes, it is an enormous blow. I guess different people have different reactions to it. So again, you have to make a decision. You take these experiences and perhaps decide simply that this activity is not worth the risk of losing your life or your limbs, no matter what you are going to get out of it. Or losing loved ones and friends.

"On the other hand, you can take the information from other people's misfortunes, examine it, try to learn as much as you can from it, and go forward. I think for me the decision was that I wanted to be involved in mountaineering long-term. For some reason, I think by the time I was climbing for eight years or so, I was very aware I had a longtime commitment to the sport. I knew by then that I was going to be exposed to both some horrible situations and some wonderful ones. And if I was going to play this game, I had to be ready and willing to accept my own demise and those of my friends. That is certainly how it has panned out."

Sometimes the reality of the sport and its possible consequences make a climber challenge tougher peaks before he is ready. Perhaps he feels that if he looks death directly in the eye and survives, he has a leg up on a long career. Carlos Buhler has experienced that aspect of examining his mortality as well.

"By the time I was twenty-two or twenty-three years old, I was trying very difficult climbs in the Canadian Rockies during the winter. Because of that, I was invited to join a mountaineering group to visit Russia in 1978, when I was twenty-three. So we climbed over there, knowing the ramifications of mistakes, and knowing that competent climbers, even better than us, and who were making more educated decision than you, were also getting killed. That led me to think that I might die before I was twenty-five years old. And I used to say, jokingly, to a lot of people, that I understood [climbing] was terribly dangerous and the risk of having a fatal accident was so great that I couldn't complain if it happened to me by twenty-five, because there were already a lot of people around me who didn't make it to twenty-five.

"I can even remember when my twenty-fifth birthday was approaching. I was on a mountain in Nepal, just my second trip to Asia. I was leading a difficult pitch on the mountain and a Sherpa was belaying me. I recall saying to myself, 'I am not going to die today. This would be too weird. I'm gonna do this safely and I'm gonna get back to camp and know that I made it to my twenty-fifth birthday.' So I think I went into this thing with my eyes open."

Having a long career in the mountains has obviously given Carlos Buhler a lot of time to think and reflect. No one truly gets used to death, or expects it, either for himself or others. But it happens, and with Buhler, that meant making a decision early on to accept the fates that live in the mountains and continue to climb. He seems to look at death in much of the same way now as when he began years earlier. Buhler knows that he could die in the mountains. Every serious climber knows that. But he goes on, learning, climbing, and accepting. That doesn't make it easier, but for him that's the way it is.

Sharon Wood, another veteran climber, has had similar experiences losing friends to the mountains. Her reactions, however, changed as she became older. "I've think I've dealt with it differently at each stage of life," Wood said. "When I was at the beginning of my ambitious run for the big mountains, I lost a very good friend. His name was John Lauchan and he was killed in an avalanche in 1982 while he was solo climbing. When John died, it was a huge shock to the climbing community and the reverberations sounded far and wide. You had to have known John to have experienced the impact. He was a very talented, very intelligent man who was into many different things. In a sense, he was a real Renaissance man and a very, very good climber. His death made me ask myself if I had lived my life as fully as possible, and whether there was anything—if I were to die tomorrow—anything I had left undone, or if there were any unrealized dreams. And there were.

"What John's death ultimately did was lead me to pick up my pace and fully immerse myself into the certification program (in Canada) that was I was going through, to get my certification and also to start climbing bigger, higher, and harder. In other words, I wanted to use my potential as fully as possible. Almost twenty years later, just last summer, I lost a friend to a freak accident. He was hit by a rock in a place where that was very unlikely to happen. In fact, the warden on the rescue team said what happened to him was as likely as a refrigerator falling out of the sky. This time, losing a friend made me pull back and not want to go into the mountains for a while and to be more fearful and more cautious, and more conservative. I think a lot of people fall somewhere in the middle after the death of a friend. They pull back for a while, and then slowly they dip their toes in and then their foot in, and then they're right into it again."

Sharon Wood still climbs, but no longer challenges the world's large peaks. She has children now and that is yet another factor in her decision. "It's a very difficult line for me to walk," she said.

"Just last summer I went out and did a little solo climb. Wasn't a huge peak, but still a situation where if I fell, there would be no chance of survival. Having children at home certainly affects what I do, but climbing for me is what makes me feel fully alive. And I think I bring that aliveness back to my children and my family, and also to my community. Because I can do that, I believe it makes life a richer place. So when death happens, it really makes you appreciate life more, and also the partners you are climbing with."

Again, Sharon Wood has obviously thought long and hard about life and death in the mountains, as well as what continuing to climb in the face of death can mean. Athletes can quit at any time, but apparently few do. Kristen Ulmer has had a number of harrowing experiences, including being caught in five avalanches. Her attitude seems to be a bit more basic, a kind of rationalization why others die and she will live.

"Yeah, I have at least one friend a year die," she said bluntly. "I think most of us are kind of stupid in how we deal with it. But we just look at the ways in which each person screwed up, and convince ourselves that we wouldn't do that, that we wouldn't be personally stupid enough to do that. It's really kind of an ignorant way to be, but I think it's a way we can also justify going back out again even though it's all very dangerous stuff."

Snowboarder Circe Wallace has also had to deal with losing friends. "We usually lose about one friend every couple of years," she said. "Mainly avalanches or cornices. Every now and then there's a helicopter crash. Then there is always random stupidity, maybe landing on something wrong. It's hard. But we all look at it as if it's life, and you lose people somehow, somewhere, whether it be that you're a participant in a sport or simply a human being who lives and breathes. When we lose a friend out in the middle of nowhere, we look at it as, hey, at least they were doing something they loved. What you hope is that they weren't doing something stupid."

Rock climber Craig DeMartino amplifies the thought that the survivors have a need to know what happened when there is a fatality and whether the climber made a stupid mistake that caused death.

"If somebody dies on a route, no matter where that route is, the traffic there suddenly picks up dramatically," DeMartino said. "People seem to want to go and see what happened. A guy fell in El Dorado Canyon about three years ago, and when you went down there on weekends, people would be lined up to climb it. I think they wanted to know what happened and were asking questions. Where did he fall? Why did he fall? Did something break? When somebody falls like that and they're killed, you never really know why and many times even his partner can't be sure. It's almost as if other climbers want to confront it, get it out in the open. Then it's not so much of a mystery because they were there, and then they can rationalize that maybe it was just a bad day for him. I guess that's just one way to deal with it. Go see where it happened.

"I'll never forget one day a few years ago. My wife and I were going ice climbing with a good friend who had just come back from Alaska. My wife realized she had forgotten her double boots, which you wear for ice climbing. Our friend said he had an extra pair in his truck and went to get them. My wife put them on and we started walking toward the base of the climb. Then she remarked that the boots really fit well and asked if she could keep them. Our friend laughed and told her she could certainly keep them because the guy who wore them had been killed. My wife completely freaked out at first because here she was, wearing a dead guy's boots. But after a few minutes she said, 'Okay, that's fine.' He had died in an avalanche in Alaska. It happens and you have to go on."

One way or another there seems to be an acceptance of death as an unavoidable consequence of the sport, a kind of it's-happened-before-and-it's-gonna-happen-again philosophy. Everyone has their own way of dealing with it, rationalizing it, and continuing to go on hoping that they are not next. Miles Daisher is just thirty-two years old and has participated in BASE jumping, sky diving, and the radical sport of rope free flying. Daisher, in fact, lost two of his mentors, BASE jumper Frank Gambalie and Dan Osman. He has talked about the possibility of his own death, and has had to deal with the deaths of his two best friends. It isn't easy.

"Shane [McConkey] and I talk about it quite often," Daisher said. "We'll say stuff like, 'Hey, man, if I ever go in, take my rigs and jump them. They're yours.' I kind of willed my stuff out to him verbally. But we know that you can totally die and I think about that a lot, especially when I'm doing something that I haven't done before and I'm not exactly sure what will happen once I step off. Even on my first ever BASE jump I was thinking, 'You can die right now, totally die right now.' But then I thought, 'If I don't jump, have I truly lived? Have I done what I really want to do?' In the end, this is what you want to do, and if you hold back, then maybe you'd rather just die because you're cheating yourself. The desire to do some of these things is so strong that it overrides any thoughts of death."

Yet Daisher's reaction to Dan Osman's death, at which he was present, seems totally out of context for him and for all the others who have talked about the ultimate price. "I was the only one there when Dano died," he said. "I didn't know how to deal with it, didn't cope with it very well. I just started drinking. A couple of friends and myself really spent a lot of time getting drunk. Sometimes I would wake up in the middle of the night or in the morning and find myself crying. Then I would drink again. Finally, I began talking about it more, explaining to my friends what had happened that day, and slowly I began feeling better. Then I started getting back into it and began to BASE jump. It put some of the fire back into me, gave me my drive back. I knew then if I quit, I would really be letting Dano down.

"When Gambler [Frank Gambalie] died, drowned in Yosemite trying to get away from the rangers who wanted to arrest him after a BASE jump, all my friends were sitting around moping, staring at the ground, crying in a big circle. But Gambler was the guy who encouraged me to do the things I really loved. So I told the guys, 'Look at you people. Frank would be so pissed if he saw you now.' I didn't want to dwell on him dying, but I didn't want to forget he died either. I would talk about it all the time. But now I had a different way of dealing with it than when Dano died. I would go out and jump because Gambler would want me to do that—keep going, keep jumping. And that fired me up. His death encouraged me to quit my job as a landscaper and just pursue the things I really wanted to do."

Again, the individual comes into play. Because Daisher was there when Dan Osman died, he seemed to take it harder than if he had heard about it from afar. The loss would have undoubtedly hurt just as much, but being there might have made him feel somewhat guilty, that perhaps he could have done something to prevent Osman from making that last, fatal jump. With Gambalie, he was angry as well as mourning the loss. Because Gambalie had made a successful BASE jump and died in such a strange and seemingly avoidable way, it just encouraged Miles Daisher to go on, to push the envelope, follow his desires, and jump some more. Though his losses have been deep and heartfelt, terrible tragedies, he can now deal with them and realize he must continue, just as Osman and Gambalie would have done.

Climber Kim Csizmazia, too, has been touched by deaths in the mountain and has yet to fully understand how to deal with it, except to keep climbing. She has seen different types of reactions in others and knows that it is very much an individual thing.

"It's really a difficult thing to deal with," she said. "I read a quote where someone said that by going back into the mountains after a death, you feel closer to the people you lost. I still can't fully explain it. We all know there's a potential for any one of us to be killed. We talk about it quite often. I just moved to a community in Canada about three years ago and there are a lot of young men who are in that statistical age group where there is a higher chance for them to get bitten off in the mountains, so to speak. You go to any kind of wilderness first-aid class, or avalanche class, and the statistics tell you the males from eighteen to twenty-four are most likely to be killed. But as I said, we all know the possibility exists and yet I really don't know how to deal with it except that you go on. There are some people who change, and they stop climbing. Some, however, become more focused and climb harder. It affects everyone differently when you lose someone close like that."

Abby Watkins, on the other hand, who often climbs with Csizmazia, put it this way: "If someone is killed that we know, a close friend, it definitely makes you think. You know it could have been you, your husband, your best friend. But you also pay tribute to their life. Usually, if they die mountaineering or climbing, you know they were doing what they loved and fully accepted the risk. So it's a good time to sit around and appreciate who they were and what they gave to the planet. Serious climbers rarely quit when someone is killed. If you have climbed enough to look the risk in the face, then you've accepted it or you wouldn't be up there. If you're naive to that risk and somebody dies, you might go either way. You might say I accept this risk, I accept that I could die doing this, or you might say okay that person died and I don't want to be next, so I'm not going to do this anymore."

Once again, all the elements that are a part of climbing come into play when someone is killed: risk and fear, the knowledge of what's up there waiting for the climbers, as well as the X-factors of avalanches, storms, crevasses, and falling rocks. Yet some climbers seem to have come to terms with all of it more easily than others. There is certainly no set formula except that those who climb and jump, and have done it for years, ultimately continue to climb and jump.

Tom Sanders, a sky diver, BASE jumper, and top aerial photographer, stood at the base of El Capitan, camera in hand, as his wife, Jan Davis, plunged to her death while BASE jumping. Her chute never opened. The story was detailed in Chapter 3. Needless to say, Sanders was devastated. Later, he made the analogy that he wouldn't stop driving on the freeway because someone was killed in a car accident, adding that his wife died doing something she loved.

Having suffered perhaps the ultimate loss, Sanders never thought for a minute that he would change his hobbies, or his career. He exposes himself to possible accidents in his work and in his lifestyle, witness a snowmobile ride he once took. "I firmly believe that when I did a four-hour ride on a snowmobile, there wasn't a moment when I wasn't in danger of being killed. At any time during the ride I could have hit a tree, even though we were under control. You have to remember what people are used to. People can accept death during a Nascar or Indy car race. Going around a track at 240 miles per hour is a great national sport. To me, though, it's not as satisfying as flying my body through the sky. But many people just don't understand what I do, or why I continue to do it."

At the age of twenty-six, Mike Metzger is considered one of the old men of the freestyle motocross circuit. Though his sport is known for the many injuries the riders suffer, there are also fatalities. He was interviewed for this book just a week after attending the funeral of a fellow rider, a youngster who had just turned eighteen.

"He lived at a local motocross track," Metzger said, "and was getting ready to race in the Mini-Olympics in Florida and he was just out at the track, warming up his bike. His bike kind of bogged off the lip of a jump and put him into an *indo,* nose down, and he landed on his neck. I don't think he suffered. He went over a double jump and landed head first. He died because he shattered his vertebrae, ripped his spinal cord. I'm a firm believer in Christianity and Jesus Christ. If it's your time to go, it's your time to go. But my faith has been a big part of my risk factor growing up. I believe if you have Jesus Christ in your heart, there is no reason to be afraid of anything. People pass on. We went to the funeral. It wasn't fun, but fortunately a good funeral, if there can be such a thing. He had a lot of friends in the motorcycle community and many people spoke about him. His family told everyone he was a Christian as well."

The two athletes who readily acknowledged the possibility of death in their sport, but didn't really talk about dealing with it, were big wave surfers Mike Parson and Archie Kalepa. Rather than talk about death, both spoke about how hard they worked to be prepared to deal with the mountainous waves they surf, adding that the waves can claim anyone at any given moment. Archie Kalepa considers himself a Hawaiian waterman, which makes surfing something that he simply continues to do. Asked about losing friends, he simply said, "Sure, it can happen," quickly adding, "That's why you try to be as cautious and safe as possible." While Parsons, confronted with a question about not being able to continue surfing, waved the question off by saying, "That thought is too difficult to think about."

❀   ❀   ❀

Injuries are something else most high-risk athletes must confront at some point in their careers. In general, they rehab and return, because an injury is just a temporary inconvenience, unless it is so serious that they can't continue. To an extreme athlete, that is sometimes a fate worse than death.

"I find that most people who BASE jump are not afraid of dying," said Mick Knutson. "I certainly don't have a death wish myself. But one thing I fully understand is the consequence of being injured. That scares me a lot more than death. Because you live with it, you're stuck with it, maybe for the rest of your life."

Knutson has been lucky. His worse injury was scraping the skin off his palms during a landing on asphalt. His mistake was not wearing gloves and the wind blew him off course. It was painful for a while, but not totally debilitating. Miles Daisher hasn't been severely injuried since childhood, but has said that if he were ever confined to a wheelchair, he would still find a way to strap a parachute on and wheel himself off the side of a cliff. Mike Metzger admits his body is full of arthritis at age twenty-six from a multitude of broken bones, but then adds he is training harder than ever and is in the best shape of his life, ready to take on the world. In fact, Metzger grew up breaking bones and getting back on his motorcycle long before the doctors gave him medical clearance.

"I was probably seven or eight when I broke my right ankle at Corona Raceway, battling with another kid," he said. "I had to have a cast on. Maybe a week or two later I was riding with my cast on, and two weeks later Dad and I were in the garage cutting it off. It's always been that way with getting injuries and getting casts. The casts don't last very long because I always get back on my bike, and whether it's a wrist or a foot, I beat the cast up until it's not doing much good anyway."

Skier and cinematographer Tom Day broke his arm in the eighth grade, missed just one day of skiing and went out for the next three weeks with one pole. Asked if the injury stopped him, Day gave a quick and succinct "No!" Kristen Ulmer has had seven knee operations and continues to ski. She says injuries are "part of the game and are to be expected," echoing the thought of others when she adds that an injury is worse for extreme athletes because it puts their lives on hold. They must be healthy to perform well, and they must perform well if they are to avoid further injuries, and survive.

Snowboarder Circe Wallace had to rehab from a pair of anterior cruciate ligament tears in the same knee. After the second one in 1996 (the first was in 1992), Wallace said she "kicked ass in rehab and got back out there in six months. But something had changed. "I kept going for a while, but my heart wasn't in it," she said. "I'll admit I was scared of it happening again. It's such an intense rehab, really nine months of your life, and it was difficult on me."

A year later, Wallace was doing a photo shoot on an extremely cold day. "We were at a place called Island Lake Lodge and it was about thirty below. The lip of the jump fell apart and I did a backside three-sixty and landed on the flat track. This time it was my other knee, the left one, and as soon as it happened, I knew. Okay, that's it, my career's over. I was twenty-six years old and part of me felt relieved. I knew I couldn't do this forever and now it was time to move on. The repeated injuries did cause something of a mental block and I just wasn't able to push myself as hard because of the physical repercussions. Before I began getting hurt, I was fearless because I didn't know what could happen."

Wallace says she doesn't think that most high-risk athletes have a real understanding of injuries until they receive one. Then, they all react differently. Obviously, that's true. Ulmer is still skiing big mountains after seven knee surgeries. Metzger still gets on his bike and does the McMetz despite having a body loaded with arthritis. So some continue, while others pull back and prepare for life after the extreme.

Perhaps it was Dr. Robert Leach, who has seen the proliferation of high-risk sports over his long career, who made the most accurate statement yet about the injuries these athletes are suffering. Said Dr. Leach, "With modern sports medicine we do great things, get people back in action, but these people won't suffer less in the long run. You're going to continue to see athletes as they age continue to have some problems. Some great studies done in Sweden on soccer players showed that even though we reconstructed their knees and they went back to playing at a high level, when they were looked at fifteen or twenty years later, they all had changes [in the areas where they had surgery]. I think a lot of these people will provide incomes for orthopedic surgeons in years to come. And I also think we are going to have an avalanche of injuries coming along the way sports are changing."

Death and injury. It's hard to talk about extreme sports without mentioning the two. They may not be the constant companions that are risk and fear, but they arise enough to make all the athletes stop, think, and then look inside themselves to perhaps reevaluate their own lives while saying goodbye to treasured friends. This is probably the single biggest by-product of high-risk sports that causes so many people to question the sanity of these special athletes and wonder how they could put their lives on the line with such frequency and without seeming to care what happens to them. But they do care, in a way that is also sometimes difficult for others to understand.

9

THE EXTREME WITH A HIGHER CALLING

The ocean for me is a totally spiritual thing. It doesn't matter if it's small surf or big surf, just being in it is the important thing. It's my place. You can have all kinds of things going on in your life, all kinds of problems and worries, and the second I begin surfing I'm completely focused on that and the rest of the world goes on hold. It's almost like someone going to church. Without a doubt, the ocean is my church.

—Mike Parsons, big wave surfer

THERE are many differences between high-risk athletes who engage in adventure sports and the conventional athlete competing in traditional sports. For openers, no mountain climber, big wave surfer, or BASE jumper today is working under a five-year, $60 million guaranteed contract. While some extreme athletes can earn a very good living with the combination of sponsors, prize money, films, and videos, none of them is becoming filthy rich, as are the majority of the athletes in the so-called major sports. There is, however, another kind of reward that some extreme athletes seem to find while pursuing their sports that also separates them from the money-laden world of traditional sports. For while they often risk their lives to climb up a mountain, ski down a mountain, ride a mammoth big wave, sleep in a porta-ledge on a 5,000-foot cliff, or BASE jump into a deep cave, many of these athletes experience a feeling no baseball or basketball player ever has, something deeper and, to them, very meaningful. Because they spend so much time dealing with the natural elements in the world, in some of the most remote, exotic, and spectacular places on the planet, they are often affected in very different ways by the environment in which they spend so much of their time.

A mountain, the side of a cliff, the oceans, the blue skies, the places they hike through and across to get to their destinations—these are not the creations of man. They were carved out of the earth over millions of years, an incredible natural history and something of which most high-risk athletes are fully aware. In fact, there is a history to almost every place they go, legends—mythologies,

stories of people who came before, not to mention the more recent triumphs and tragedies that often go hand in hand with each
locale. Not surprisingly, the athlete who stands atop a huge mountain, navigates down a tricky, snow-covered slope, or rides his surfboard into the tube of a giant wave often has a special feeling not
only for what he is doing, but also for the place in which he is
doing it. It is a kind of special reverence some have for the things
they see, the places they go, and one that well could be a motivating factor for the athletes to continue their sport despite the risks
and dangers.

The mountains provide an especially powerful stimulus for this
kind of spiritual effect. High peaks have been looked upon as the
homes of gods for many centuries and by many different peoples.
In Greek legend, for example, Mount Olympus served as a home
for the gods. Both the Judaic and the Christian religions have significant mountains connected to key events in the unfolding of
their respective revelations. Native Americans from the Cheyenne
and Sioux groups on the North American plains still travel in pilgrimage to Bear Butte, their sacred mountain. In addition, many
of the world's peoples, including the Sherpa and Nepalese, have
not considered their mountains as things to be mastered or conquered.

Over the years, many climbers have returned from difficult
treks, perhaps even from near-death experiences, with tales of experiencing a special inner peace and comfort as conditions deteri-
orated and they were fighting for their lives. However, before
anyone reads the intervention of a higher power into this, there
might be something of a scientific explanation. Environmental
psychologist Bernard S. Aaronson has an explanation for "the traditional association of mountaintops with the abode of Diety."

He believes that in this environment, any feelings of com-
muning with a higher being are often caused by people being de-
prived of oxygen in the death zone, and especially by people who
have survived close encounters with death. Perhaps this is the
mind's way of lessening the fear, explaining why they survived, and
allowing them to climb again. But instead of drawing conclusions

based on conjecture, let's look at the feelings of some of those who have been there.

Carlos Buhler, who has been going into the mountains for more than two decades, has thought deeply about every aspect of his long career, including the places he has been and what they mean to him on every level. Because of the nature of his sport, he feels that there is definitely a kind of bonding with nature that transcends the ordinary, everyday experience. "Nature is the overriding force in these types of activities," Buhler explained, "unlike wrestling, or soccer, or football, or ice skating. Even alpine ski racing isn't like climbing because skiers are blitzing down a slope at top speeds. In these kinds of environments, where you are traveling for weeks to get into the mountains and often walking for days and days just to approach the peak, nature becomes the surrounding influence. When you begin talking about the rarity of standing on a piece of real estate that's twenty-five, twenty-six, twenty-seven thousand vertical feet above the planet, there's only a few square feet on the entire planet like that. Some of these peaks are extremely remote geographically. To me, it's almost a pinnacle of achievement, not only in terms of what you do, but in terms of what nature has created.

"I can remember climbing to the summit of the Matterhorn in the Italian Alps, a pointy little mountain with a knife-edge bit of snow on the top. My friend was belaying me upward toward him up the ridge, to this tremendously exposed little bit of land. Thousands and thousands of people have crossed that little bit of land because the mountain is a popular destination. But that point is very special, and to say that there is no spirituality there, you would be lying. It's very special, and for several reasons. One because of the achievement of reaching it, touching it, and physically being there under your own power. The other side of it is the enormity of the peak itself, that this is the culminating point where every face and every ridge terminates.

"To the people in Tibet, and in many parts of the world, South America as well, gods were the people who lived on these summits. And you are naturally climbing in that environment, spending many months there, and you begin to understand the way the gods in the mountains become alive for you. The idea of thinking back to where the early beliefs put those gods as home, well, it's an incredible thing. You're in somebody's home when you're on that summit. It's a moment of brief gifts from the gods."

Buhler is probably not speaking about gods being literally alive for him, nor is he claiming to have seen anything out of this world. But his feelings undoubtedly are real. He regards mountaintops as special places—godlike in their appearance and remoteness, and the way they jut toward the heavens, culminating in a small, pristine, snow-covered peak. It is certainly the kind of thing that the average person cannot conceive of and possibly not even imagine. You simply have to be there and not many people can say they have.

Sharon Wood reveres the mountains for what they are, but is hesitant to go beyond that. "I really can't put a label on my climbing," she said. "I think each time you climb those mountains and you're there with good people with whom you really have to work to pull it together, you find something deep within yourself that you don't usually find in everyday life. I think that's very humbling. You can see it in people's eyes, people who have been through a lot, whether it's in a war or whether it's an epic in the mountains. There's a certain degree of wisdom, but a spiritual feeling, no, not really. I have tremendous reverence for the mountains, almost a fear. It makes me feel very small and unimportant. I'm very thankful for good health and strength, and the companionship I've had climbing the mountains. But nothing beyond that."

For climber Kim Csizmazia, there is a sense of spirituality based on the timelessness of the mountains themselves. "Climbing connects you," she said. "I was asking a friend recently why he climbs and he said it makes him feel more alive. What does that mean? I guess it is because it connects you with the mountains. For me . . . it's that they have been there such a long time and they will continue to be there long after we're gone. It kind of puts things in perspective. Things will change and the seasons will change, but the mountains don't care what you are doing. They don't have a consciousness. Man can climb, but can't change the mountains, can't tell them what to do or how to act. There's something in nature that puts you in your place, and it's a good place. I think that with all risk sports, at some level, there is an artistic element. In a way, it's a performance art. A climber that has a feel for the sport sees a line, sees a direction, as artists do, and then tries to complete it. It almost as a painter would do, seeing something different and changing his color selection of painting sequence. The same things happen in these sports.

"But the bottom line I have found is that what matters with climbing is what the individual finds. Climbing is about personal experience. For me it sharpens the colors of life. It has taught me about living life fully and about death. Climbing helps to express the beauty of life by immersing me in the small things like the green lichen on pink granite, the smell of early morning July air on a high teton ridge or the sound of hoar crystals shattering under thick plastic boots. Losing friends and mentors to the mountains has taught me deference. The most important thing is the feeling in my heart as I walk away each time: strong, confident, and beautiful."

The modern climber is, in most cases, someone who thinks very deeply about his sport. No longer does George Mallory's explanation, "Because it's there," suffice as the reason most people climb. Today's athletes have a more total appreciation for what remains untouched and unspoiled. Abby Watkins explains her thoughts on her own climbing and sports-filled life.

"Climbing to me is understanding how to negotiate a natural feature," she said, "one that has been weathered by time and water, and all the natural forces. That's what you climb. If you were climbing a cliff that had no weathering, it would be impossible. What you are climbing are weathered weaknesses, if it's a mountain or a waterfall being created by gravity and freezing to ice. I feel small, but essentially linked to my environment, aware of the natural processes of weather, time, and nature. I love unlocking the choreography of a climb, how my body fits in to the weathering of the stone, the suspended flow of a frozen waterfall or an ancient, powerful glacier. It all means having an affinity for nature and the processes of the planet."

Rock climber Craig DeMartino equates his climbing and his place in nature with enabling him to get close to God.

"I have always felt that when you're climbing, you're in this place a lot of people don't get to see," he said. "I grew up with a strong religious background, so I have a real affinity for the natural state, and I've always felt the closest I ever get to God is when I'm climbing. You're in this place that not many people can go, and that really makes it special. Now that I'm older, I'm more focused on where I climb. If I'm three-quarters of the way up a route and sitting on a ledge maybe a thousand feet off the ground, relaxing and watching the birds play in the thermals on the cliff, it's just a great place to be. For maybe sixty percent of the climb you're virtually alone, even when climbing with a partner. It's a great time to get perspective in your life."

Kevin Quinn, who has been on the mountains as a skier, a jumper, and by running a heli-skiing service, explains his reaction to spending so much time amid nature. "I have a hundred percent special feeling about spending so much time in the mountains and in natural surroundings," he said. "There's a peak that we have named the Sphinx, because it looks just like one of the seven wonders, and every time I get on it, I shed tears because it's so special. It's on top of a nine-thousand-foot peak looking over the Chugach Mountains. When I'm not there, I still dream about standing on it. You can see for thousands of miles. You look to the south and you see the ocean; you look to the west and see more mountains. It's just incredible. It is definitely spiritual, a totally WOW feeling. We always carry a cell phone and call our mothers from the top peak."

Remember, Kevin Quinn was once a professional hockey player. His role was that of an enforcer. He enjoyed the fighting, the rough stuff, a carryover from a high-risk childhood. Taking chances and following a whole bevy of extreme sports followed. Yet here he is, an avowed tough guy, admitting to being brought to tears by the sheer beauty of a mountain, dreaming about it, and calling his mother from a cell phone. He says it's spiritual. Any way you look at it, it's special.

Kristen Ulmer, too, thinks about the places she has been and in quieter moments puts them within the context of her always-exciting life. "I'm a very spiritual person and I've studied religion very intensely," she explains. "I didn't get involved in skiing because of the aesthetics of the mountains, their natural beauty. I got involved in skiing because of the sport. Same with climbing. I love rock climbing probably eighty percent because of the gymnastics and twenty percent because of the view. But as I said, I am also very spiritual. Of course, it all depends on the situation, but if you're helicopter skiing, for example, there are moments when you just look around and see how beautiful the mountains are. That can be an extremely spiritual moment.

"At the same time I can feel that same kind of spirituality in very simple things, such as a single pink rose hanging on in November outside my front walkway. But I can tell you it's pretty incredible standing on the top of a mountain in the Himalayas and taking a big, long look. There are some pretty tremendous moments in Alaska, too. That's just a bonus, an extra, because I didn't get involved in the sport for that reason."

Ulmer has found her own spirituality without consciously looking for it. There was no long search for the meaning of life, or for the beauty of nature. She's a radical skier as well as an outstanding climber, and she courts excitement and danger. In doing that and surviving to do it again, she has also found something else, something that makes what she does just a little more satisfying.

Spiritual feelings seems to surface more frequently when the sport is practiced in a remote place or a place where nature has control and man is simply a visitor, sometimes an intruder. That's why the mountains evoke such strong feelings from the athletes who go there. Another place where, not surprisingly, the athlete has an affinity for the environment that transcends his sport is the ocean, where the big wave surfers challenge killer waves. This kind of surfing, as we have learned already, is one of the most radical of the extreme sports owing to the power and potential violence of the big waves that the surfer rides. Yet surfers don't think twice about going in. To those we spoke with, the ocean represents a lot more than just a place that produces the waves they need.

Archie Kalepa, a native Hawaiian, has a special feeling for the water that comes from the long history and tradition of his people.

"It's a totally spiritual connection," he said. "It is like sailing on the traditional Hawaiian canoe, which has helped to revive the Hawaiian people. We never knew who we were or where we came from. But through the canoe, and voyaging back to where we came from before we discovered Hawaii, we discovered who we were as a people. It has taught not only me but the Hawaiian people to be connected with the ocean, which Hawaiians are so much a part of."

Kalepa is referring to the history of the islands. It is felt by historians that between 400 and 900 A.D., Polynesians from the Marquesas Islands as well as Tahiti settled some of the Hawaiian Islands after traveling across the ocean in large sailing canoes. That's why Kalepa feels the tradition of the sailing canoe is so important, even to modern-day Hawaii. He also feels that this spiritual connection to the ocean should be a part of nearly every Hawaiian's life, but says that many have forsaken the life for other things. "There are so many talented Hawaiin surfers, but many of them end up going in other directions and lose sight of what they could have been. You feel kind of sad because you see a lot of them, instead of being in the water surfing, they're off somewhere drinking beer. For a Hawaiian, to keep at it and continue to excel in the water is sometimes a difficult thing because of distractions, and many fall by the wayside."

Californian Mike Parsons doesn't have the same kind of historical roots as Kalepa, so his focus is upon the ocean. Yet the same kind of connection exists. "The ocean for me is a totally spiritual thing," Parsons explained. "It doesn't matter if it's small surf or big surf, just being in it is the important thing. It's my place. You can have all kinds of things going on in your life, all kinds of problems and worries, and the second I begin surfing, I'm completely focused on that and the rest of the world goes on hold. It's almost like someone going into church. Without a doubt, the ocean would be my church. In some ways, it becomes for me a total escape from the day-to-day things, but most importantly is the fact that the ocean is where I want to be and what I want to be doing. There's the physical part of it, of course. If you surf first thing in the morning, you have a great day, no matter what. I wake up and check the surf. I know the times for high and low tides every day of my life. No doubt about it, my life revolves completely around the ocean."

Spiritual feelings in extreme sports surface mostly in the remoter venues, where nature can be both beautiful and deadly, such as the mountains and the oceans. Those who espouse them seem to be the athletes who have pursued their sports over long periods of time and have traveled to many different locales. Perhaps having survived for years in sports that have taken many lives plays a role in the advent of a spiritual feeling or connection. More likely, because these people have spent such a great deal of time on the mountains, skiing the slopes, flying through the air, perched on cliff tops, or surfing in the ocean, they have had the time to learn, understand, and fully appreciate firsthand both the power and the beauty of nature and the earth itself.

10

WHY SMART PEOPLE SOMETIMES DO STUPID THINGS

To me, it's all about trophy hunting. Everybody wants to be a hero. Everest attracts the worst values in our society—the greed, the avarice, the ambition. People don't go there in teams now. Each individual is there and out for himself. It's a dangerous dynamic, I think, on a mountain like that.

—Sharon Wood, expedition climber

VERY few people not involved with extreme sports will, out of the blue, decide to jump off a cliff, be towed into a huge wave, or swing off the side of mountain on a long rope. Nor will they ride a motorcycle off a ramp and fly seventy-five feet through the air. There are, however, some sports that have exhibited a new kind of seductiveness to people who might be restless in their daily lives, find themselves looking for a challenge, or simply decide to do something they consider extreme so they can tell their friends, neighbors, and business associates. At the turn of the new century, Americans were getting themselves into trouble in increasing numbers as they came closer to the edge with brief forays into sports that can be extreme. Hiking and camping, for example, have long been leisurely vacation activities for people who want to be outdoors and commune with nature. Only now many of those hikers are looking at the likes of Mount Rainier, or dreaming about the ultimate, a trek up Mount Everest.

There are literally thousands of recreational skiers and snowboarders in the United States, taking to the slopes in the winter and seeking out new venues in which to have fun. Some have begun emulating the more skilled practitioners of the sport by going out of bounds or skiing higher in the mountains than their ability dictates. Others simply overestimate their skills and become too reckless. With so many extreme-sports videos available, young skiers and snowboarders may suddenly feel they can do the same types of things as a Kristen Ulmer or Rob DaFoe.

Today, more people than ever seem to be looking for outdoor adventures of one form of another. A 1998 survey by the Travel

Industry Association of America reported that 98 million Americans had taken an adventure-travel trip within the past five years. Those numbers continue to increase and served as the impetus for adventure-travel pioneer Richard Bangs to make the statement that he is "continually amazed that people will spend enormous amounts of money up front to go places that are defined as risky, with people they have never met and guides they know nothing about." Adventure travel is a growing industry and there can be nearly as many bad stories as good ones, including unprepared people, travel guides that don't do their job, outfitters that fail to provide the proper equipment and provisions. Larry Habegger, an editor of the Travelers' Tales Books, said there are many stories of dream vacations becoming nightmares.

"There's nothing worse than being out in the middle of nowhere with an outfitter who doesn't deliver," Habegger said.

Just read the papers every day and you'll see all-too-familiar stories about hikers lost on a mountain and having to spend the night in near-freezing temperatures, or someone injured in a fall while climbing relatively easy (for a skilled person) rock faces, or a family losing a small child while hiking or camping, necessitating a huge search mission with fingers crossed. More often than not, these are intelligent people who just didn't take the proper precautions, didn't bother to learn even the basic skills needed for what they were doing, or simply bit off just a little bit more than they could chew. In any case, many of these incidents are examples of smart people doing stupid things.

What, exactly, is adventure travel? Paul Muir, the organizer of a 2002 trade show on the subject, gives the following definition of the term: "The better definition for us is experiential—people who wish to have an experience when they're on vacation," he said. "That experience can be the challenge of climbing Mount Everest, or going on a tour of cultural or historical sites in Peru or Thailand."

It is the Mount Everest part of adventure that has been causing the most concern. For some reason, more and more people are attracted to climbing the big mountains, perhaps the one place where the margin disappears quickly and the odds of going too far out to the edge rise dramatically. It isn't only Everest. In the Introduction, there was the story of three California women who decided they wanted to climb a mountain. They considered Everest, but settled on Mount Rainier in California, a 14,000-foot-plus peak that doesn't go into the death zone, but has many of the same harsh conditions as the high peaks in the Himalayas. After a three-day mountaineering course and some physical fitness training, they set out as part of an organized party of sixteen climbers. All made the summit, but on the descent were caught by the same X-factor—an avalanche—that has claimed so many of the world's best climbers. The three women survived with various injuries, while one member of their party was killed. Two of the women said they had had enough. That was it; no more mountains. The third, who had been the most seriously injured, said she wanted to climb again.

Rainier, with the unforgiving nature of much higher mountains, has continued to take a toll. On May 30, 2002, it was announced that an international party of four climbers had reached the summit of Mount Rainier, but three of them died when high winds and whiteout conditions lashed the peak. A twenty-one-year-old Oregon woman and a German man and woman were the victims. The body of the American woman was brought down by rescuers before swirling snow and 60-mile-per-hour winds drove rescuers off the mountain. A helicopter rescue team brought the other two bodies down the following day. The story said that the four climbers had no experience on Rainier, but did have ice- and rock-climbing experience. They were also climbing without a guide.

After reaching the summit, the climbers set up a camp near the peak when the severe weather hit. Their tent was destroyed by the winds. They tried to build snow caves for shelter, but the caves apparently collapsed. Authorities said they were on the northeast side of the mountain, known as the Liberty Ridge route. It is a demanding, difficult route that is usually attempted only by experienced climbers. The conditions on Rainier and its rapidly changing weather have led the mountain to be called a miniature

Everest. Mike Gauthier, the lead climbing ranger on Rainier, put it this way: "The weather was bad, considered to be terrible. Mount Rainier makes its own weather. You can see sunny skies, and five minutes later see clouds come in, and the weather change very, very quickly."

Cliff Mass, a University of Washington meteorologist, was even blunter in his assessment: "These [people] essentially committed suicide by not looking at the weather forecasts," Mass said. "The computer models were very good . . . predicting heavy snow and strong winds for the period. It was absolutely crazy to go up there with the clearly forecast extreme conditions."

It certainly sounds as if it was a tragedy that could have been avoided. Experienced climbers check everything, try to leave as little to chance as possible. On the other hand, inexperienced climbers can neglect things. Because Rainier can be climbed in a day and doesn't go up into the death zone, people seem to overlook the dangers much too often. Ironically, the Rainier tragedy wasn't the only one. Just a day later it was announced that nine climbers had fallen into a crevasse on Mount Hood in Oregon, with three of them killed and two more critically injured. To make matters worse, an Air Force helicopter crashed while trying to rescue the survivors. Fortunately, all four crewmen survived, though one was also seriously injured.

There were three separate groups of climbers some 800 feet from the 11,240-foot summit of the mountain, which is about 100 miles south of Rainier, when the tragedy occurred. The accident apparently occurred when two climbers at the front of the pack slipped and fell into the climbers behind them. They all then crashed into the next group of climbers and everyone tumbled into the crevasse.

"The only thing I can compare it to is hockey players who throw themselves on the ice to block a shot," said Cleve Joiner, who was among the group and called for help from a cell phone. "Everybody was sliding on the ice, and then they disappeared."

Mount Hood is a popular climbing site, with some 40,000 people filling out permits to climb every year. The climbers who fell were on a very well-traveled route and were on the mountain during what is considered prime climbing season. Keith Mischke, executive director of the Mazamas, a Portland climbing magazine, said that the crevasse was about twenty-five to thirty feet deep, explaining that climbers normally go around it or cross one of the snow bridges that naturally form across the gap. "They go across the bridges one at a time usually," he said. "A snow bridge can be between two feet and fifteen feet wide, but if somebody falls, they could pull the others in."

Both Hood and Rainier have checkered histories. Eleven people died on Rainier back in 1981 when they were caught in a massive storm, while in May 1986, nine teenagers and two teachers from the Oregon Episcopal School in Portland froze to death on Mount Hood while trying to escape a storm during an annual climb by students and staff. Statistics show that during the last ten years there have been an average of thirty climbing deaths per year in the United States. It may not sound like a great many, but how many could have been avoided? Still, the people continue to come, and some of the successful ones aspire to more, usually Everest.

Everest, of course, stands as a symbol for the ultimate extreme adventure, and its allure continues to grow. In effect, the mountain has become a symbol for smart people doing foolish things for the wrong reasons. On May 16, 2002, Everest recorded the most crowded day ever at its summit. Climbers broke four records as fifty-four Westerners and Napali Sherpa guides took advantage of good weather and scaled the mountain. One of those to make it was Tashi Wangchuck Tenzing, the grandson of Sherpa Tenzing Norgay, who along with Sir Edmund Hillary, was the first to reach the summit back in 1953. Also on the mountain in a separate group was Hillary's son, Peter, who hoped to meet Tenzing at the summit to begin a year of celebrations in the countdown to the fiftieth anniversary of their forefathers' ascent.

Nepal's Tourism Ministry said there were eleven teams of about a dozen climbers each on the slopes, with many others expected to try for the summit in the coming days. Among those reaching the top that busy Thursday was a veteran Sherpa guide named Appa, who set a record by reaching the mountain's summit for the twelfth time, and Ellen Miller of Asheville, North Carolina, who climbed from the southern side a year after reaching the summit from the northern side: this made her the first American woman to reach the top from both sides. Phil and Susan Ershler of Bellevue, Washington, also made the summit, and in doing so became the first married couple to climb the highest peaks on each of the world's seven continents, according to the couple's spokesman. These were just a few of the agendas that people took with them to Everest. The above mentioned climbers are certainly all legitimate, trained mountaineers with track records of going into altitude. How many of the others on the mountain are veteran climbers, well, that's always open to question. The sudden increase in the popularity of the mountain all seems to stem from the 1996 tragedy that was chronicled in Jon Krakauer's *Into Thin Air*.

"Everest was becoming a has-been, a tired, old mountain," said David Breashears, a codirector of a film about the mountain made that same year. "The tragedy of 1996 has resurrected Everest."

Suddenly, more people with little or no climbing experience decided they wanted to climb Everest. By 1998, the people continued to come, paying up to $70,000 to go on an organized, guided trip up the mountain. Ed Viesturs, a guide and world-class climber who had taken people up Everest, saw the numbers of climbers increasing and didn't think it was a very good idea. "You go up there now, there are eighteen other expeditions, and half of them shouldn't be up there," Viesturs said. "I have too much respect for Everest to want to drag anyone up there again."

The most recent statistics say that Everest has been climbed more than 1,000 times with some 180 fatalities. That doesn't include injuries, frostbite, hypotheria, hypoxia, near-death experiences, and perhaps some permanent mental and physical disabilities that climbers take off the mountain with them. Why, then, do people have this obsession with climbing Everest . . . or maybe just being able to say they climbed Everest? Sharon Wood, the first North American woman to reach the summit, feels that something is very wrong with the current scenario, beginning with the aftermath of Krakauer's book on the 1996 tragedy.

"[Krakauer] was in a great place at the right time for a writer," Wood said, "but other than that, I was disgusted by the feeding frenzy that went on over that debacle. You shouldn't be surprised when people die when you set out with agendas like that. Everybody wants to be a hero without putting any real investment into it, and Everest has become so accessible. To me, however, it's all about trophy hunting, people climbing for the wrong reasons. Everest attracts the worst values in our society—the greed, the avarice, the ambition. People don't go in teams now. Each individual is there and out for himself. It's a dangerous dynamic, I think, on a mountain like that. You really have to be looking out for each other. You really need to be caring for each other. Some of these people are literally dragged to the top. The whole thing has certainly desecrated what was once an icon of human achievement. Now these guides take great pride in getting nearly everyone to the top. They have great success formulas, as long as nothing goes wrong."

Wood's last phrase is the operative one. *As long as nothing goes wrong.* As we have already learned, on a big mountain, especially climbing in altitude, there is plenty that can go wrong. Even the most experienced climbers have died, and yet they have a much better chance of surviving since their experience has taught them how to deal with many different dilemmas. So for inexperienced and one-time climbers, the risk is increased tremendously.

Carlos Buhler also feels that there is something very much skewed about the way people are flocking to Everest. "I often run into people who have dreams of climbing big mountains," Buhler said, "and that is a wonderful dream to have. I always encourage people to have big dreams. But the question about Everest in particular is an interesting one, because then you have to ask yourself, what are these people really after? There is a tremendous achievement in climbing Makalu, but you never hear about anyone just going to climb Makalu. There is tremendous achievement in climbing Kanchenjunga. It's more difficult than Everest. But you don't hear about people in New York social circles saying I'm training for Kanchenjunga. Well, why? Is it because they want to have the feeling of achievement, or it is because they're chasing something else? That is what make Krakauer's experience and the whole experience of people on that trip so catastrophic. It's another example of people confusing their own desires with how others perceive them as people, and that's when you run the risk and it gets out of hand.

"All people have egos. Different people find different ways to express themselves in life. In Krakauer's book you begin to see the various motivations the people brought with them. Perhaps they were financial. Those who were already financially successful didn't care about the money. They wanted the cocktail party impact. That's what they were after and I think this is what Krakauer was trying to say. The only reason they're on Everest is to go home and put a trophy on the shelf. It's a trophy hunt and this is what confuses people's decision making when they're four hundred feet from the top of a big problem."

Buhler is referring to the obviously bad decisions made by the 1996 expeditions to continue to the summit beyond the agreed-upon turnaround time. Shortly after, the storm came in and the tragedy unfolded. Experienced climbers such as Buhler and Wood have talked about how exhausted and depleted mountaineers become when they near the summit of a major mountain. Teams of climbers have worked their way slowly up a mountain, acclimating to the thinning air, helping each other, pulling together as a team. Yet when they get close to the summit, sometimes only two or three of them are strong enough to make the final try. If someone gets in trouble at that point, it is extremely difficult to help that person, and it could take much too much time to get a rescue mission underway. Yet groups of inexperienced climbers led by experienced guides will be even more helpless if problems arise.

Dr. Morten Rostrup, senior research fellow in emergency and intensive care medicine, in Oslo, Norway, and a Himalayan climber, writing in the *British Medical Journal* in January 1998, described a number of situations in which climbers in trouble either couldn't be helped or wouldn't be helped by fellow climbers on Everest.

Sometimes climbers were simply too exhausted to help, but other times they were too concerned with making the summit themselves. With mixed expeditions, climbers thrown together, there is often a lack of group solidarity, which is important if and when a rescue is needed. Many people who pay to be taken to the summit in commercial groups are part of these mixed expeditions. "The experience of some of these climbers is sometimes questionable," Dr. Rostrup said.

In addition, he says that climbers develop a kind of narrow-mindedness that shuts out everything except reaching the summit. "High on the mountain, the only things that matter [to these people] are reaching the summit, keeping warm, and having enough oxygen," claimed Dr. Rostrup. "During such a mental change, climbers may avoid helping each other, they do not see descent as an alternative, they push to the summit too late, and eventually they die."

It isn't a pretty picture. The story in the *British Medical Journal* was titled, "Mt. Everest: A Deadly Playground," and to people like Morten Rostrup, as well as Sharon Wood and Carlos Buhler, that's what Everest has become. Dr. Rostrup closed by sending a message to the new breed of climber who is often on Everest. "When passing climbers who are sick or in danger on your way to the summit, you should always try to do something, even though it might seem hopeless and your own summit attempt has to be abandoned. To keep on climbing to the summit under such circumstances shows lack of humanity. It should not happen."

Indeed, it should not. The veteran climbers interviewed here have said repeatedly that reaching the summit is not the most important element in a climb. Sure, it bothers them when they come very close and make the decision to stop and turn, but they are fully aware that the summit is just a part of the whole. Many climbers coming to Everest today do not think that way. They are not familiar with the total climbing experience, do not have the same affinity and respect for the mountains, are unaware of the total process that is expedition mountaineering. Many of them are, without a doubt, trophy hunting. It may be a self-desired trophy. Some people are doing it for themselves. Others, as Carlos Buhler suggested, are looking to corner the bragging rights at cocktail parties. In either case, these people are not doing the brightest thing. Though more and more people continue to flock to Everest, sometimes at great personal expense, financially and otherwise, the rational reasons for climbing these mountains could be receding further into the background.

Many of these people are interested in *firsts*, doing something that hasn't been done before. In June 2001, Dr. Sherman Bull, a surgeon from New Canaan, Connecticut, at age sixty-four became the oldest man ever to reach the summit of Everest. At the same time, Erik Weihenmeyer, thirty-two, of Golden, Colorado, became the first sightless man to reach the summit. Dr. Bull was in a party that included his thirty-three-year-old son, a thirty-one-year-old climber from Colorado, and eight Sherpa guides. That's a far cry from how the real alpine mountaineers do it, but it shouldn't dampen the achievement. Dr. Bull still had to climb up to the summit. Then, just a few days after Bull and Weihenmayer completed their climbs, a fifteen-year-old Sherpa boy named Temba Tsheri, who had lost five fingers from frostbite during an attempt to climb Everest a year earlier, became the youngest ever to reach the summit. He broke a record set way back in 1973 by another Nepalese climber, a seventeen-year-old. It seems now as if everyone is after a record.

Dr. Bull, for instance, had broken a more recent record. In 1999, a Soviet Georgian climber named Lev Sarkisov reached Everest's summit at age sixty-one. A year later, the record was broken by sixty-three-year-old Toshio Yamamoto, a Japanese climber. Almost as quickly as Dr. Bull completed his climb, a seventy-two-year-old man from Chicago announced that he was planning to try to break the newly set record. Al Hanna has already tried and failed three times to reach the summit of Everest, coming within 300 feet of making it during a climb in 2000. He didn't begin climbing until he was fifty-eight "because I felt stale," and over the years has climbed the highest peak on every continent . . . except Everest. Despite his age, he is a legitimate climber and obviously has a chance to make it. Hanna trains arduously, going outdoors five nights a week from 2 A.M. to 5 A.M. and carrying a sixty-pound pack of weights up and down a hill maybe fifty times.

"I don't know if there is another person who does that kind of day-in and day-out rigorous training that isn't a professional mountaineer," said Gordon Janow of Alpine Ascents International, a Seattle-based guide service.

Hanna said he will make one more try. Fortunately, he has apparently been able to bear the huge costs of his mountainous excursions, being the owner of a mortgage banking company in Chicago. Like Dr. Bull, Al Hanna is a successful professional who has set some very ambitious personal challenges. Despite his rigorous training, he isn't a professional mountaineer. That, combined with his age, still makes the risk exceedingly great.

Any time these new and first-time records are set, however, lifelong climbers can't help but wonder what it's about. "You have to ask yourself why did a Sherman Bull go to Everest?" Carlos Buhler asked. "Why didn't he choose a mountain like Kanchenjunga? In the climbing world, that would have been a much greater achievement, but he wouldn't have been as recognized for it. That being the case, you've got to ask what it is he's really chasing?"

Weihenmeyer, the sightless climber, admitted he went for Everest because of its name. "Everest is so famous, that you read and hear so much about, that I wanted to try it out," he said. Having already climbed Mount McKinley in Alaska, Mount Aconcagua in Argentina, and Mount Kilimanjaro in Tanzania, Weihenmeyer is no novice. He climbs by following the sounds of bells tied to the jackets of his climbing partners and Sherpa guides. It has to be considered an incredible achievement.

Everest, apparently, has become *chic*, the place to go. At the end of May 2002, the tourism and civil aviation ministry of Nepal announced that the price to join a guided expedition up Everest will be slashed dramatically. Whereas the cost was upwards of $70,000, the price has been slashed to a paltry $25,000 for a solo climber to scale the mountain. With the cost slashed to nearly a third, the mountain has been made more easily accessible to a whole new socioeconomic group, and putting even more people in harm's way on a peak that was not made for the average man to climb.

So they keep coming. A story hit the papers on the morning of May 19, 2002, detailing how five Americans, who had hoped to become the first all-women team to climb Everest, were forced to turn back just short of the summit. The reason given was health problems and weather. At the time they turned around, the story said, they were just 285 feet from the summit. This was yet another guided expedition. Eric Simonson of International Mountain Guides of Tacoma, Washington, had reported to his wife on Saturday that things were going well. "Everything was going beautiful," Simonson's wife, Erin, said. "Twenty minutes later, I'm getting this distress call."

Among the climbers was fifty-eight-year-old Midge Cross, a grandmother who hoped to become the oldest woman to scale Everest. She turned back on Friday due to fatigue. Four others, Alison Levine, Kim Clark, Lynn Prebble, and Jody Thompson, began making the final summit push. The story said the group began running into problems about 6:40 A.M., Nepal time, when Levine collapsed from exhaustion and the effects of altitude. The other three continued along a thin ridge of snow that led to a steep pitch called the Hillary Step. Then another climber began experiencing difficulties. At the same time, clouds began gathering and the wind began picking up. At least cooler heads prevailed to some degree and the party started down. Once again, however, the recipe for disaster had climbed toward the top of the menu. And the motivations continue to change. People seem to want to be the first this and the first that. Whatever the goals might be, they are a far cry from those of veteran mountaineers.

Even those in other sports can see what is happening on mountains such as Everest, where people are taking major risks for all the wrong reasons. Asked about the motivations of those who want to take a major risk for which they are unprepared, sky diver Jim McCormick immediately referred to the ill-fated Everest expedition described in *Into Thin Air.* "I'm really not in a position to answer the question about motivation," he said. "I'd just be guessing.

But my guess, if you delved into it, would be that these people have something to prove. You remember in Krakauer's book, there was a New York socialite who was dragged up the mountain. He believed she was trying to do it to impress her socialite friends. It was a nonexperience for her because they dragged her up there like a dog on a leash, then dragged her back down. What kind of accomplishment is that? She was probably pissed off that it was so well documented. Otherwise, she could have told friends she did it on her own."

There is obviously a big difference between high-risk athletes who have worked hard to learn their sport, then take it to the limits of their ability, and even push a little farther out when the mood strikes, and those who step onto the edge with hired help to show them the way, even assist them in getting there. According to Jim McCormick and others, the real sense of accomplishment is lost, and the experience, which should be uplifting in the long run, becomes—at least to the real athletes—a nonevent.

Since the mountains seem to be the medium that attracts the most first-timers, one-timers, and those who just decide to spend a day out hiking in the hills, that seems to be the place where people often find themselves in trouble. It doesn't have to be Everest or Makalu, just a moderately sized mountain that doesn't have a lot of traffic. Veteran mountaineers have made a list of the eight major blunders that people make when climbing without the proper training and preparation. Here are the most common ways inexperienced mountaineers can quickly get themselves in trouble.

1. Fail to pay attention. "One of the main reasons people get lost is that they just don't keep looking around and striving to maintain a constant awareness of their surroundings," said Rocky Henderson, president of the Mountain Rescue Association. People should always be aware of their surroundings and, as Henderson says, "try to save the extraordinarily stupid moments for when they're at home in front of the television set."

2. Leave behind the ten essentials. People simply don't pack the proper gear. The ten things any climber should take, according to the Mountain Rescue Association, are map and compass, flashlight/headlamp, extra food and water, extra clothes, sunglasses, first-aid kit, pocketknife, waterproof matches, fire starter, and emergency shelter. It may sound like a lot of gear, but by having it with you, it might save your life, or at least a trip to the hospital.

3. Don't learn how to read a map and compass. If you're wise enough to take a map along, be wise enough to learn how to read it.

4. Panic. Veteran tracker Hannah Nyala puts it very simply: "When people get lost, their brains start running so fast they forget the simple things like putting one foot in front of the other. This leads to injuries that just compound the problem of being lost." In other words, keep a cool head. You don't have to find your way again in the first five minutes.

5. Succumb to summit fever. This is a trap that even veteran mountaineers can fall into. One reason is that whenever someone returns from a climb, they are usually asked immediately if they made the summit. Those who feel the only successful climb is one that culminates on the summit often make bad decisions and pay the price.

6. Enter a cave without the right equipment. People who climb on mountains for fun will sometimes come upon a cave and immediately go inside. This can be extremely dangerous and once again the proper equipment is needed, including safety gear, a backup light, and the right footwear. Falls, rather than getting lost, are the most common pitfall in a strange cave. Just having a headlamp as opposed to a handheld flashlight as well as the proper footwear can prevent trouble.

7. Don't tell a responsible person where you are going. This is often the thing people neglect the most when they set out for a day in the mountains. Always make sure that someone responsible knows exactly where you are going and when you expect to return.

8. Move too quickly. Even veteran climbers can find themselves exhausted and depleted. People who suddenly find they are lost tend to almost start running in an attempt to find their way. This is similar to the panic response. Instead of moving, moving, moving, and becoming tired, someone who finds they are lost should stop first. Sit down, take stock, think things through, observe the area around, and then make a plan.

There is no one set rule for being totally safe in the mountains. That rule just doesn't exist. X-factors can happen on small mountains as well as large ones, and people who are not fully aware of what they are doing can quickly find themselves in trouble.

Yet there have been people doing dangerous and risky things for years now. Single events and stunts are now often done with huge contingents of media invited, sponsors brought in, with the individual taking the risk getting a huge amount of publicity and creating the potential to earn a great deal of money for himself. That is often a motivating factor when someone decides to try something that is exceptionally dangerous or something that he is not fully equipped to do. In 2001, a former Australian army commando said he wanted to sky dive from the edge of outer space. He planned to fall nearly twenty-five miles to the earth in what would be the highest sky dive ever.

The Australian Press said the man would wear an astronaut's suit to protect his body from extreme pressures, would ride a hot air balloon to reach the proper altitude, and then would free fall for some seven minutes at speeds up to 1,100 miles per hour before opening a parachute. If the man succeeded, he would also break the sound barrier on the way down. It was a harrowing thought and still, to our knowledge, has not been tried. But there are people willing to risk their very lives for a few minutes of fame.

There are also, of course, people who simply want a challenge. They may do something very dangerous and not totally intelligent because they want to see if they can. These people aren't looking for fame or fortune. However, for something to really come under the heading of smart people doing stupid things, you would probably have to take the person's entire life into consideration. For example, if a family man with several children, a good job, and a number of people depending on him suddenly refinances his home to raise the money needed to go on an expedition to Everest, where his life could end in a storm, a fall, or an avalanche, he isn't doing the brightest thing for himself or his family. If he does it because of an innate need, a challenge, something he feels has absolutely has to do, then something is apparently missing from the life he has been leading.

Extreme sports haven't exactly provided the only vehicles for people to suddenly step out on the edge without rhyme or reason. But by being there, by growing, by becoming a television event, they have helped. That isn't to say that someone with a fairly sedentary lifestyle can't decide to do something dangerous or extreme. They should simply take it slow, become fit, train for their specific discipline, and work with those who know the sport and have done it before. By doing that and going about it slowly and methodically, at least they are leveling the playing field somewhat and lessening the odds of bad things happening.

The brace of reality shows, beginning with *Survivor,* that have been proliferating on the television screens, is also providing impetus for people to become involved with danger. Some of these shows play on people's curiosities about elements such as fear, as they ask participants to do things that are totally frightening and foreign to most people. Others, such as those with race themes, are actually combining a number of extreme sports as participants attempt to navigate mountains, rapids, and other forms of difficult and dangerous terrains. Most of the contestants are young and single, and maybe looking to jump-start careers, or simply win a pile of money. But this type of risk for television is growing as well and, as long as the ratings are there, will continue to proliferate.

All of this leads to speculation for the future. After all, more kids are beginning to look to the extreme, as events such as the X Games and Gravity Games feed off young audiences. It has been said that more young kids now are likely to know of someone such as skateboard champion Tony Hawk than the top baseball, football, or basketball players. Kids are growing up with these former alternative sports that are quickly becoming mainstream. They skateboard, snowboard, in-line skate, and show a propensity to take risks. How many of them, once grown, will be pushing the envelope on a regular basis, and how many may decide to step out on the edge just occasionally, doing something they are ill prepared to do, but doing it nevertheless?

11

EARNING AN EXTREME

LIVING

I would never characterize sponsorships as negative. They allow a sport like sky diving to get to a level of professionalism that it hasn't been able to achieve in the past.

—Jim McCormick, sky diver

THERE was a time when those participating in alternative adventure sports basically toiled in anonymity. Like Olympic athletes from days past, they had to pay their own way—buy their own equipment, foot the bill for traveling, train on their own time, and find a way to earn a living as well. They pursued their hobby whenever they could, didn't look for publicity, and had few critics or labels. No one called mountain climbing or sky diving an extreme sport then. It was simply what it was—mountain climbing, skiing, rafting, or parachute jumping. Now there are labels for everything, many more sports, and others still evolving. The extreme has become respectable, marketable, viewable, and loaded with sponsors. Television events are proliferating, major corporations are jumping on the extreme bandwagon, and both clothing and equipment used in all the sports have become big business. In a nutshell, much of what was formerly extreme has gone mainstream.

As with so many things, there is both a good and a bad side to the public's embracing of the extreme. The opportunities to receive publicity and win money have brought many new participants out, taking risks for the wrong reasons. Injuries and fatalities have undoubtedly risen because the numbers of participants are increasing, many of them taking excessive risks with a percentage not fully prepared for what they are attempting to do. On the other hand, the real high-risk adventurer, the person who pursues his sport with intelligence and fervor, and continues to do it for long periods of time, these people now have increased opportunities to earn a living within the context of their sport, allowing them to be involved full time.

Let's first take a look at how the entire extreme sports industry has grown in recent years. Some feel that the modern extreme sports movement, if you want to use the most popular label, began in the early 1980s with the skateboarding culture developing in California. In the early days, when skateboarders and in-line skaters showed up doing their *gnarly* tricks whenever there was room to skate, these new sports were quickly associated with rebellious teenagers who wore different kinds of clothes, created new hairstyles, and often dabbled in light drugs. Despite the outward accoutrements, these young athletes were doing amazing things on their boards, showing skills and daring, and seemingly ignoring pain and injuries. It was the MTV generation, later called Generation X, and it soon spawned other sports. Many of the early skateboarders took up snowboarding, and before long the mentality that went along with these sports expanded to still others. The athletes began moving closer to the edge, where other athletes—such as mountaineers—had already been for years.

It was a man named Ron Semiao, the program director for ESPN2, who got the idea for the X Games back in 1993. He began looking for magazines that featured only extreme sports and found there were none. There were some specialty magazines that he purchased and, flipping through them, saw that a few companies were already using extreme sports images to cater to twentysomething consumers. The seed had been sown and Semiao began hatching the idea that would become the Extreme Games. Still in charge of the games today, Semiao says he prefers sports that "have a whole culture attached to them, a specific attitude and a group of people who live and die for that sport."

Interesting choice of words. In any case, it was the ESPN Extreme Games that brought some of these sports to a wider audience and created new opportunities for the athletes and sponsors as well. The Summer X Games began in 1995, with the Winter X Games having their inaugural two years later. The Games have continued to be a successful yearly event. Some of the new specialty magazines now call the X Games too commercial, that they have lost the rebellious spirit that the sports first evoked. Ron Semiao, however, is not fazed by the criticism. He addressed his answer specifically to the skateboarding industry, which is not one of the sports covered as extreme here, but nevertheless still represents the idea of the extreme.

"A lot of the insider magazines feel a moral obligation to trash the X Games because ESPN is a large corporation," he said. "But when I see more kids buying skateboards, and more skaters doing ads for Pepsi and AT&T, I think that's a good thing for the skateboard industry. There's nothing wrong with it."

Though some of the athletes covered here have been X Games winners, such as Kim Csizmazia in ice climbing, the Games have often served to promote and legitimize new sports. Skiboarding, which didn't exist until 1995, features miniature snowboards, which strap on the boots so that practitioners can easily carve down a mountainside and do a myriad of tricks, jumps, spins, and flips. The sport made its X Games debut in 1998 and that made Jason Levinthal, the twenty-five-year-old founder of Line Skiboards of Albany, New York, able to double his production staff.

"I was psyched," he said. "I knew from the get-go that I had to get in the X Games. If you don't get on there, you're nowhere."

While the X Games are certainly not considered the apex of extreme sports by most of the athletes interviewed here, they definitely have a place in the mainstreaming of alternative sports, and have created something of a groundswell for companies looking to sponsor athletes and those who manufacture clothing and equipment. Soon, new companies were springing up and older ones were adding new products and lines, all designed to cater to alternative sports. Just by sheer numbers, the effects of the X Games can be seen. The 1998 games in San Diego drew an estimated 250,000 spectators and a television audience estimated at 74 million. It created an economic impact on the city of San Diego of some $35 million. So the dollars were flowing. In the 1999 Games in San Francisco, prize money alone totaled more than $1 million. Major companies that were beginning to jump on the alternative sports bandwagon and cater to Generation X consumers (mostly males under twenty-five) were The Gap, Mountain Dew, Taco Bell, and Volkswagon.

"The X Games have done a lot to open people's eyes about what type of alternative sports are out there," said Gina Staffiery, who was serving as marketing director for her family's business, Extreme Adventures, a company selling extreme sports merchandise. "Most people can't do the tricks you see on the X Games, but it has sparked the fantasy."

It is the fantasy, or the dream, that often leads to reality for many people. So the number of participants has been increasing, as we have learned, not always for the right reasons. For the industry's economy, however, the reasons didn't always matter, only the dollars did. At and after the turn of the twenty-first century, things continued to mainstream. In April 2000, Broadband Sports, a leading producer of proprietary sports content and commerce on the Internet, announced the launching of FreestyleDirect, which would provide official web sites for extreme athletes. The FreestyleDirect destination was to provide action sports viewers with detailed information about their favorite athletes, new information, and exclusive Broadband Sports interviews and full-motion action clips.

There was little doubt about the commercial growth now. The 1999 Harris Interactive Survey reported that there were approximately 57 million action sports participants in the United States, with some $13 billion worth of action sports equipment purchased. According to the Sporting Good Manufacturers Association, that figure represents one third of overall sporting goods sales. Granted, the people participating and buying equipment and gear are not all living on the edge, or even close to it. But there's little doubt that just by the magnitude of the numbers, some of these people will begin to creep a little closer and eventually adopt the lifestyle of the real extreme, high-risk athlete. It's just a natural progression, especially when so many young people are becoming involved at various levels. The reason for that is simply marketing and exposure.

The video industry has also grown tremendously and has provided another vehicle to get more people, especially youngsters, into extreme sports. The best and most radical of the skiers and snowboarders, as well as the freestyle motocross and stunt motor-cycle athletes, are all into making videos, which now have wide-spread distribution and growing audiences. Youngsters just starting in some of these sports have an opportunity to see the best doing the most gnarly and dangerous maneuvers. If they dream enough, which many do, the next generation of envelope pushers will soon be on the way. Before the advent of the VCR, these kinds of films were available to very few. Instead of television giving birth to the video, in the case of extreme sports, the growth of the video has been responsible for getting these sports on television.

Another prime example of how extreme sports has mainstreamed is in the marketing scheme put in place for the 2002 Winter Olympic Games at Salt Lake City. The previous Summer Olympic games from Australia had the worst television ratings ever, and NBC executives made a conscious decision to use extreme sports and what they called "edgy" advertising to attract a younger demo-graphic.

"We're calling this phase Extreme," said Vince Manze, a co-president of the NBC Agency. "We are going to focus on the fact that the Winter Olympics are a little wilder, a little more extreme. The popularity of extreme sports is not just with snow, but skate-boarding, street luge, in-line skating, and all of the rest, have just taken off over the last several years."

Aerial photographer Tom Sanders was part of the Olympic buildup. The shots he filmed were even more to the point of the extreme than those described by Manze. "I shot a BASE-jumping team for a Nike commercial which [ran] during the Olympics," he said, "and I just shot a guy coming out of an airplane on skis for NBC that they will serve to point out that the incredible accelera-tion a downhill skier generates is somewhat like a sky diver in free fall. By doing that, they [put] some cool little comparisons to these different Olympic sports."

Before the Olympics actually began, NBC ran twenty different extreme-type spots focusing on everything from aerial skiing to snowboarding. High-risk extreme sports are not part of the Winter

Olympics, yet in an effort to boost ratings and capture a younger audience, NBC made these sports, or at least images evoking the sports, a major part of their promotional package. That certainly says something about the increasing popularity of the sports as well as the perceived mentality of the viewing audience. Their attention is apparently captured by risk and by the edge. NBC was using it in an attempt to generate more dollars.

Extreme sports took yet another step toward mass-market distribution and a wider audience in the summer of 2001. During the days when the X Games were held in late August, ESPN experimented with broadband sports-video distribution. The programmer, Comcast Corporation, and streaming media distribution provider, Aerocast, Inc., gave 50,000 of the Philadelphia area's cable-modem subscribers a virtual seat at the Summer X Games via their computers. It was ESPN's first broadband event, which enabled people to watch the Games on their computer monitors.

"The concept was that we wanted to keep the interface consistent but we wanted to cut the content in a bunch of different ways, because the idea is you want to differentiate and you want to serve the sports fans," said ESPN vice president of affiliate sales development and operations, Manish Jah. "The X Games was just where we wanted to prove the concept."

How far the concept will go isn't known, but it's certainly interesting that once again, extreme sports, or at least the ESPN version of them, were used as the test vehicle. In addition, the Games continue to grow. The regular television audience was up 48 percent from the year before across all the company venues, ESPN, ESPN2, and ABC, with an average audience of 465,905. The extreme is a secret no longer. In fact, some of the sports are now trickling down to an even lower age group via the toy manufacturers. As always, toy manufacturers watch the trends before developing new lines and they began to get the notion that alternative sports were no longer taking back seats to traditional ones. Sporting goods is a $65 billion industry and in recent years one alternative sport (if it can still be called that), in-line skating, has surpassed the former national pastime, baseball, in the number of youthful participants. Mike May, director of communications for the Sporting Goods Manufacturers Association (SGMA), estimated that 10 million Americans played baseball in 2000, while 27 million participated in in-line skating in 1999.

"A new kid on the block challenging a traditional athletic pastime is worth acknowledging," May said.

The feeling also was that year-round exposure on television was continuing to increase mainstream interest in these sports. The SGMA added that sports such as snowboarding and motocross racing were already appealing to the masses, as well as finding a new audience in young boys. Kids were also watching cartoons which were said to "spotlight adrenaline seekers," such as Action Man and Max Steel. Toy likenesses of these kinds of heroes were always coming out on the market.

Now even the toy industry was moving into alternative sports. ESPN licensed the name *X Games* to toy manufacturer JAKKS Pacific's Road Champs line of action figures, vehicles, and accessories. The new line showcased sports such as street luge, snowboarding, and freestyle motocross. It also set up licensing agreements with seventy athletes. Another toy company, X Concepts, has built its business around extreme sports licenses by manufacturing miniature action sports collectibles. A company spokesman said its mission is to team up with any extreme sport athletes who are recognized as being cool in the field. Other companies were following suit. In 2000, Spin Master was selling 300,000 diecast replicas of real BMX bikes each week. Miniature skateboards have also appeared on the market, as well as longboards, snowboards, wakeboards, Tech and motocross bikes. In addition, fast-food restaurants such as Taco Bell are including extreme sports figurines in their kids' meals.

In summing up everything that has been changing on the alternative sports scene, Mike May of the SGMA said this: "The whole thrill-seeking adventure caters to the average American," adding that viewers continue to admire the carnage and guts the athletes display, no matter what they are riding.

There's still more. In June 2001, SightSound.com, which has reached agreements with a number of studios for electronic video rights, made twenty-four music and extreme sports videos from

Woodhaven Entertainment available via download from its website. Again, it seems to be an appeal to a young audience. An example would be *All My Crazy Friends*, which is described as a
crossover between the two genres (music and extreme sports) and
features the world's top jet skiers, wakeboarders, motorcyclists,
and snowboarders performing some of their most amazing stunts
to heavy metal music.

The business of extreme sports is growing in many directions,
from the ESPN X Games, to new lines of toys, to a blend of music
and videos. It stands to reason that kids growing up with and
around these sports, watching them, trying them, having heroes
who move to the edge, will only encourage more continued participation and an entire new generation of extreme athletes may be
on the way, ready to dwarf the present generation by both their
numbers and the kind of adventurous risks they may take in the
years to come. If that happens, it will be the result of aggressive
marketing, media exposure, and an industry that has grown into
the mainstream, leading to the acceptance of the sports and their
consequences by a much greater segment of the population at
large.

And what about today's athletes? How have they profited from
the way the business of extreme sports has grown? What have they
done to ensure earning a living while pursuing their sports, and
perhaps at the same time giving back, using what they have learned
to help others improve their lives and lifestyles? Let's take a look.

A number of athletes have used their experience with high-risk
sports to become speakers and lecturers, sometimes conducting
seminars and self-help programs. Sky diver Jim McCormick has
been providing motivational talks for five years. His talks and seminars
deal with controlling fear and taking calculated risks in making important decisions, as well as the importance of self-confidence and
assertiveness. He feels quite well qualified for this because of what
he has gained from his sport.

"I can tell you with absolute certainty," he said, "that I would
not have had the confidence to go into business for myself were it
not for the confidence I gained sky diving. You can look at these
things and say that they are very, very different. But there is an in-

nate confidence that I have gained by virtue of my doing the things I do in sky diving that has truly made me into a different person than I was before I started. As I travel around the country making presentations to groups, it's not uncommon for people to approach me afterwards and want to share an experience with me. They'll tell me they did a sky dive last year or last month, or five years ago, and when I ask them how it affected them, the answer, without exception, is that it made them more confident. They say they felt if they could do that, they could do anything. It's a common response.

"I tell people they should always try something—whether it be sky diving or river rafting—something they find frightening but have some interest in. I tell them not to deprive themselves of the experience because it will affect them, impact their lives in a positive way. I also tell people to carefully assess the things they are contemplating. Suppose it is a job change to perhaps a less secure position. I tell them not to make an impulsive decision, to be methodical, to do it the same way I prepare for a high-challenge sky dive. Write down the benefits, the downside, the best-case scenario, the worst-case scenario. I tell them to ask themselves if it is survivable. If all the bad things happen, are you still okay with it. If not, you don't make the decision.

"But this is one of my core beliefs, something I always emphasize in my talks. When you take risks, you add vibrancy to your life. I'm not only talking about physical risks, but just a risk such as telling someone you love them. That's a huge risk. You may get profound rejection. But there's a vibrancy that will enter into your life when you're willing to do that, a vibrancy you will not experience otherwise."

McCormick continues to sky dive while giving his talks and seminars. When he was interviewed for this book, he was at a large East Coast university, dealing with thirty-two higher education professional fund raisers. He spoke with them as a group, and met with them individually, and he fully credits his success in his speaking career to his success as a sky diver.

Once Sharon Wood stopped challenging mountains like Everest, she decided to forge a second career as a motivational speaker.

This was another challenge for her at first. "I just wanted to overcome another fear and I thought public speaking would be a great skill to have," she said. "It has always been a goal for me to express myself more effectively in many mediums. If I overcome that fear, well, then I have more freedom. Less fear has always meant more freedom for me. I had done some guiding before, but I can earn more in one day of speaking than in two months of guiding. I wasn't convinced that I had a message in the beginning. I was more out there for my own growth and development. Now, however, it's more meaningful for me. I think I have a good message that I feel worthy of delivering."

The essence of Wood's talks is that ordinary people are capable of doing extraordinary things, that everyone has untapped potential. "I tell people that we often define ourselves and our lives by our limitations, but that life looks a lot different if you define it by your possibilities," she explains. "The goal is to do more with less. I speak from my own experience in the mountains, surviving in environments of adversity, finding resources and opportunities wrapped in strange packaging that you normally wouldn't recognize. I also speak about the value of diversity, the value of people seeing things differently, of people having different personalities. It's about striving as an individual, but still teaming with others and how the two must go hand in hand together."

Wood speaks to a diverse number of groups, from nonprofit organizations, kids groups, school groups, and women's groups to corporate entities such as Hewlitt-Packard, IBM, Bristol-Meyers Squibb, ITT, and others. She is not only enjoying her newfound career, but making a good living while still climbing whenever she has the chance. Sometimes, the rewards come from unexpected sources and don't have to be financial.

"I had a woman stop me in the middle of the street in Canmore [Alberta, Canada] recently," she said. "I was walking with my kids and she says, 'Sharon, I've been meaning to tell you this for the last two months. My daughter heard you speak at a benefit recently and she remembered one part of your story when you were climbing and didn't feel as if you could go on, but that you had given it everything you had and pushed through it. She was in a race the other day and her ski pole broke. She just wanted to give up, but then she thought of your story and how you went on. That's when she pushed on and won the race.' The woman was crying and hugging me. That's why I do what I do now, to be able to influence one kid, one girl. It makes it all worthwhile."

Snowboarder Circe Wallace, no longer riding big mountains or making videos after blowing out a knee for the third time, has become a sports agent, concentrating on working with other high-risk athletes. She learned a great deal about acquiring sponsors and making movies as an athlete, so she can now steer her clients in the right direction. Until recently, these athletes didn't have enough opportunities to require an agent. Now that has changed. "I work with athletes who surf, skateboard, snowboard, ride BMX, and now I have one motocrosser," Wallace said. "The opportunities have grown because of the popularity and acceptance of these sports in mainstream culture. We owe a lot to the ESPN Extreme Games and the media. Skateboarding has been around forever, but in the last few years has really become a legitimate sport. Some people say the skating parks have become the ballparks of the twenty-first century. All of a sudden there is local legislation in many communities supporting the sport and the parks have actually been able to come to life.

"What I do mainly is secure and maintain endorsements for my clients. I do a lot of public relations, some counseling, and give them a real friend to talk with. So it's an all-around experience. It's about licensing, merchandising, and helping clients to build a brand. A lot of these young athletes can benefit from having someone who understands the big picture."

As an agent, Wallace is self-taught. "A lot comes from my own experience negotiating my contracts. I was involved in a lawsuit and learned a lot about that after a sponsor let me go. I won and they settled. The experience allowed me to learn a lot about contract language as well as what you have to do to protect yourself. I think I always had an entrepreneurial spirit as a young kid and always wanted to be a businesswoman. So I really paid attention to all the things going on around me because I always knew there would be an end to my riding career. Now I am where I want to be."

Sound familiar? Sound mainstream? These are situations closer to what happens in the traditional sports than what used to happen in extreme sports. The gaps are certainly closing.

Some athletes who don't want to completely abandon the outdoors have started businesses that keep them on the edge, working in the same environments in which they so often played. Kevin Quinn, who went from playing hockey to skiing, to sky diving and BASE jumping, as well as big game guiding, now has a heli-skiing business in Alaska. He, too, has come a long way, thanks to his sports experience.

"I'm a high school dropout," Quinn admitted. "I left school in the eleventh grade to pursue a hockey career. But I came back to get my GED and my college of life has been my experience and travel through my sports. I made some great contacts, put a business plan together, acquired some investors, and created a heli-ski operation, which is now probably the largest in Alaska. We started Points North Heli Adventures in 1998 and have probably taken a thousand skiers up in the last three seasons.

"We have a diverse clientele from world-class skiers to average intermediate weekend skiers, and we take them to the Chugach Mountains in Alaska, which is one of the best ranges for heli-skiing. I'm owner-operator and lead guide. I have twenty-two employees and twelve additional guides."

Running this kind of business is a huge responsibility because people's lives are in our hands. "Our clients don't have to be high-end skiers," Quinn explained, "but I tell them they have to be competent in all conditions. We're basically their lifeline. We tell them where they can and can't go and mitigate all hazards that are out there—avalanches, glaciers, crevasses, ice falls, big holes. We obviously have them on a very short leash. Most times the guide will go first, maybe go halfway down. Guides will check the snow to detect whether there is an avalanche hazard on every run. From there, the guide sends the first person down to a safe zone or pickup zone. Everybody skis with radios, so there is constant communications."

This sounds like an ideal business for Kevin Quinn. He has lived a high-risk, rough life, taking chances, going to the edge, and controlling his fears. Now he has a business that can be construed as high risk, and he's approaching it as he has everything else in his life—head on.

Tom Day's business is simply an extension of his sport. He was, and still is, an extreme freestyle skier. Now he is a cinematographer who still goes on high-risk adventures, filming other extreme skiers, often under extremely difficult conditions, such as he did on a harrowing journey to South Georgia Island near Antarctica. Today, Day is continuing to do what he has always done, working out on the edge. Only this time he's chronicling it with his camera, as well as living it.

Mike Metzger's whole life has been motorcycles, whether it is racing or doing the dangerous freestyle motocross. Looking to the future, he has started Metzger Motors. "Right now the business is run by my mom, Sharon, and my aunt Cathy Armstrong," he said. "We make graphic kits for motorcycles, T-shirts, and hats. Hopefully, we'll be able to expand in the future, but right now I'm trying to stay focused on my racing."

Speed climber Chris McNamara had one of the most interesting businesses for someone who loves being on the sides of a mountain. The name of his business is Super Topo. His company produces guidebooks for other climbers to follow.

"I was climbing El Cap for about six years," McNamara said, "was almost addicted to it. Then I began to feel that there was a lot to be improved upon in the guidebooks. There had to be more accuracy. I also thought it would interesting if people could read about the history of the various routes because many of them are legendary across the world. El Cap is really the center of big wall climbing. I wanted to figure out what were some of the untold stories and called a lot of people who had first climbed the routes. It has been a real project to obtain better information.

"I started by self-publishing an El Cap guidebook. After that, I met up with Randy Furrier, who had this idea to start offering some of these guidebooks on the web. That's what we have been doing the last few years, creating guidebooks. The first was the Yosemite free climbs, shorter ones, and now we're creating books for other areas around the country. They're called Topo maps. Climbing Topo maps for a rock give the climber a view looking straight at it, and they tell him where the cracks and bolts are, where you should stop and belay. They're very detailed. Our whole plan is to create more detailed Topos than have ever been done by selecting routes that are more popular, that are the most classic, and putting a whole lot of energy into it. We learn about the history, have outstanding photos, and give a lot of important details that other books have omitted.

"We've done it for about two years now and have received some great response. It's the climbing industry, so we'll probably never make big money. But this is fun to create and nice to hear from people who have benefitted from the information. We've also heard from people who aren't climbers and aren't planning to climb."

McNamara is just twenty-four years old and attending the University of California at Berkeley, studying geography. He wants to continue to put his education to use within the climbing industry. In addition, McNamara founded the American Safe Climbing Association, a group that regularly replaces old, worn, and dangerous anchor bolts on the side of El Capitan. "Bolts are only visible to climbers, yet on El Cap there must be 100,000 bolts," he explained. "The oldest were put in around 1958, and some of them must be replaced."

Shane McConkey, still active in skiing and BASE jumping, continues to make his living like many athletes, finding sponsors and endorsing products. "Skiing is a relatively large industry," he said, "and there are many products you need when you go skiing. All these companies that make the products need athletes to promote them. I have a number of sponsors and consider myself lucky. If I was a runner, I might be able to get a shoe sponsor, but that would be it.

"I still compete for prize money as well, but most of my income is from sponsorships and endorsements. Using the products, being in the ads, skiing with them every day. It's really great today with all these extreme, adrenaline, and alternative sports out there. In the past you weren't able to make a living doing it unless you were an auto racer. Now all the little kids want to be skateboarders, skiers, BMX riders, snowboarders. So this whole side of sports now enables you to make a living. The kids want to buy the products, so you find sponsors and you can make money."

Surfer Mike Parsons, still active at thirty-six, also earns a living by working with sponsors and competing in contests. It allows him to surf every single day, which he has an overwhelming desire to do. "I compete in about twelve to fifteen contests a year," Parsons said. "I'm also involved with the Billabong Odyssey, a three-year search for the world's biggest wave. We travel around the world looking for the storms that could create the largest waves. Billabong is an apparel company sponsoring the Odyssey and they are one of my sponsors as well."

Archie Kalepa revels in being a Hawaiian waterman and is a lifeguard when he isn't surfing, canoeing, or looking to be towed into giant waves. He's never very far from the ocean.

Abby Watkins's entire life continues to revolve around climbing. She is sponsored by various companies and had plans to compete in the Ice Climbing World Cup in 2002. There are five events held in Russia, Austria, Italy, Switzerland, and Quebec. Watkins says the prize money is very good and she has additional incentives from her sponsors. "We also have some local corporate sponsorship, local oil brokers from Calgary who are helping to pay our way to Europe this year."

In addition, Watkins is working to become a certified mountain guide in Canada. It is work, an extremely difficult course, but something she wants to complete. "It's a very well looked upon profession," she said. "Becoming a certified guide in Canada would mean I would be internationally certified. It's a long, difficult process, and those who make it through really know what they are doing. It's something I really aspire to, to pass tests in front of my peers, the examiners. They don't give it away."

Watkins explained that there are five exams, as well as various other avalanche courses the candidates have to take. "The exams are assistant rock, assistant alpine, full alpine, assistant winter (ski), and full winter. So you have to be a very well-rounded mountaineer and fully understand every aspect of it. Taking somebody who knows nothing about the mountains into the mountains is a huge responsibility, and it adds a whole new dimension to what you are doing. I've already done a lot of guiding in the States, where you don't need certification. I enjoy it immensely, so becoming certified takes guiding to a whole new level of professionalism."

Watkins is also one of the founders of a group called Ascending Women. Its purpose is to inspire women into the sport of climbing. "We want to give them the opportunity to get into climbing in a positive way and develop their skills," she said, "helping to bring them to a place where they can feel that climbing is for them and they believe they can do it. So we conduct clinics in various locations and we would like to interest more women in climbing, believing in themselves, and fulfilling their potential. My good friend, Kim Csizmazia, is also part of the group. We both share the same beliefs, feel quite empowered by climbing, and would like to pass that down to as many women as possible."

Besides working with Abby Watkins in the Ascending Women program, Kim Csizmazia still competes in contests, has sponsors, and also guides. For the past two years she has been teaching climbing and guiding in the Grand Teton National Park. Her life also revolves completely around her sport. "I work for a company called Exum Mountain Guides. They have been around for some seventy years, the oldest guiding service in the United States," she said. "They're located in the Grand Teton in Moose, Wyoming, and they have very high standards for hiring their guides. They base it on your proven survivability in the mountains."

Seth Enslow's business is his sport. He gives exhibition motorcycle jumps and continues to do stuntwork in films. His is a tough way to make a living, and while he has always loved jumping motorcycles, he admits that he directs his jumping to where the money is. "It's all about business for me now," he said. "I want to make money. Sure, I have some goals, like breaking the world distance record before I retire. When I made a video of my attempt at the world record, I did it for two reasons, to break the record and to make money from the video. I didn't break the record, but the video worked out well.

"When I do an exhibition, I charge a fee for a jump, an appearance fee, and I also get paid from sponsors, the gear that I wear. I'm under contract, so I have a salary, photo incentives, and sponsors for my videos. This is a job I created for myself so I have to keep doing it. I can see the light at the end of the tunnel, but I always want to stay connected with sports. Maybe I'll eventually go into car or truck racing, or speed bike racing. I like going fast and I couldn't hack it with a desk job."

Scott Feindel works as a welder during the winter, seventy or eighty hours a week, so he can paddle and jump waterfalls all spring, summer, and fall. He also makes some sponsorship money from boat companies. "The more exposure you get, the more you're gonna make," he said. But in a relatively obscure sport, it isn't a lot. Miles Daisher works as a sky-diving instructor and jumps whenever he can. Kristen Ulmer continues to ski. Because she is one of the best, and always willing to ski radical and difficult routes, she has always been well paid by sponsors, magazines, film companies, and photographers.

BASE jumper Mick Knutson is a trained engineer who has his own software company called Base Logic. "We build Internet middleware applications for companies like Discover Financial, IBM, Intel. I've been doing this now for twelve years, and some of the things we do include online banking and customer service applications." But that isn't all. Because of his love for BASE jumping, Knutson has also started a website called BLINC, which stands for Base Logic, Inc. It was started in 1994, providing articles and information on BASE jumping. "It has been very successful," Knutson said. "We have increased traffic twenty to fifty percent each year, have over 215,000 hits a day, and are in eighty-three different countries with a unique user base of around 30,000."

Though he has a large, busy, and successful software business, Mick Knutson has done what most of the other athletes have managed to do—combine the love of their sport with a business, so they can spread the word about what they do and encourage other people to try it. In one sense, it comes under the realm of business, but it is really about sport and love.

There can be little doubt now that extreme sports are here to stay, a part of the culture that is continuing to grow, finding new audiences, and developing new athletes. If the mainstreaming of the various sports continues at its present pace, there will be a whole new generation of athletes who will become involved with alternative and high-risk sports. For these people, the potential to earn money from their sports should be greater than ever before, giving them perhaps another incentive to take the necessary risks and brave the dangers they will encounter.

12

LIVING ON THE EDGE— THE LIFESTYLE OF THE EXTREME

Climbing is about personal experience. For me it sharpens the colors of life. It has taught me about living life fully and about death. . . . Losing friends and mentors to the mountains has taught me deference. The most important thing is the feeling in my heart as I walk away each time—strong, confident, and beautiful.

—Kim Csizmazia, climber

THERE is a kind of fraternity among high-risk athletes, whether it be climbers, skiers, BASE jumpers, or big wave surfers. In many ways, they feel they are special, doing something that few people can or are willing to do. By the same token, they welcome others into their sports and help newcomers all they can. Because alternative and extreme sports are figuratively still the new kids on the block, and because the reputations of a number of the sports continue to be somewhat negative, the athletes also act as ambassadors as often as they can.

There continues to be a big difference between those who go out to the edge just occasionally and those who do it constantly. As some of the full-timers have said, their agendas and motivations are different. The extreme can take you out very quickly and often without warning. That's what makes the full-time extremists so different and, yes, special. These people not only are pursuing a sport, but are living a lifestyle. For whatever their reasons—and they do vary somewhat—nearly all the athletes interviewed for this book have chosen to pursue a way of life that is often foreign to most of us. Sure, money is involved. It always is. But the two operative words that keep surfacing time and again are *love* and *life*.

How many people have heard of a man named Royal Robbins? Probably very few outside of the climbing community. Yet Robbins is described as one of the most influential American climbers of the twentieth century. Robbins grew up on the streets of Los Angeles, quit school at age sixteen, and went to work at a ski resort, which introduced him to the mountains. In 1950, he began climbing at Stony Point in the San Fernando Valley of California, the beginning of a climbing and adventuring career that has lasted more than a half-century.

By 1952 he was making first ascents in the mountains of California, long before routes were bolted and mapped out. In 1961, Robbins met his wife, Liz, in Yosemite, and they have been climbing partners ever since. By 1965, Robbins and his wife were teaching skiing and climbing in Switzerland. He continued to make first ascents and that same year became climbing editor of *Summit* magazine. A year later he developed the Royal Robbins Yosemite climbing shoe for a French company called Galibier. Then in 1968, Robbins made the first solo ascent of El Capitan in Yosemite, and the same year he and his wife established the Rockcraft Climbing School.

The Robbinses' accomplishments have continued unabated. The number of rock-climbing routes they have established are too numerous to mention, but it has been said that Royal Robbins defined a new era of mountaineering in which the sky was the limit for the climbing culture. Today, the Robbinses have a clothing company and promote various educational programs, as well as campaigning for the protection of the environment. Both have had a long and active life taking risks outdoors. Ask Royal Robbins why he chose to live as he does, and he'll tell you it's all about life.

"That's what I've always loved about adventure," he said. "It forces you to be alive, and that's something we all want."

Why tell the story of Royal Robbins? Simple. His long life and career climbing on the mountains, combined with all his other ventures, lead up to a single conclusion—his is not just a love for climbing or adventure, not just a willingness to take risks and court danger, not just the ambition to make first ascents and get his name in the record books. No, Royal Robbins has chosen a lifestyle of living on the edge, of being in the mountains and on the cliffs, of seeking a high-risk adventuresome existence. His thoughts about adventure forcing him to be alive echo what many of today's athletes are saying. It is what separates Sharon Wood's climb of Everest from the New York socialite who made it to the top in 1996 as part of the ill-fated expedition chronicled in *Into Thin Air.* It is what separates Archie Kalepa from any average surfer who cruises the beaches looking for girls and good waves. It is what makes Jim McCormick and Tom Sanders very different from the person who finds the courage to make a single sky dive, then brags that he did it.

There are many active people who pursue sports that can go into the extreme, or who go on what can be called extreme vacation trips, or who find a major challenge, work to conquer it, and then retreat into their previous everyday lives. There is nothing wrong with that, but there is also nothing wrong with the people who continue to push the envelope and live their lives courting danger with extreme sports. For most of them, the sport is more than an adventure, more than a challenge, more than picking up sponsors and making videos. For most of these athletes, extreme sports have become a way of life, the lifestyle that they have chosen of their own free will. If someone calls them crazy or nuts, that isn't their problem. They simply don't care what others think.

Carlos Buhler, who has already had a mountaineering career of more than twenty years, says that his way of life eventually spread to his family, especially his mother who, instead of worrying about him from afar, would often come to the base of the big mountains he climbed.

"My mother was a tremendous influence on my life," he said. "We became very close when we would take walks together at the base of mountains. She knew as well as I did that when I left base camp, it could the last goodbye. She understood better than anyone the risks of Himalayan climbing. She saw people one season and suddenly they were no longer there. We learned to appreciate the moments we had together and the moments we were still alive. It gave us both tremendous strength and she continued to come with me until 1996, when she began feeling ill and was diagnosed with cancer. There's no getting around it, we're all on this planet for a limited time.

"As for my own climbing, I certainly don't have a specific date when I plan to stop. The activity continues to be rewarding, even on small peaks. I have already removed most of what I do in mountaineering from the competitive side of things. I can't keep up with the new, young generation of climbers, though I certainly would like to, but you have to take your age with grace. To a certain degree, you can still do a lot because you have so much experience and that makes up for strength. In the end, you do more things because it's rewarding for you, and less competitive. I think that will evolve over the next twenty years and I plan to still go into the mountains when I'm sixty-five. I just won't be climbing at the same level. But then I'll get satisfaction out of small peaks, which I already do now."

In other words, Buhler doesn't expect to change his lifestyle, only alter it a bit to accommodate his age and physical abilities. As dangerous as it is, climbing is one sport in which you can do that. Sharon Wood is part of the same generation as Carlos Buhler, and has also tapered off with her major climbs. She has her second career as a motivational speaker, but that doesn't mean she has forsaken the lifestyle and camaraderie she loves so much.

"I still rock climb and have some very special people in my life with whom I climb regularly," she said. "I reached the summit of a mountain last year with Lauri Skresnik, this man who's been in my life since the 1970s. We both looked at each other and said, can you imagine us doing this in our late forties? Now I have kids and a whole new dimension to living, learning, and loving. But I wouldn't have been able to be this satisfied if I hadn't pushed myself in the beginning and climbed the way I did."

For these two veterans, climbing has simply been their life and their lifestyle, something they will never give up entirely, despite the sometimes cruel toll the mountains take. Rock climber Craig DeMartino, citing similar feelings, notes that climbers usually wind up in a rather closed circle, spending much of their time with those who have similar interests.

"One thing I've noticed that most climbers have in common is that they are pretty independent," he said. "They are not real crowd followers and seem very happy to do their own thing. It isn't that they have a loner mentality. Rather they travel in the same circle of people, and are normal in every respect. But they are very independently spirited. Most of my wife's and my friends are climbers. We're all completely immersed in it."

For Mike Metzger, there was never a doubt what course his life would follow. Both his father and grandfather rode and raced motorcycles, and he was riding while still in diapers. His lifestyle has never wavered for an instant, despite all the injuries, broken bones, and a body becoming more arthritic every year. No, riding is a tradition that has overtaken his family and he has always been a willing part of it. "I know there are many injuries in my sport," he said. "But the pain does go away, you will be healed, and you will ride again. That's always the way it has been."

Kevin Quinn, who now has a heli-skiing business to go with his many extreme sports activities, has noticed that there has been a rather unexpected reaction to his lifestyle, especially from those who live more conservatively. "It's funny," Quinn said, "when I began to seek investors for my business, I would meet with potential business backers, all usually college graduates in suits. I'd be wearing jeans and a nice shirt, with my long hair. After they heard something about me, a lot of these guys would come up to me and say something like, 'How can I have your life?' Many of them were really intrigued by it. All of a sudden there is all this respect for what we are doing and a lot of these guys are becoming clients."

Because there is such an outward freedom to the extreme lifestyle, an almost carefree attitude that many mistake for insouciance, it can appear attractive from afar to those who live by the old rules . . . to have a secure job, a family, and not take too many unnecessary chances. It's easy to call extreme athletes crazy, or reckless, or any other name. But perhaps more people than anyone fully realizes have a side of them that wishes they were outside, climbing mountains, skiing slopes, riding big waves. It's difficult to cite numbers, but the reactions the "suits" have to a Kevin Quinn makes you wonder. How many people would chuck their lifestyle to go to the extreme, if they really felt they could?

The surfing lifestyle is another that seems attractive, because it means being on the beach around good-looking, physically fit people, and spending a great deal of time in the ocean. Big wave surfers, as much as anyone in the extreme world, always seem to make their sport a total lifestyle. If a day goes by when they aren't in the water, not surfing to some degree, they aren't happy. The tow-in surfers have so few days when the waves are just right that they will go almost anywhere to find them. Other than that, just being around the total atmosphere—the beach, the water, surfboard, other surfers, and listening to the waves crash on the shore—that's what it's all about. As Mike Parsons said, "My life revolves around the ocean. It's all about who I am as a surfer. I'll never stop surfing until the day I die and I'm incredibly thankful that's the case."

Miles Daisher, who has said that if he lost the use of his legs, he would roll his wheelchair off the end of a cliff and BASE jump in it, is another who simply loves the lifestyle he has chosen. Once he took Frank Gambalie's advice, gave up a mundane day job, and put all his efforts into the sports he loves, he knew there was no other way. "I meant what I said about BASE jumping in a wheelchair if it came to that," he said. "In fact, I know a guy now who sky dives and is paralyzed from the waist down. So it is definitely our choice, the way we want to live. I love to jump and fly and I'll do everything I can to keep it going strong. It's definitely a way of life for me. You can't deny the heartache of losing friends but I still want to do all kinds of different things because I love it so much."

BASE jumper Mick Knutson knows he belongs to a rather closed circle, since his sport still hasn't found widespread acceptance. Because he spends so much time with other jumpers, he knows what real camaraderie is and says there is something special about spending time with others who follow the same dream. "There is a camaraderie that isn't even talked about," Knutson said. "It's like another jumper is your comrade. It's known and understood. We all know the consequences of our actions and we teach people how to jump. But it's kind of weird. You see another BASE jumper and you know immediately that you'll trust that guy with your life, simply because he knows exactly what you go through when you jump. You know that person is thinking the same thing you are when he stands up there on that edge. Even when I'm jumping in Germany or Italy, with people who don't speak English, I totally trust them with my life. I just have this strong feeling that I understand what is going through his brain and he understands me. It's all part of the same lifestyle."

Kristen Ulmer admits she loves excitement, and it is the radical sports she follows that provide her with the excitement she craves. Her lifestyle has evolved because of that. "I got into ski-mountaineering because it enabled me to combine my two favorite sports," she said. "I made it into one and it increased the challenges and the excitement. I can see beauty in so many different things that I'm sure I would have found a different type of lifestyle that would have been very satisfying had I not enjoyed excitement and challenges so much. I know I thought about things a lot after the terrorist attacks in New York on September eleventh. Even before that, I'd done a lot of traveling and realized how fortunate we are in what we have in this country. There are so many people out there who have so much hate and who are angry and carrying grudges, that they don't see the beauty of the world as I do. It makes me feel personally so much happier that I get to live this dream life of being American and being able to do whatever the hell I want to do, and still have a lifestyle of skiing and climbing."

Love and life. The ongoing themes. How many of these extreme, radical athletes, these people who are so often called crazy, have said that they only feel totally and truly alive when following their sport and their dreams, that they are living life to the fullest and wouldn't want it any other way? Nearly all of them. They have taken on lifestyles that go against the cultural grain, against a society that says stay warm, stay safe, don't take chances, be careful. Ironically, extreme athletes, for the most part, are very careful. They just can't fully control the environments in which they work, play, and compete.

Will the current trends continue and see more people adopt this kind of lifestyle? All indications are that they will. The mainstreaming of so many previously alternative and extreme sports in the last decade has helped create a new generation that looks away from the traditional sports and to the alternative, with a leg up on the extreme. Then there are the kids of the next generation. In one sense, kids have already contributed to the extreme sports movement. Freestyle motocross developed from freestyle BMX, with young bike riders doing the tricks and setting the trend that eventually moved on to motorcycles. Snowboarding, especially tricks done in the halfpipe, is a direct descendent of skateboarding, another sport in which the kids led the way, doing gnarly maneuvers on the streets and in the parks. Gradually, more snowboarders began moving up the mountains and getting into the extreme sport of freestyle or free riding.

There is more evidence to show that the next generation of young people may also move out to the edge in increasing numbers. While kids continue to play the traditional sports, more of them are moving over to individual sports, showing their creativity on their bikes, in-line skates, and skateboards. By doing gnarly things early, they get accustomed to risk, and to wiping out, dealing with injuries at an early age. It's not that different from some of the athletes interviewed here, who spoke of high-risk childhoods that carried over to the extreme. Only many more seem to be doing it now.

One thought is that kids are rejecting the structure, coaching, rules, and pressure of organized traditional sports. The increased pressure on kids to excel coupled with more parental violence against officials and other parents at games and competitions could be serving to drive kids toward the individual sports. That, coupled with some natural rebellion and the desire to do their own thing, points the way to alternative sports. In addition, the first generation of BMX/skateboard/in-line skating kids will soon be raising families of their own and could bring a decidedly different attitude toward their children and the sports they pursue. Paul Vail, a twenty-nine-year-old BMX freestyle rider, explains why. "Today's kids," said Vail, "who have been riding skateboards or BMX bikes since they were twelve-year-olds will become the parents who say, 'Yes, skateboarding and bike riding are perfectly acceptable sports for my kid to do. And don't tell me they have to play football or be on the basketball team to be accepted, because that's no longer true.'"

It has also become more socially acceptable for girls and women to take to the slopes, skies, mountains, cliffs, and surf. The women who participate in radical high-risk sports today are also pioneers, and are constantly encouraging more women to follow them. Avid climbers Abby Watkins and Kim Csizmazia have even set up an organization to encourage women to take up climbing, and hold clinics for that purpose at locations all around the country and in Canada. Women also seem to be drawn to sports that have fluidity, and which require balance and coordination. Surfing, snowboarding, and climbing are sports that have been attracting more and more women in recent years and should continue to do so.

Traditional sports have long had a star system, with the best players getting most of the accolades and respect, as well as showing the most confidence. Those who struggle along often have confidence and self-esteem problems. Yet the individual alternative sports have been shown to empower youngsters with independence, individuality, and confidence. This sounds very similar to the thoughts and feelings of the top performers today, who have all said that by participating and excelling at their sports, they have gained a strong sense of self, a total feeling of confidence, and the powerful feelings of being different and special.

The future of high-risk sports and adventurous lifestyles certainly seems secure. There will continue to be injuries as well as some fatalities. The nature of the sports dictate that. But since a major part of forging an extreme lifestyle is conquering and controlling fear, it stands to reason that neither injuries nor the possibility of death will stop people in the future just as they haven't stopped people in the past or those who are active in the sports today. For these people, the rewards of pursuing their sport, being one with nature and the environment, challenging themselves to push higher, faster, and farther, and living a lifestyle that is far from the so-called norm, are worth any risk that might appear on the horizon. Extreme athletes are skilled, intelligent, courageous, and different. What they do often shocks people unfamiliar with their sports and their lifestyles. Yes, they spend a great part of their lives on the edge, and for that call them adventurous, extreme, radical, or thrill seeking—but they are the very best at what they have chosen to be.

WEBSITES

A number of people who helped with the preparation of material for this book and who were gracious enough to consent to lengthy interviews have websites associated with their businesses or their exploits. Additional information can be obtained by accessing the following sites.

Carlos Buhler—www.carlosbuhler.com

Kim Csizmazia and Abby Watkins—www.ascendingwomen.com

Shawn Frederick—www.frederickphoto.com

Mick Knutson—www.blincmagazine.com *and* www.baselogic.com

Jim McCormick—www.takerIsks.com

Chris McNamara—www.supertopo.com

Mike Metzger—www.metzgermotorsports.com

David Nagel—www.nagelphoto.com

Kevin Quinn—alaskaheliski.com

Tom Sanders—www.aerialfocus.com

Kristen Ulmer—www.kristenulmer.com

Sharon Wood—www.canspeak.com

INDEX

Aaronson, Bernard S., 220
Acclimatization, 84–86
Acute mountain sickness (AMS), 84–86
Addiction of the rush. See Adrenaline rush
Addison, Corran, kayak waterfall jumping, 153
Adrenaline rush, 185–200
    climbers and, 194–96
    jumpers and flyers and, 188–94
    personality types, 32–33
    riders and, 197–200
    theories, 187–88
Adrenal medulla, 189
Adventure Network International, 51–52
Adventure travel, 7, 231–33
Aerated water, 154–55
Age
    adrenaline rush and, 200
    fear and, 168
    risk taking and, 35
Aid (rock) climbing, 113
All My Crazy Friends (video), 258
Alpine climbing, 83–108
    adrenaline rush from, 194–96
    altitude sickness and, 47, 84–86
    deaths, 86–87, 94–96, 204–8, 210–11
    decision to turn back, 96–98, 101, 239–40
    fear and, 174–79
    history of, 19–20
    ice climbing and, 110–11
    major blunders, 243–45
    personal stories, 87–94, 99–108
    risks associated with, 84–87
    spirituality and, 220–23
    women and, 120–22, 278–79
Alps, 88–89, 95
    Eiger Nordwand, 10–11, 90–91, 95

Matterhorn, 95, 221
Altimeters, 45
Altitude sickness, 84–86
American attitude toward risk, 37–39
American Safe Climbing Association, 264
Amundsen, Roald, 18
Andrews, Bob, 67
Angel Falls (Venezuela), BASE jumping, 65
Anker, Conrad, 94
Antarctica, 51–52, 140. See also South Pole
Appa (Sherpa guide), 236
Apter, Michael, The Dangerous Edge: The Psychology of Excitement, 31
Armstrong, Cathy, 263
Art, extreme sports as, 223
Ascending Women, 266, 278–79, 280
Asshole magnet (AM), 35
Attention getter, risk taking as, 34–35
Automatic-activating devices, for sky diving, 45–46
Auto racing, 128
Avalanches, 86, 94, 130–31, 133–34, 142, 233
Aviation, 16–17, 20. See also Flying and jumping

Bad risks, 25–26, 30–31
Baffin Island, 115
Ballard, Jim, 96
Bane, Michael, Over the Edge: A Regular Guy's Odyssey in Extreme Sports, 31
Bangs, Richard, 7, 232
Barron's Dictionary of Medical Terms, 189
BASE jumping, 53–69
    adrenaline and endorphin rush from, 191–93

BASE jumping (*cont.*)
   care and preparation, 56–57
   deaths, 54, 62–68, 208–10, 213
   description of, 54–55
   fear and, 168, 169–70, 171–72
   guidelines for, 60–61
   injuries and, 213
   legal issues, 37–38, 53–54, 59–62
   lifestyle, 276
   number of jumpers, 57–58
   outlaw image of, 59–69
   sky diving compared with, 56, 70
   in wing suits, 77–78
Base Logic, 267
Big wall climbing, 117, 122–24
Big wave surfing, 128, 143–48
   adrenaline rush from, 197–98
   deaths, 212
   fear and, 183–84
   lifestyle, 275–76
   spirituality of, 225–27
Billabong Odyssey, 265
Black Canyon of the Gunnison, 117
BLINC (Base Logic, Inc.), 267, 280
Blunders, climbing, 243–45
BMX bikes, 156, 277, 278
Boger, Henry, BASE jumping, 58
Bono, Sonny, 143
Bonzai Pipeline (Hawaii), 151
Boofs, 153, 154
Bouldering, 111, 112, 117
Bowen, Scott, 67
Brain (brain function), 188
Brando, Marlon, 156
Breashears, David, 236
Bridge Day (Fayetteville, West
   Virginia), 58
Bridges, Dave, 94
British Medical Journal, 238–39
Broadband distribution, 256
Broadband Sports, 254
Buhler, Carlos, 88–91
   on adrenaline rush, 194–95
   climbing, 87, 88–91, 96–99, 102,
      105–8
   on death and mortality, 5, 90–91,
      204–6
   on fear, 175–76
   on the lifestyle, 273–74
   personality traits, 30
   on spirituality, 221–22
   on trophy hunting, 237–41

   Web site, 280
Bull, Sherman, 240, 241
Bungee jumping, 70–71

Camping, 231
Camping Magazine, 25
Can-can trick, 157–58
Candlestick Park (San Francisco), 171
Canoeing, 153, 226
Carelessness, risk taking and, 39
"Catching air," 20, 29, 134
Cave of the Swallows (Mexico), BASE
   jumping, 58–59
Caves, 244
C.C. and Company (movie), 156
Cerebral edema, high-altitude
   (HACE), 85–86
Child development, risk taking and,
   25–26, 30–31
Chugach Mountains, 262–63
Cima Grande (Alps), 95
Cinematography, 138–42, 263
Clark, Kim, 242
Climbing, 81–124. *See also* Rock
   climbing
   adrenaline rush from, 194–96
   altitude sickness and, 47, 84–86
   big wall, 117, 122–24
   deaths, 86–87, 94–96, 204–8,
      210–11
   decision to turn back, 96–98, 101,
      239–40
   fear and, 174–79
   history of, 19–20
   ice, 108–12, 115, 117–18
   major blunders, 243–45
   oxygen and, 84–86
   personalities, 87–96
   risks associated with, 84–87
   speed, 113–15
   spirituality of, 220–24
   women and, 120–22, 278–79
Coffin zone, 81, 111
Cold Fusion videos, 138, 139
Comcast Corporation, 256
Compasses, 244
Congdon, Dwayne, climbing, 97–98,
   99–102
Corona Raceway, 157, 213
Cortez Banks, 146
Creature comforts, risk taking and,
   31–32

Creeking, 153, 155
Cross, Midge, 242
Crusty Demons of Dirt (movie), 163
Csizmazia, Kim, 111–12
   Ascending Women, 266, 278–79,
      280
   climbing, 109–10, 111–12, 121–22,
      123, 269
   on death and mortality, 210
   on earning a living, 266
   on fear, 174, 178–79
   personality traits, 28, 111
   on spirituality, 222–23

DaFoe, Rob
   on risk, 13, 31
   snowboarding, 11, 137–38
Daisher, Miles
   on adrenaline rush, 4, 192–93
   BASE jumping, 56, 57, 58, 63–64,
      192–93
   on death and mortality, 208–10
   death of Dan Osman and, 5, 75–76,
      208–10
   on fear, 171–72
   on injuries, 213
   on the lifestyle, 276
   personality traits, 26–27
   rope free flying, 71, 74–77
   sky diving, 52–53, 56, 63
Dalai Lama (13th), 19
*Dangerous Edge, The: The Psychology
   of Excitement* (Apter), 31
Danosecond, 72
Dans Triple Crown (1999), 159–60
Daredevils, 6, 49
Da Vinci, Leonardo, 20
Davis, Jan, death of, 5–6, 38, 54, 64–66,
   211
Day, Tom
   on adrenaline rush, 199–200
   on earning a living, 263
   on injuries, 213
   personality traits, 29–30
   skiing, 138–42
Death, 3–6, 201–13
   climbing and, 232–43
   of Dan Osman, 5, 75–76, 208–10
   of Frank Gambalie, 54, 63–64, 208,
      209–10
   of Jan Davis, 5–6, 38, 54, 64–66, 211
Death wish, 49, 58, 213

DeMartino, Craig
   on adrenaline rush, 196
   climbing, 81, 111, 116–19, 122–23,
      124
   on death and mortality, 207–8
   on fear, 179
   on the lifestyle, 274
   on spirituality, 224
DeMartino, Cyndy, 117
Dhaulagiri (Nepal), 105–7
Dill, John, 67
Ditter, Bob, 25
Dopamine, 188
Double-can trick, 158
Double-knack trick, 158
Double XL Award, 146
Downclimbing, 104–5, 106–7
Drop Zone (movie), 50
Drus, the (Alps), 95

Earhart, Amelia, 17
Earning a living, 258–68
   business opportunities, 262–64,
      267–68
   motivational speaking, 258–61
   sponsorships, 249, 253–54, 257, 261,
      264–65, 267
   sports agent, 261–62
Eckhardt, Nadia, 51
Eiger Nordwand (Alps), 10–11, 90–91,
   95
El Capitan, BASE jumping, 53–54, 59,
   60–68
   fatalities, 5–6, 38, 54, 63–66
El Capitan, rock climbing, 112–13,
   114–15, 264, 272
El Capitan guidebooks, 263–64
El Dorado Canyon, 116, 208
Endless Summer, The (movie), 143
Endorphins (endorphin high), 189,
   191–92
Endorsements, 264–65. *See also*
   Sponsorships
Endurance (ship), 140
Enslow, Seth
   on earning a living, 266–67
   on fear, 167, 182–83
   motorcycle jumping, 160–63,
      182–83
Epinephrine, 189
Ershler, Phil, 236
Ershler, Susan, 236

ESPN, 256–57. *See also* X Games
Esteem, risk taking and, 34–35
Everest. *See* Mount Everest
Everest, George, 19
Exhaustion, 115, 245
Exhibition sky dives, 47–48
Expedition climbing, 83–108
    adrenaline rush from, 194–96
    altitude sickness and, 47, 84–86
    deaths, 86–87, 94–96, 204–8,
        210–11
    decision to turn back, 96–98, 101,
        239–40
    fear and, 168, 174–79
    history of, 19–20
    major blunders, 243–45
    personalities, 87–96
    personal stories, 87–94, 99–108
    spirituality of, 220–23
    women and, 120–22, 278–79
Expedition kayaking, 155
Explorers, early, 15–16, 17–18
Extreme Adventures, 254
Extreme Games. *See* X Games
Extreme Sports Channel, 59
Extreme vacation trips, 273
Exum Mountain Guides, 266

Falkland Islands, 139–41
Family traditions of risk taking, 29–30
Farley, Frank, 12, 32
Fatalities. *See* Death; Injuries
Fatigue, 115, 245
Fear, 165–84
    climbers and, 174–79
    jumpers and flyers and, 169–74
    riders and, 180–84
Federal Aviation Administration (FAA),
    45
Feindel, Scott
    on earning a living, 267
    on fear, 184
    kayak waterfall jumping, 153–55,
        184
Fifi Buttress (Yosemite), 74
Filippino, Adam, 55
Finch, Peter, 38
Fisher, Scott, 8–9
Flossing the sky (rope free flying),
    71–77, 189
Flying and jumping, 41–79
    adrenaline rush from, 188–94

BASE jumping, 53–69, 70
    fear and, 169–74
    rope free flying, 71–77
    sky diving, 43–53
    wing suits, 77–78
Ford/Stettner route (Grand Teton),
    132
Formation sky diving, 52
48 Hours (TV show), 66–68
Frederick, Shawn, 280
Free climbing
    ice, 110–11
    rock, 111, 113
Free falling, 44, 45, 52–53, 70. *See also*
    Sky diving
Freeskiing, 134–35, 180–81
Free soloing (rock climbing), 111, 113,
    116
FreestyleDirect, 254
Freestyle motocross, 128, 156–60, 277
    adrenaline rush from, 200
    deaths, 212
    fear and, 180, 182
    injuries and, 213
Freestyle snowboarding, 136–37
Freestyle snowmobiling, 135
Friedman, Bobby, 148–49
    on fear, 184
    tandem surfing, 143–44, 148–52,
        184
Frostbite, 86, 204
Furrier, Randy, 264

Galibier, 272
Gambalie, Frank ("Gambler"), 57,
    62–64, 73, 276
    death of, 54, 63–64, 208, 209–10
Gauthier, Mike, 234
Gear. *See also* Parachutes
    climbing, 243–44
Gediman, Scott, 66
Gender (women), 278–79
    climbing and, 120–22, 278–79
    skiing and snowboarding and, 131
Generation X, 252, 254, 277–78
Genetics (genes), 187–88
Glen Canyon Dam, 61
Golden Gate Bridge, 112
Gosling, Alistair, BASE jumping, 59–60
Government interventions. *See* Legal
    issues
Grandes Jorasses (Alps), 95

Grand Teton National Park, 266
  skiing, 132–33, 181–82
Gravity Games, 159, 246–47
Great Escape, The (movie), 156
Great Trigonometrical Survey (India),
  19
Ground rush, 46
Guidebook publishing, 263–64
Gymnastics, 28–29

Habegger, Larry, 232
HACE (high-altitude cerebral edema),
  85–86
Half-pipe snowboarding, 129, 136,
  277–78
Hall, Rob, 8–9
Hall, Susan, 9–10
Hamilton, Laird, 3
Hanna, Al, 240–41
HAPE (high-altitude pulmonary
  edema), 85–86
Hargreaves, Alison, climbing, 94–96, 122
Harris Interactive Survey, 254
Hart, Kerry, 159
Hartfield, Chris, BASE jumping, 67–68
Hawk, Tony, 246
Head-down sky diving, 52
Healthy risks, 25–26
Heli-skiing, 262–63
Henderson, Rocky, 243
Hersey, Derek, 66–67
High-altitude cerebral edema (HACE),
  85–86
High-altitude pulmonary edema
  (HAPE), 85–86
High-altitude sky diving, 48–49
Higher calling. *See* Spirituality
High-risk personality types, 23–40
Hiking, 231, 232
Hillary, Edmund, 6, 20, 96, 235
Hillary, Peter, 95–96, 96, 235
Hillary Step (Mount Everest), 242
History of risk taking, 13–21
Hockey, 234
Hooper (movie), 27
House, David, freestyle motocross,
  158–59
Hypoxia, 47, 84–86

Ice axes, 109
Ice climbing, 108–12, 115, 117–18,
  179, 208

Ice Climbing World Cup, 109, 265
Injuries, 201, 213–15
International Mountain Guides, 242
Into Thin Air (Krakauer), 8–9, 236,
  237, 238, 242–43
Irvine, Andrew "Sandy," 19–20, 87

Jacobi, Cameron, 67
Jah, Manish, 256
JAKKS Pacific, 257
Janow, Gordon, 241
Jet skis, for big wave surfing, 144–46
Jiri, Nuru, 105–7
Johnson, Keith, 187–88
Joiner, Cleve, 234
Jones, Mike, freestyle motocross, 159
Jordan, Michael, 91
Jumping and flying, 41–79
  adrenaline rush from, 188–94
  BASE jumping, 53–69, 70
  fear and, 169–74
  rope free flying, 71–77
  sky diving, 43–53
  wing suits, 77–78

Kalepa, Archie
  on adrenaline rush, 198
  big wave surfing, 145–48, 183
  on death and mortality, 23, 212
  on earning a living, 265
  on fear, 183
  on spirituality, 225–26
Kanchenjunga (India), 95, 105, 237–38,
  241
Kayaking, 128, 152–55
Kayak waterfall jumping, 128, 153–55,
  184
Kennedy, Michael, 143
Khan Tengri International Speed
  Climbing Competition (1993),
  92–93
Knack-knack trick, 158
Knievel, Evel, 6, 49, 128, 156, 161
Knutson, Mick
  on adrenaline and endorphins, 185,
  191–92
  BASE jumping, 20, 37, 54–61, 64,
  66, 68, 69
  on death and injuries, 213
  on earning a living, 267–68
  on fear, 169–70, 171
  on the lifestyle, 276

Knutson, Mick (*cont.*)
  personality traits, 29
  sky diving, 46, 169
  Web site, 280
Krakauer, Jon, *Into Thin Air,* 8–9, 236,
    237, 238, 242–43
K2 (Kashmir), 95–96, 98, 99–107

Ladies Home Journal, 10
Lauchan, John, 206
Leach, Robert, 39, 193, 214–15
Leaning Tower (Yosemite), rope free
    flying, 74–76
Legal issues
  BASE jumping and, 37–38, 53–54,
      59–62
  risk taking and, 36–38
Levine, Alison, 242
Levinthal, Jason, 253
Liberty Ridge route (Mount Rainier),
    233–34
Licensing, 256–57
Lifestyle, 269–79
  risk taking and, 35–36
Lindbergh, Charles, 17
Line Skiboards, 253
"Living on the edge," 6
Lover's Leap (South Lake Tahoe),
    BASE jumping, 57
Lowe, Alex
  climbing, 5, 91–94
  personality traits, 36
  skiing, 132–33
Lowe, Dottie, 92
Luebben, Craig, ice climbing, 110
Lynn, Deborah, 9–10

McConkey, Shane
  on adrenaline rush, 192
  BASE jumping, 57, 135
  on death and mortality, 209
  on fear, 173
  personality traits, 29, 40
  skiing, 134–35
  sponsorships, 264–65
McCormick, Jim
  on adrenaline rush, 190–91
  on fear, 170–71
  on motivational speaking, 258–59
  personality traits, 29, 34–35
  on risk, 4–5, 242–43, 259
  sky diving, 44, 45, 47–49, 258–59

  on sponsorships, 249
  Web site, 280
McDowell, Mike, 51–52
McGlynn, Dennis, BASE jumping, 58
McMetz trick, 159–60, 214
McNamara, Chris
  guidebook publishing, 263–64
  rock climbing, 112–16
  Web site, 280
McQueen, Steve, 156
Mainstreaming of extreme sports,
    253–58
Makalu (Himalayas), 5, 97–98, 99, 101,
    237
Makauskas, Dainius, climbing, 105–7
Mallory, George, 19–20, 87, 223
Manze, Vince, 255
Maps, 244, 264
Marketing, 254–58
Marshall, Rich, 120–21
Mass, Cliff, 234
Matterhorn (Alps), 95, 221
May, Mike, 256–57
Mazamas, 235
Media exposure, 6–8, 256–57. *See also*
    ESPN
Merced River, 63–64
Mescola, Riccarda, 64
Metzger, Fritz, 157, 275
Metzger, Mike
  on adrenaline rush, 200
  on death and mortality, 212
  on earning a living, 263
  on fear, 182
  freestyle motocross, 157–60, 182
  on injuries, 201, 213, 214
  on the lifestyle, 274–75
  personality traits, 30
  Web site, 280
Metzger, Ted, 157, 275
Metzger Freestyle Frenzy, 158
Metzger Motors, 263, 280
Miller, Ellen, 236
Miller, Warren, 138, 139
Mischke, Keith, 235
Mixed climbing, 111, 113
Money. *See* Earning a living
Monoamine oxidase B (MAO B), 188
Motivational speaking, 258–61
Motocross, freestyle, 128, 156–60, 277
  adrenaline rush from, 200
  deaths, 212

fear and, 180, 182
injuries and, 213
Motocross racing, 128, 156, 157
Motorcycle jumping, 160–63, 182–83
Mount Aconcagua (Argentina), 241
Mountain climbing. *See* Climbing
Mountain guides, 265–66
Mountain Rescue Association, 244
Mountains, spirituality of, 220–23, 224
Mountain sickness, 84–86
Mount Everest, 232–33, 235–43
    Hillary and Norgay expedition, 6, 20, 235
    Mallory and Irvine expedition, 19–20, 87
    obsession with firsts and, 236–43
    Into Thin Air and, 8–9, 236, 237, 238, 242–43
    Wood and Congdon expedition, 84, 97–98, 99–102, 177, 236–37
"Mt. Everest: A Deadly Playground" (Rostrup), 239
Mount Hauscaran (Peru), 177–78
Mount Hood, 234–35
Mount Kilimanjaro (Tanzania), 241
Mount McKinley, 10, 241
Mount Olympus (Greece), 220
Mount Rainier, 9–10, 83, 231, 233–34, 235
MTV generation, 252, 277–78
Muir, Paul, 232

Nagel, David, 280
Namath, Joe, 156
National Park Service (NPS), 60, 61
Nature, bonding with, 220–21. *See also* Spirituality
Nature Genetics, 187–88
Navy Seals, 72
NBC, 255–56
Negative (unhealthy) risks, 25–26, 30–31
Nepal, 241–42. *See also* Mount Everest
Network (movie), 38
Nike, 255
Noonan, Fred, 17
Norgay, Tenzing, 6, 20, 235
North Col (Mount Everest), 19
North Pole, early exploration of, 17–18
Nyala, Hannah, 244

Ocean, spirituality of, 225–27
Odell, Noel, 19
Old West, 15–16
Olympic Games, 129, 130, 255–56
Oregon Episcopal School, 235
Osman, Dan, 71–77
    death of, 5, 75–76, 208–10
    on endorphin high, 189
    rock climbing, 71, 72
    rope free flying, 43, 71–75, 171–72
Osman-Brown, Andrea, 75, 76
Outlaw image, of BASE jumping, 59–69
Outward Bound, 87–88
Over the Edge: A Regular Guy's Odyssey in Extreme Sports (Bane), 31
Oxygen, climbing and, 84–86

Panic, while climbing, 244, 245
Parachute jumping, 43–44. *See also* Sky diving
Parachutes, 50–51
    reserve, 45–46, 49
Park and huck, 155
Parsons, Mike
    on adrenaline rush, 197–98
    big wave surfing, 144–45, 146, 147–48, 183–84
    on death and mortality, 212
    on fear, 183–84
    on the lifestyle, 276
    personality traits, 29
    on spirituality, 217, 226–27
    sponsorships, 265
Pencils, 153
Performance art, risk sports as, 223
Personalities of risk takers, 23–40, 187–88
Pioneers, early, 15–16, 17–18, 86–87
Piz Badile (Alps), 95
Point Break (movie), 50
Points North Heli Adventures, 262–63
Poop tubes, 123
Porta-ledges, 122–24
Powell, Lake, 61–62
"Power trips," 10–11
Prebble, Lynn, 242
Prize money, 264, 265
Psychology of risk taking, 23–40

Pulmonary edema, high-altitude
(HAPE), 85–86
Puppet Masters (movie), 65

Quinn, Kevin
on adrenaline rush, 193
on earning a living, 262–63
on fear, 167, 172–73
on the lifestyle, 275
personality traits, 29
rope free flying, 41
sky diving, 172–73
snowboarding, 138
on spirituality, 224
Web site, 280

Racquetball, 149
Reality TV shows, 7, 246
Rebellious personality, 27
Rectangular parachutes, 43, 50–51
Redman, Nina, 9–10
Reserve parachutes, 45–46, 49
Rewards, 219. *See also* Spirituality
Reynolds, Burt, 27
Riding, 125–63
adrenaline rush from, 197–200
big wave surfing, 128, 143–48
fear and, 180–84
freestyle motocross, 128, 156–60
kayak waterfall jumping, 128,
153–55
motorcycle jumping, 160–63
skiing, 127, 129–35, 138–43
snowboarding, 127, 129, 135–38,
143
spirituality of, 224–27
tandem surfing, 148–52
Risk aversion, 3–32
Risk taking, 11–12
history of, 13–21
psychology of, 23–40
Road Champs, 257
Robbins, Liz, 272
Robbins, Royal, 271–72
Rock climbing, 71, 111–24, 271–72
adrenaline rush of, 196
big wall, 117, 122–24
death and, 207–8
fear and, 174, 179
free soloing, 111, 113, 116
personalities, 111–19
sleeping and, 122–24

speed, 113–15
spirituality of, 224, 225
women and, 120–22
Rockcraft Climbing School, 272
Rope free flying (flossing the sky),
71–77, 189
Rostrup, Morten, 238–39
Round parachutes, 50–51, 55
Royal Robbins Yosemite climbing shoe,
272
Rush, addiction of the, 32–33, 185–200
climbers and, 194–96
jumpers and flyers and, 188–94
riders and, 197–200
theories, 187–88

SAG (Screen Actors Guild), 64–65
Sanders, Tom
BASE jumping, 61–62, 64–65, 68
on big wave surfing, 143
death of wife and, 5–6, 38, 54,
64–66, 211
on fear, 173–74
Olympic Games and, 255–56
on risk, 38
sky diving, 46, 50–51, 52, 53, 79
Web site, 280
wing suit, 77–78, 79
Sarkisov, Lev, 240
Schlissel, Charles, 10–11
Schoene, Robert, 84–86
Schreiber, Peter, 88–89
Scott, Robert, 18
Screen Actors Guild (SAG), 64–65
Scurvy, 18
Self-esteem, risk taking and, 34–35
Self-mastery, 195
Semiao, Ron, 252, 253
Sensory overload, 44–45
Seven Summits, Frank Wells and, 11
SGMA (Sporting Goods Manufacturers
Association), 254, 256–57
Shackleton, Ernest, 140
Sherpas, 86, 235
Shishapangma (China), 94
SightSound.com, 257–58
Simonson, Eric, 242
Simonson, Erin, 242
Skateboarding, 149, 261
snowboarding and, 129, 277–78
early culture of, 252–53
Skiboarding, 253

Skiing, 127, 129–35, 231
    adrenaline rush from, 198–200
    fear and, 180–82
    deaths, 143
    personalities, 130–35, 138–42
    injuries and, 213–14
    spirituality of, 224
Ski mountaineering, 131–32, 276–77
Skreslet, Lauri, 87–88
Skresnik, Lauri, 274
Sky diving, 43–53
    adrenaline rush from, 190–91
    BASE jumping compared with, 56
    fear and, 169, 170–71, 172–74
    high-altitude, 48–49
    minimizing risks, 47–49
    safety of, 45–46, 50–51
    sensory overload and, 44–45
    at the South Pole, 51–52
    static line, 69–70, 77
    in wing suits, 77–78
Sky surfing, 70
Slab fractures, 142
Slater, Rob, 96
Small-T personalities, 32
Smoke canisters, for sky diving, 47
Snowball tests, 57
Snowblindness, 86
Snowboarding, 135–38
    adrenaline rush from, 198–200
    deaths, 143
    fear and, 182
    freestyle, 136–37
    half-pipe, 129, 136, 277–78
    injuries and, 214
    skateboarding and, 129, 277–78
    stupidity and, 231
Snow bridges, 234–35
Snowmobiling, 135
Snurfer, 129
Soccer injuries, 214–15
South Georgia Island, 139–41, 263
South Pole
    early exploration of, 17–18
    sky diving at, 51–52
Speed (rock) climbing, 113–15
Sphinx, the, 224
Spin Master, 257
Spirit of St. Louis, 17
Spirituality, 217–27
    of climbing, 220–24
    of riding, 224–27

Sponsorships, 249, 253–54, 257, 261,
    264–65, 267
Sporting Goods Manufacturers
    Association (SGMA), 254,
    256–57
Sports, traditional, 16, 121–22, 187,
    278, 279
Sports agent, 261–62
Staffiery, Gina, 254
Static-line sky diving, 69–70, 77
Stearns, Cheryl, sky diving, 49
Stony Point (San Fernando Valley),
    271–72
"Struggle responses," 85
Stupidity, 229–47
    eight blunders of climbing, 243–45
    mountain climbing and, 233–43
Summit, 272
Summit fever, 244
Sunburn, 86
Sunset Beach (Hawaii), 145
Super Topo, 263–64, 280
Surfboards, 146–47
Surfing, 127–28, 143–52
    big wave, 128, 143–48
    fear and, 183–84
    lifestyle, 275–76
    sky, 70
    spirituality of, 225–27
    tandem, 148–52
Survivor (TV show), 246

Taco Bell, 257
Tandem surfing, 148–52, 184
Tanzing, Tashi Wangchuck, 235
Television exposure, 6–8, 256–57
Test pilots, 16–17
Thomas, Tiare, tandem surfing, 150–52
Thompson, Jody, 242
Tibet, 19. *See also* Mount Everest
Topo maps, 264
Tow surfing, 144–47, 198
Toy marketing, 256–57
Traditional rock climbing, 113
Training, 7, 8
Travel Industry Association of America,
    231–32
Trespassing, 60
Troll Wall (Norway), BASE jumping, 63
Trophy hunting, 229, 236–37, 239–41
Tsheri, Temba, 240
Type-T personalities, 32

Ulmer, Kristen
  on adrenaline rush, 32–33, 198–99
  on death and mortality, 5, 207
  on fear, 180–82
  on injuries, 125, 213–14
  on the lifestyle, 276–77
  personality traits, 26, 32–34
  on risk, 4, 38
  skiing, 130–34, 180–82
  on spirituality, 224–25
  Web site, 280
Unhealthy risks, 25–26, 30–31
United States Parachute Association
    (USPA), 60, 61
United States Ski Team, 130

Vail, Paul, 278
Video industry, 254–55, 257–58,
    266–67
Viesturs, Ed, 236
Vietnam War, 55

Wallace, Circe
  on adrenaline rush, 199
  on death and mortality, 207
  on fear, 165, 182
  on injuries, 214
  personality traits, 27–28
  snowboarding, 135–37, 182
  as sports agent, 261–62
Wall climbing, 117, 122–24
Water, aerated, 154–55
Waterfall jumping, 128, 153–55, 184
Watkins, Abby
  on adrenaline rush, 195–96
  Ascending Women, 266, 278–79,
    280
  climbing, 119–22, 123
  on death and mortality, 210–11
  on earning a living, 265–66
  personality traits, 28–29
  on spirituality, 223
Webber, Joe, BASE jumping, 58
Web sites, 280

Weight training, 117
Weihenmeyer, Erik, 240, 241
Weisner, Fritz, 98
Wells, Frank, 11
Wild One, The (movie), 156
Wind River Mountain Range, 88
Wing suits, 77–78
Winter Olympic Games (2002), 255–56
Women. *See* Gender
Wood, Sharon, 87–88
  on adrenaline rush, 195
  climbing, 84, 87–88, 97–98, 99–107
  on death and mortality, 206–7
  on fear, 177–78
  on the lifestyle, 274
  on motivational speaking, 259–61
  Mount Everest expedition, 84,
    97–98, 99–102, 177, 236–37
  personality traits, 27
  on spirituality, 222
  on trophy hunting, 229, 236–37
  Web site, 280
Woodhaven Entertainment, 258
World Cup, 109, 110, 129, 265
World Tour, 135
Wrangell Saint Elias Range, 142
Wright Brothers, 16, 20

X Concepts, 257
X-factors, 18, 94, 211, 245
X Games, 8, 246–47, 252–54, 256–57
  freestyle motocross, 159
  ice climbing, 109–10
X Games (toy), 257

Yamamoto, Toshio, 240
Yosemite National Park, 66–67, 68
  climbing, 112–13
  El Capitan, BASE jumping, 53–54,
    59, 60–68
  El Capitan, rock climbing, 112–13,
    114–15, 264, 272
  Leaning Tower, rope free flying,
    74–76